COMBINATORIAL HARMONY

CONCEPTS AND TECHNIQUES
FOR COMPOSING AND IMPROVISING

BY JULIO HERRLEIN

COMBINATORIAL HARMONY

JULIO HERRLEIN

Original edition registered at Biblioteca Nacional ESC Direitos Autorais (Rio de Janeiro, Brazil) under the register number 524.225 (Biblioteca Nacional) Livro 995 Folha 221
Copyright© 2011 by Julio Herrlein

CREDITS
Acoustic / Electric Guitars and Compositions: Julio Herrlein
Chord Diagrams (Chapter 3 and 4): Guilherme Barros
Cover art by Julio Herrlein and Luciana Etchegaray
English Translation: Thais Gonzalez
English Revision and Proofreading: Emily Hurst and Ben Monder
Musical Editing and Musical Notation Revision: Julio Herrlein
Recording and Mixing: Julio Herrlein
Coordination and Graphic Production: Julio Herrlein
Assembly and Artwork: Julio Herrlein
Executive Production: Luciana Etchegaray
Author's Photo Credit: Lucio Chachamovich

COMBINATORIAL HARMONY

CONCEPTS AND TECHNIQUES
FOR COMPOSING AND IMPROVISING

BY JULIO HERRLEIN

- *Essential reference for guitarists, arrangers, composers, improvisers and harmony students*
- *The most complete fingerboard mapping*
- *All four-note chords (35 types) with diagrams*
- *All three-note chords (18 types) with diagrams and mnemonic exercises in the included CD*
- *24 different voicings for each four-note chord including Closed, Drop 2, Drop 3, Drop 2+4, Drop 2+3 and Double Drop 2 + Drop 3*
- *Functional Harmony and Musical Set Theory*
- *Combinatorial Voice Leading (New Concept)*
- *Pentatonic Exercises*
- *Hexatonics and triad pairs exercises (for all instruments)*
- *How to build chord progressions (97 cadential models)*
- *Electric and acoustic guitar compositions*

"This book is unique in that it applies combinatorial approach to harmony with materials generally known to the jazz improvisor, thus casting a new and exciting light on a familiar subject. It is also the only book I have seen of its kind to be so guitar-friendly. I am finding a vast store of possibilities here, and I am very grateful to Julio Herrlein for providing them."

Ben Monder

"Julio Herrlein has put together a very comprehensive overview of his approach to harmony and improvisation. His text is filled with useful and practical tools that will be very valuable to any serious student. Highly recommended."

John Stowell

"Julio Herrlein's Combinatorial Harmony book reveals all the possible combinations of notes and harmonic situations you'll need in order to be a creative and unique musician, regardless of the style you play. One of the best things about this book is that it really inspires you to come up with your own ideas. It shows the student all the different colors and canvases you have available, but you're the one that has to paint it! I'm sure many serious guitarists (and other musicians) will benefit from this definitive work!"

Gustavo Assis-Brasil

TABLE OF CONTENTS

ACKNOWLEDGEMENTS 9

FOREWORD by Nelson Faria 10

PREFACE by the Author 10

INTRODUCTION 11

WHO S THIS BOOK FOR 12

HOW TO STUDY THIS BOOK 12

CHAPTER 1

1.   INTERVAL CLASSES 13
1.1   DIATONIC STEP 14
1.2   ACOUSTIC INTERVAL ROOT 14
1.3   INTERVAL GEOMETRY 15
1.3.1   CIRCLES (Chromatic and of Fifths) 15
1.3.2   CYCLES 15
1.3.2.1 DITONE CYCLE 15
1.3.2.2 SESQUITONE CYCLE 15
1.3.2.3 WHOLE TONE CYCLE 15
1.3.2.4 TRITONE 17
1.4   MAPPING THE GUITAR 18
1.4.1   GUITAR FRETBOARD (Notes in Standard Notation) 18
1.4.1.1 CHORD DIAGRAMS 18
1.4.1.2 SCALE/CHORD DIAGRAMS 18
1.4.1.3 GUITAR FRETBOARD (notes in standard notation)........................... 19
1.4.1.4 GUITAR FRETBOARD (notes on tablature)....................................... 19
1.4.1.5 FINGER POSITIONS 20
1.4.2   FIVE ACTIVITY AREAS (CAGED) 20
1.4.3   FRETBOARD (Set Theory View)... 21
1.4.4   FRETBOARD (Intervallic View) 22
1.5   NOTATION CONVENTIONS 24
1.5.1   NUMBERING MELODIC DEGREES.. 24
1.5.2   NUMBERING HARMONIC DEGREES 24
1.6.1   DEGREE CONVENTIONS... 25
1.6.2   CHORD SYMBOLS CONVENTION 26
1.7   MODULATORY CHARACTERISTIC OF DIATONIC SCALE 27
1.7.1   CYCLE OF FIFTHS KEY SIGNATURES OF TONAL CENTERS.................. 27
1.8   SCALE SUPERIMPOSITION 27

CHAPTER 2

2.   FUNCTIONAL HARMONY 29
2.1   FUNCTIONAL NOTATION... 31
2.2   SUPERIMPOSITION OF THIRDS CHORD MODEL 31
2.3   TONAL SYSTEM – AXES 33
2.3.1   TONAL CYCLE / CHORD PROGRESSION 33
2.4   MAJOR TONALITY – FUNCTIONAL AXES.. 34

2.4.1   TONIC AXIS IN [C:] 34
2.4.2   DOMINANT AXIS in [C:] 35
2.4.2.1 TRITONE (LEADING TONES) 36
2.4.3   SUBDOMINANT AXIS in [C:] 37
2.5   MINOR TONALITY - FUNCTIONAL AXES 38
2.5.1   TONIC AXIS IN [a:] 39
2.5.2   DOMINANT AXIS IN [a:] 40
2.5.3   SUBDOMINANT AXIS IN [a:] 41
2.6   SYMMETRICAL AXES 42
2.6.1   OCTATONIC DOMINANT AXIS 42
2.6.2   OCTATONIC DIMINISHED AXIS 42
2.6.3   WHOLE TONE DOMINANT AXIS 43
2.7   USUAL CHORD SYMBOLS RELATED TO HARMONIC FUNCTION 44
2.8   SCALE/FUNCTION RELASHIONSHIP 45

CHAPTER 3

3.   CARDINALITY 3 – THREE NOTE CHORDS 47
3.1   "A" TYPOLOGY – TRIADS 47
3.2   "B" TYPOLOGY – QUARTAL CHORDS 47
3.3   "C" TYPOLOGY – SEVENTH WITHOUT THE FIFTH CHORDS 47
3.4   "D" TYPOLOGY – SEVENTH WITHOUT THE THIRD CHORDS 47
3.5   "E" TYPOLOGY - CLUSTERS (THREE NOTE SEGMENTS) 47
3.6   CARD 3 – TYPOLOGY 48
3.6.1   7-35 DIATONIC SCALE 48
3.6.2   7-32a HARMONIC MINOR SCALE 49
3.6.3   7-34 MELODIC MINOR SCALE 50
3.6.4   7-32b HARMONIC MAJOR SCALE 51
3.6.5   8-28 OCTATONIC SCALE 52
3.6.6   9-12 NONATONIC SCALE 53
3.6.7   AUXILIARY SCALES TYPOLOGIES 54
         6-35 WHOLE TONE SCALE 54
         6-20 AUGMENTED SCALE 54
3.6.8   TRICHORDS – GENERIC INTERVALS 55
3.6.9   TRICHORDS – GENERIC INTERVALS THROUGH DIATONIC STEPS 56
3.6.10   TRICHORDS - STEPS THROUGH SYMMETRICAL SCALES 57
         TRICHORDS - STEPS THROUGH 8-28 OCTATONIC SCALE STEPS 57
         TRICHORDS - STEPS THROUGH 9-12 NONATONIC SCALE STEPS 57
3.7   CARD 3 – THREE-NOTE CHORDS 58
         See the Pitch Class Sets Index on page 309

CHAPTER 4

4.   CARDINALITY 4 – FOUR-NOTE CHORDS 95
4.1   "A" TYPOLOGY – SEVENTH CHORDS 95
4.2   "B" TYPOLOGY - QUARTAL CHORDS 95
4.3   "C" TYPOLOGY – TRIADS WITH AN ADDED NINTH OR IN THE BASS (SUS) ... 95
4.4   "D" TYPOLOGY – TRIADS WITH AN ADDED FOURTH OR IN THE BASS 95
4.5   "E" TYPOLOGY - T 3 7 + (9) FOUR-NOTE SEGMENTS 96
4.6   VOICING THEORY 96
4.6.1   CLOSED POSITION CHORDS 97
4.6.2   OPEN POSITION CHORDS 97
4.6.2.1 DROP 2 VOICINGS 97
4.6.2.2 DROP 3 VOICINGS 97
4.6.2.3 STRING TRANSFERENCE 98

4.6.2.4   VOICINGS (SUMMARY TABLE) 99
4.7   THEORY OF GENERIC INTERVALS 100
4.7.1   TABLE OF GENERIC INTERVALS 102
4.8   GENERIC INTERVALS FORMULAE 103
4.8.1   GENERIC INTERVALS FORMULAE TABLE 105
4.9   CARD 4 – TYPOLOGY 106
4.9.1   7-35 DIATONIC SCALE 106
4.9.2   7-32a HARMONIC MINOR SCALE 107
4.9.3   7-34 MELODIC MINOR SCALE 108
4.9.4   7-32b HARMONIC MAJOR SCALE 109
4.9.5   8-28 OCTATONIC SCALE 110
4.9.6   9-12 NONATONIC SCALE 112
4.9.7   AUXILIARY SCALES TYPOLOGIES 114
            6-35 WHOLE TONE SCALE 114
            6-20 AUGMENTED SCALE 114
4.10   CARD 4 – FOUR-NOTE CHORDS 116
            See the Pitch Class Sets Index on page 311

CHAPTER 5

5.   CARDINALITY 5 - TYPOLOGY 159
5.1   7-35 DIATONIC SCALE 159
5.2   7-34 MELODIC MINOR SCALE 160
5.3   7-32a HARMONIC MINOR SCALE 161
5.4   7-32b HARMONIC MAJOR SCALE 162
5.5   CARD 5 – MELODIC EXERCISES 163
5.5.1   PENTATONIC SUBSETS OF 8-28 SCALE 166

CHAPTER 6

6.   COMBINATORIAL VOICE LEADING OF HEXATONICS 169
6.1   MELODIC AND HARMONIC EXERCISES 172

CHAPTER 7

7.   CADENCES AND CHORD PROGRESSIONS 243
7.1   TONAL AXES 243
7.2   CADENTIAL GRAVITY 243
7.3   ALL TONAL CENTERS - FUNCTIONAL SUMMARY 244
7.4   CADENTIAL MODELS 246
7.5   LIST OF CADENTIAL MODELS 247
7.6   CONNECTING CADENTIAL MODELS 253
7.7   CHORD PROGRESSIONS 254
7.7.1   SAME CHORD TYPE THROUGH THE SESQUIDITONE CIRCLE 254
7.7.2   V-I THROUGH THE SESQUIDITONE CIRCLE 255
7.7.3   V-I THROUGH THE DITONE CYCLE 256
7.7.4   V-I THROUGH THE SESQUITONE CYCLE 256
7.7.5   V-I THROUGH THE WHOLE TONE CYCLE 257
7.7.6   II-V THROUGH THE SESQUIDITONE CIRCLE 258
7.8   HARMONIC PLURALITY 259
7.9   HARMONIC ANALYSIS 260
7.9.1   SECONDARY DOMINANTS 260
7.9.2   SECONDARY SUBV7 261

7.9.3   SECONDARY II – V 263
7.9.4   SECONDARY II – SubV7 263
7.9.5   EXTENDED DOMINANTS 263
7.9.6   INTERPOLATED CHORDS 264
7.9.7   ADJACENT II – V´s 264
7.9.8   MODAL INTERCHANGE 265
7.9.8.1   MODAL BORROWING 265
7.9.8.2   CHROMATIC MEDIANTS 265
7.9.9   DIMINISHED CHORDS 266
7.9.10   AUGMENTED CHORDS 267
7.10   SCALE FINGERINGS (GUITAR) 268
7.10.1   SCALE 7-35 (DIATONIC) 268
7.10.2   SCALE 7-32a (HARMONIC MINOR) 269
7.10.3   SCALE 7-32a (MELODIC MINOR) 270
7.10.4   SCALE 7-32b (HARMONIC MAJOR) 271

CHAPTER 8

COMPOSITIONS 273
        SONATA (to Ben Monder) 274
        AINDA NÃO (NOT YET) 283
        SERIAL MATRIX USED ON "AINDA NÃO" COMPOSITION 291

TECHNICAL APPENDIX (MUSICAL SET THEORY) 293

A.   BASIC DEFINITIONS 294
A.1   PITCHES 294
A.2   PITCH CLASSES 295
A.3   CIRCULARITY 296
A.4   PITCH CLASS SETS 296
A.5   PRIME FORMS 297
A.6   INTERVAL VECTOR 297
A.7   FORTE´S TABLE 298
A.7.1   REDUCING THE SCOPE 300
A.7.2   THE 3-1 SET (0,1,2) 300
A.7.3   REMOVING THE 3-1 (0,1,2) THRICORD FROM THE SYSTEM 300
A.7.4   TABLE OF THE SETS WITHOUT THE 3-1 TRICHORD 301
A.7.5   SETS WITHOUT THE 3-1 302

END NOTES 303

REFERENCES 305

ABOUT THE AUTHOR 307

PITCH CLASS SETS INDEX 309

CD TRACKS INDEX 311

ACKNOWLEDGEMENTS

I would like to thank the people who have supported me and worked on this project: the great guitarist and pioneer of the brazilian guitar teaching Nelson Faria, for writing the foreword of this book, lending credibility to this project; to Gustavo Assis-Brasil for all the inspiration and support; to Emily Hurst who did a first class revision of my english text together with the guitar genius Ben Monder; to Vinícius Grossi and José Carlos de Oliveira at Freenote Store (São Paulo, Brasil) to make contact with Bryndon Bay and make this edition a possibility. To Fumproarte Staff (Porto Alegre). And the most special thanks must go to my wife Luciana Etchegaray, who has always been by my side in good times and also in difficult moments of our lives. Without Luciana this task would have been impossible.

I would like to thank all the people who have been my students at any time; the list is too large to put here. Many of these people have become great musicians, which brings me joy and pride.

To fellow musicians who have written quotes in support of this project: John Stowell, Gustavo Assis-Brasil and Ben Monder.

I would like to thank Dmitri Tymoczko (Princeton University) for his application software "chord geometries," on Max/Msp; Paul Nelson for his very useful site www.composertools.com.

FOREWORD
by NELSON FARIA

HEAVY ARTILLERY!

What we see in this book is heavy artillery! Valuable information, deeply detailed and illustrated in order to bring both the student and the experienced musician the opportunity to experience harmony and all its combinatorial relations in a logical and effective way.

A good tree is one that produces good fruit, and the musical examples presented by Julio Herrlein in this book prove that. The tasteful exercises in this book demonstrate the genius of this virtuoso guitarist, who has now generously shared with us his knowledge.

Örebro, June 15, 2011

Nelson Faria

PREFACE
by THE AUTHOR

The basic premise of this book, since the first edition (2011), is to be a catalog of possibilities. We do not deal with specific styles. Students will be able to incorporate the ideas presented here into their own music.

Some people can make great music using only two basic chords, while others may use complex combinations of hexachords generated from an octatonic scale. The value of music lies in its expressiveness and communication rather than in the complexity of the theory surrounding it. Theory is a tool to explain and organize, but it does not make music by itself.

Therefore, i hope you, dear reader, make the best use of the material gathered here and use it wisely.

Julio Herrlein
Porto Alegre, February, 2013

INTRODUCTION

When we explore musical material, we look for ways to create new sound combinations. Pitch organization is part of the compositional process. With the production of atonal music, the Second Viennese School composers (Schoenberg and his disciples) started using unusual harmonic structures that could not be represented by familiar chord symbols.

These composers used twelve-tone rows with inverted and retrograde forms, employing all sorts of combinatorial manipulation, and introducing a new way of looking at harmony. The combinations generated by twelve-tone rows (serialism) created complex sound sets that could not be expressed in common terms like C major or G7 (b9).

As these new compositions were based on combinations (12-tone rows) and produced unusual harmonic structures, a new harmonic analysis needed to be considered. How many combinations of chords are possible using the 12 tones of the equal temperament system? How do we name these chords?

The idea of using musical set theory, as developed by Allen Forte, was an analytical solution for this new repertoire. Elliott Carter also managed to list the possible combinations of sets, especially for his compositional purposes. The fact that all possible combinations of sounds in the temperament system fit on only two pages is amazing (see Appendix).

However, these two pages are a succession of numbers which at first glance may seem daunting to musicians not familiar with this language.

On the other hand, jazz and popular songs created a series of procedures and codes that we call "common practice," the "modus operandi" of music that is not just the music itself but the way musicians work and communicate with each other. The harmonic repertoire of this music tends to be based more on the use of chord symbols than in the writing of each particular chord in standard notation.

In "common practice," musicians are implicitly required to master this language, and be able to convert chord symbols in real time, utilizing a unique harmonic vocabulary (END NOTE 1).

Songwriting, and its use as a vehicle for improvisation, inspired the practice of an extended tonality. The use of fixed forms (12-bar blues, rhythm and changes, 32-bar songs) led to the expansion and reharmonization of song structures, with musicians contributing their own individual solutions to familiar harmonic progressions ("Coltrane changes," for example). All this material is widely discussed and available in several sources (songbooks, jazz methods), and is part of the daily routine of jazz musicians.

One of the goals of this book is to connect these two worlds: the abstraction of combinations and "the common practice."

As a guitarist for over twenty-five years, I have always been interested in how I could use these aforementioned concepts in my practice. Currently, there is a tendency towards intervallic phrasing in improvisational music, based on specific combinations of sounds, modes of limited transposition, and other techniques such as hexatonics (six-note sets).

In preparing this book, all three-note and four-note sets have been mapped with their possible usage as harmonic function. When I mention "all sets," I mean those which are not subsets or supersets of trichord 3-1 ("chromatic cluster"). As non-tonal sets, they are out of the scope of this book (see Technical Appendix). This mapping includes fretboard diagrams for acoustic and electric guitars and exercises to memorize these patterns. I have also attempted to simplify the musical set theory approach, using a more familiar chord typology.

WHO IS THIS BOOK FOR

ARRANGERS

Each four-note set (totaling 35) has 24 different voicings, totaling 798 different chords. The arranger can see all the possibilities of the chord, helping to arrange, for example, a four-note chord for a string or brass quartet.

ACOUSTIC / ELETRIC GUITAR PLAYERS

For the 798 possible four-note chords and for the 100 possibilities of voicings of three-note sets, the guitarist will also find a diagram for each set voicings (24 voicings per four-note set), plus a general diagram with geometric location of each set on the fretboard. Bass players can use the four bass strings of the diagrams to view notes on the four string bass.

COMPOSERS

Composers who are interested in having a "friendly" compendium on musical set theory will find a useful reference here, as it is presented in a way accessible to musicians familiar with traditional functional harmony.

NON-GUITARISTS COMPOSERS

Composers who do not play the acoustic or electric guitar may use this book as a guide to the fretboard, making the work of finding the most idiomatic fingerings much easier.

IMPROVISERS

Hexatonics (six-note sets) are fully explored in this book. All possible combinations of hexatonics are applied both in melodic form and in combinatorial voice leading between trichords, which is a very innovative concept in the literature. This great range of ideas can be used for composition and also for improvisation. For all instruments.

HARMONY AND ANALYSIS STUDENTS

This book presents a theory of harmony, with relationships between chords and scales, suggesting the harmonic function in each of the 35 four-note chords (Chapter 4) within the same tonality, making possible the understanding and analysis of chord, degree, and function of all these structures. Each chord has a list of functional possibilities that may be used. Chapter 3, with 18 trichords, is also organized in the same way.

SIGHT READERS

Students interested in sight reading can use the hexatonics chapter for this purpose.

HOW TO STUDY THIS BOOK

Most of the content of this book is self-explanatory. It is important to apply these concepts to your own repertoire and compositions, making the content familiar to your musical reality. Exercises are suggested along the way. The compositions apply, in a practical way, many of the concepts dealt with in the book. For a better understanding of the structure of the book and on naming sets, I suggest reading the Technical Appendix (at the end of the book) before starting Chapter 1.

1. INTERVAL CLASSES

CLASS	STEP	Normal Form	Inverted Form
SEMITONE (st) *	2/7	Minor Second	Major Seventh
WHOLE-TONE (wt)		Major Second	Minor Seventh
SESQUITONE (m)	3/6	Minor Third	Major Sixth
DITONE (M)		Major Third	Minor Sixth
SESQUIDITONE (P)	4/5	Perfect Fourth	Perfect Fifth
TRITONE (TT)		Augmented Fourth	Diminished Fifth

* For easy reference, let´s use some abreviations for interval classes:

(st) SEMITONE CLASS   (M) DITONE CLASS
(wt) WHOLE-TONE CLASS   (P) SESQUIDITONE
(m) SESQUITONE CLASS   (TT) TRITONE CLASS

1. INTERVAL CLASSES

We will use proper names for the six classes of intervals (SEMITONE, WHOLE-TONE, SESQUITONE, DITONE, SESQUIDITONE AND TRITONE), in order to not confuse them with the intervals, which are generated by the classes (seconds, thirds, fourths, etc.). So, we have six interval classes, each of which generates two complementary intervals (page 13).

1.1 DIATONIC STEP

Intervals are named based on diatonic step, i.e. how many degrees are covered within the diatonic scale. Thus, the steps corresponding to the seconds are listed below:

7-35 [C:]	´C	´D	´E	´F	´G	´A	´B

Whole Tone Class:	´C-´D, ´D-´E, ´F-´G, ´G-´A, ´A-´B
Semitone Class:	´E-´F, ´B-´C

Each interval class creates two dyads. The dyad in normal form is the one represented by the shortest path between two notes. For example, between the notes 'C-'D, there are two steps ('C-'D) or the path of seven steps ranging from' D to 'C (' D 'e' f 'g' a ' b 'C). The Normal and Inverted forms are always complementary. Thus the concept of inversion is linked to the complementarity within the same interval class.

Although the second major interval 'C-'D belongs to the whole-tone class and the second minor interval 'E -'F belongs to semitone class, both can be expressed with two notes in the diatonic scale, and for this reason, the semitone and whole-tone class are at the same diatonic step 2 / 7 (see interval classes table).

Besides being represented in the chromatic circle, we have examples of dyads corresponding to each interval in standard notation. The white notes correspond to the acoustic interval root.

1.2 ACOUSTIC INTERVAL ROOT

According to the harmonic theory of Paul Hindemith (END NOTE 2), each interval has a root, but it is not always the lowest note of the interval. This phenomenon can be experienced in practice. When the interval classes are played, pay attention to the note that stands out, that is, the note that is acoustically enhanced by adding up the sounds of the interval.

1.3 INTERVAL GEOMETRY

Note that the interval classes (page 13) are represented by geometric figures. The choice of these figures was due to the nature of the cycle created by each interval class.

1.3.1 CIRCLES (Chromatic and of Fifths) - (please refer to page 16)

A "Circle" means a cycle formed by the same type of interval that runs through all the notes of the chromatic scale.

There are two circles: the Semitone circle (or chromatic) and the Sesquiditone circle (or of Fourths/Fifths).

For intervals of the Semitone class (2m and 7M) and for Sesquiditone class (Perfect Fourth and Fifth) we use the circle because the repeated application of these intervals goes through all the notes (12 tones).

1.3.2 CYCLES - (page 16)

Other intervals classes do not form circles, but "cycles." The difference between circles and cycles is that the cycles do not pass through all 12 notes.

1.3.2.1 DITONE CYCLE

For intervals generated from the Ditone class (3M and 6m,) we use the triangle because the repeated application of this interval creates a cycle of three notes.

1.3.2.2 SESQUITONE CYCLE

For intervals generated from the Sesquitone class (3m and 6M) we use the square because the repeated application of this interval creates a cycle of four notes.

1.3.2.3 WHOLE TONE CYCLE

For intervals generated from the Whole Tone class (2M and 7m) we use the hexagon because the repeated application of this interval creates a cycle of six notes.

1.3   INTERVAL GEOMETRY

Interval Circles and Cycles

1.3.1   Semitone Circle   Sesquiditone Circle

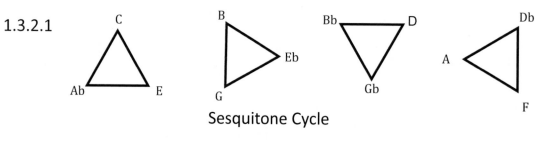

Ditone Cycle

1.3.2.1

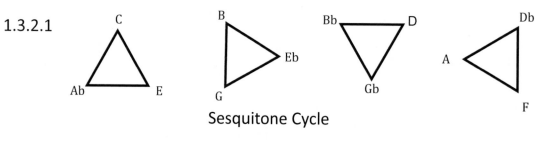

Sesquitone Cycle

1.3.2.2

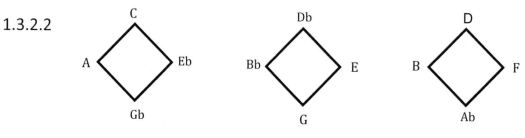

Whole-tone Cycle

1.3.2.3

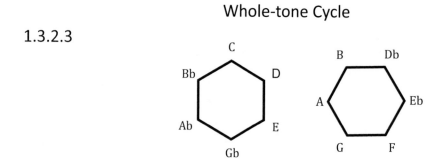

1.3.2.4 TRITONE

The tritone does not generate a cycle, but it divides the octave exactly in the middle and can be part of both Whole Tone and Sesquitone cycles. It also divides the Chromatic Circle, separating the Normal and Inverted Forms from the interval classes.

The figure 1.3.2.4 shows the Chromatic Circle using intervals classes represented by geometric figures, using the Tritone right in the middle of the circle, dividing the Normal Form from the Inverted Form.

The Chromatic Circle is a way of representing the 12 notes of the equal temperament system. The initial note (R, or root) can start at any note. In the figure below, on the left, we have the Chromatic Circle starting at ´C and on the right, beginning at ´Gb.

1.3.2.4

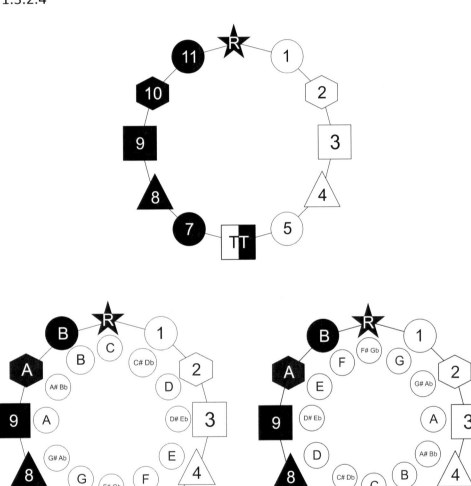

1.4   MAPPING THE GUITAR

1.4.1   GUITAR FRETBOARD (Note names and Positions)

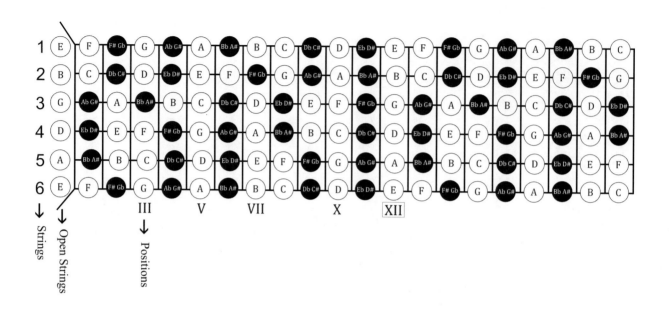

1.4.1.1 CHORD DIAGRAMS

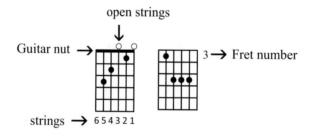

1.4.1.2 SCALE/CHORD DIAGRAMS

Diatonic C Scale with C major triad chord tones in
white and other tones in black:

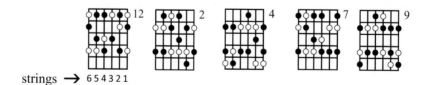

1.4.1.3 GUITAR FRETBOARD (notes in standard notation)

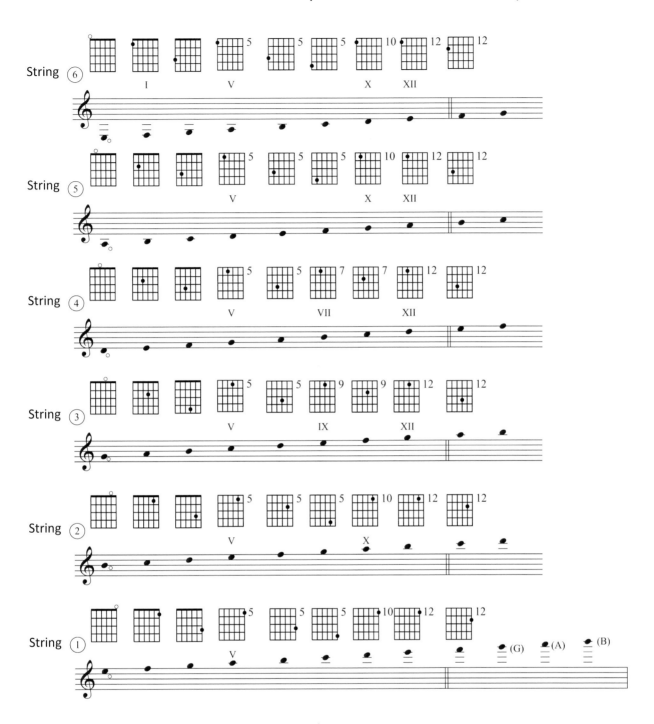

1.4.1.4 GUITAR FRETBOARD (notes on tablature)

1.4.1.5　FINGER POSITIONS

Basic Position

Frets	I	II	III	IV	V	VI	VII
(Fingers) Position II		1	2	3	4		
(Fingers) Position IV				1	2	3	4

Extended Position (stretch finger 1 and 4)

Frets	I	II	III	IV	V	VI	VII	VIII
(Fingers) Position II	(1)	1	2	3	4	(4)		
(Fingers) Position IV			(1)	1	2	3	4	(4)

1.4.2　FIVE ACTIVITY AREAS - CAGED SYSTEM

Most of the material in this book is mapped using the CAGED system, splitting the fretboard in five areas, according to the basic shapes of the major triad.

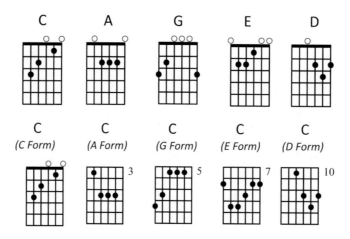

Diatonic scale in the five CAGED areas

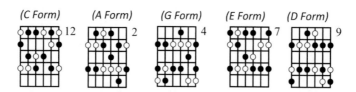

1.4.3 FRETBOARD (Set Theory View)

The most used form of diagrams in this book is the set theory view. Due to the multiple functions that a chord may have (harmonic plurality), this is the most neutral form of representing the intervallic relations on the fretboard:

1.4.3

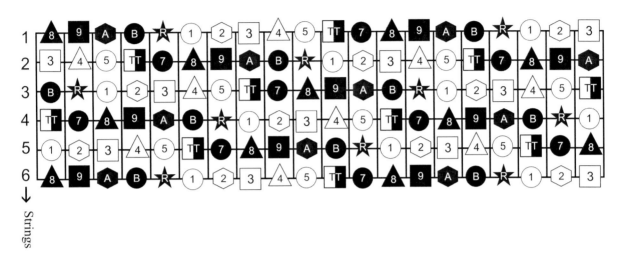

Strings

In this way of representing the fretboard there are not fret numbers, so you can choose whatever note you want to be the root note (R) and find the relation with the remaining notes. The same holds true with the Intervallic View.

The intervallic view of the guitar fretboard shows the intervallic relationship between any of the notes.

Thus, a major triad (R, 3M, and 5J) may be represented equally starting at any note, for example, in C (`C,`E, `G), Gb (`Gb, `Bb,`Db) or E (`E, `G#, `B). See the figures below, with the interval classes represented on the guitar fretboard.

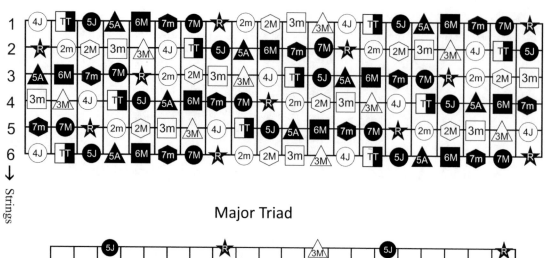

Major Triad

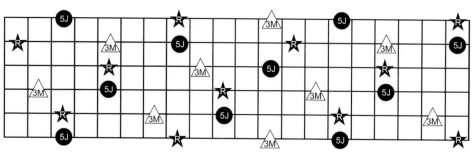

Perfect Fourth / Perfect Fifth Intervals
Sesquiditone Class

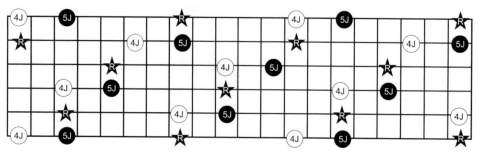

Minor Second / Major Seventh Intervals
Semitone Class

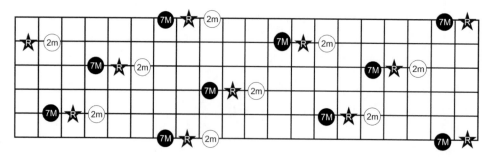

Major Second / Minor Seventh Intervals
Whole-Tone Class

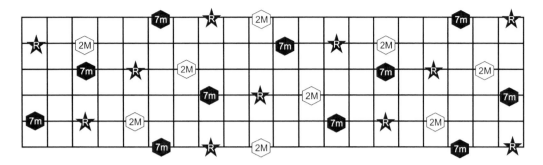

Minor Third / Major Sixth Intervals
Sesquitone Class

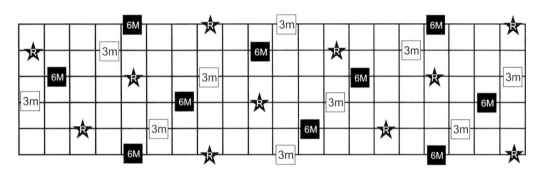

Major Third / Minor Sixth Intervals
Ditone Class

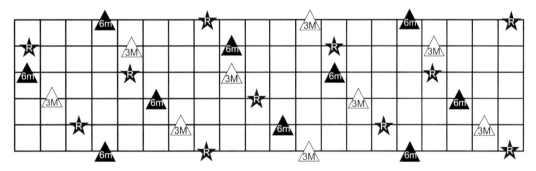

Augmented Fourth / Diminished Fifth Intervals
Tritone Class

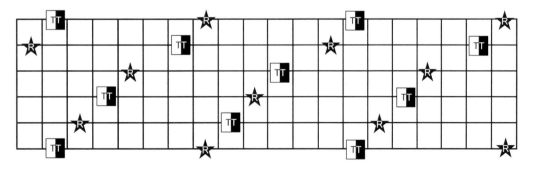

1.5.1 NUMBERING MELODIC DEGREES

From now on, we will think of the diatonic scale numbering its degrees. We will number the melodic scale degrees with Arabic numerals preceded by an acute accent ('). Throughout the text, when we mention the notes, we will also use the acute accent (') before each note (e.g. the note C will be referred to as ' C, D flat note as ' Db, and so on). In the process of numbering the melodic degrees, there will be no difference between major and minor mode. The first note of the diatonic scale will be designated by the number one ('1).

1.5.1   NUMBERING MELODIC DEGREES

Melodic Degrees

'1	'2	'3	'4	'5	'6	'7
'C	'D	'E	'F	'G	'A	'B

Melodic Degrees (Chromatic)

'1	'#1	'b2	'2	'#2	'b3	'3	'4	'#4	'b5	'5	'#5	'b6	'6	'bb7	'b7	'7
'C	'C#	'Db	'D	'D#	'Eb	'E	'F	'F#	'Gb	'G	'G#	'Ab	'A	'Bbb	'Bb	'B

1.5.2 NUMBERING HARMONIC DEGREES

The harmonic degrees, on which we will build chords and functions, appear as Roman numerals. For analysis purpose we differentiate between the major (capital letter) and minor (lower case letter) modes in the harmonic and functional degrees convention. See 1.6.1.

1.5.2   NUMBERING HARMONIC DEGREES

Harmonic Degrees

I	II	III	IV	V	VI	VII
C	Dm	Em	F	G	Am	Bdim

We will deal with the degree conventions from the diatonic scale on (7-35). The degrees are represented by Roman numerals. When dealing with the major scale, capital numbers will be used in opposite to lower case Roman numbers when referring to the minor scale.

The major tonal centers will be represented by a capital letter followed by a colon and brackets, thus [C:] means Tonal center of C major.

The minor tonal centers will be represented by a lower case letter followed by a colon and brackets, thus [a:] means Tonal center of A minor.

The natural minor scale can be thought as a major scale where III, VI and VII degrees have been lowered and therefore the third, sixth and seventh degrees of the minor scale appear as biii, bvi and bvii.

1.6.1   DEGREE CONVENTIONS

[C:] means C major tonal center.
[a:] means A minor tonal center.

1.6.2   CHORD SYMBOLS CONVENTION
(Intervals used in Chords)

Name	Scale *	Chord Symbol **	Semitones	[C:]	[F#:]	[Ab:]	[E:]
Unison	1	-	0	C	F#	Ab	E
Minor Second	2m	(b9)	1	Db	G	Bbb	F
Major Second	2M	(9)	2	D	G#	Bb	F#
Augmented Second	2a	(#9)	3	D#	Gx	B	Fx
Minor Third	3m	m	3	Eb	A	Cb	G
Major Third	3M	-	4	E	A#	C	G#
Diminished Fourth[1]	4d	not used	4	Fb	Bb	Dbb	Ab
Perfect Fourth	4j	4, (11)	5	F	B	Db	A
Augmented Fourth	4a	(#11)	6	F#	B#	D	A#
Diminished Fifth	5d	(b5)	6	Gb	C	Ebb	Bb
Perfect Fifth	5j	-	7	G	C#	Eb	B
Augmented Fifth	5a	(#5)	8	G#	Cx	E	B#
Minor Sixth	6m	(b13)	8	Ab	D	Fb	C
Major Sixth	6M	6, (13)	9	A	D#	F	C#
Diminished Seventh	7d	0	9	Bbb	Eb	Gbb	Db
Minor Seventh	7m	7	10	Bb	E	Gb	D
Major Seventh	7M	7M	11	B	E#	G	D#
Perfect Octave	8j	(8)	12	C	F#	Ab	E

* Interval as a melodic device (in a scale or melodic pattern).

** Interval in a chord symbol.

[1] This interval is not normally used in chord symbols, but it´s convenient to understand the concept of interval inversion.

1.7 MODULATORY CHARACTER OF DIATONIC SCALE

The major scale, among the scales that do not contain the trichord 3-1 (see the Technical Appendix at the end of the book) is the only scale at which it is possible to obtain, through a minimum change, an equal set with the same properties (however, in different transposition). That way, the key signatures introduce one note at a time, progressively. This is the main reason why the diatonic scale is a reference to the tonal organization: the possibility of an objective measurement of the distance between two tonal centers, based on the Cycle of Fifths.

1.7.1 CYCLE OF FIFTHS KEY SIGNATURES OF TONAL CENTERS

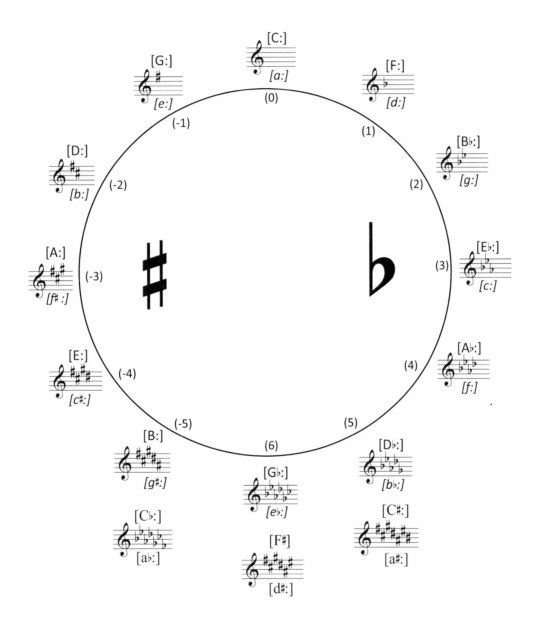

1.8 SCALE SUPERIMPOSITION

We will use a system of scale superimposition to create our tonal organization system (END NOTE 3). Other forms of the minor scale (harmonic minor and melodic minor) and the harmonic major scale will be considered as variations of the diatonic scale, derived from the modification of one of its notes. These four scales (7-35, 7-34, 7-32a and 7-32b) form the most important core of the tonal system, producing all the four-note chords that do not have the chromatic cluster (0,1,2), Forte number 3-1, that is, the entire tonal harmonic material.

DIATONIC SCALE

```
[C:]  I   II   III  IV   V    VI   VII      [a:]  i    ii   biii  iv   v    bvi  bvii
[a:]  biii iv  v    bvi  bvii i    ii       [C:]  VI   VII  I     II   III  IV   V
```

HARMONIC MINOR SCALE

```
[a:]  i    ii   biii  iv   v    bvi  vii
[C:]  VI   VII  I     II   III  IV   (#V)
```

HARMONIC MAJOR SCALE

```
[C:]  I   II   III  IV   V    bVI   VII
CHM:  I   II   III  IV   V    bVI   VII
```

MELODIC MINOR SCALE

```
dM   i    ii   biii  iv   v    vi   vii
C:        II   III   IV   V    VI   VII   #I
```

SCALE SUPERIMPOSITION - SUMMARY - [C:] and [a:] Tonal Center

	C	C#	D		E	F		G	G#/Ab	A	B
[C:]	I	bII	II		III	IV		V	#V/bVI	VI	VII
[a:]	biii	(iii)	iv		v	bvi		bvii	vii	i	ii
	´1	´b2	´2		´3	´4		´5	´#5/´b6	´6	´7
7-35	C		D		E	F		G		a	B
7-34		C#	d		E	F		G		A	B
7-32	C		D		E	F			G#	a	B
7-32b	C		D		E	F		G	Ab	A	B

7-35 (**C**) Diatonic (major) scale and (**a**) natural minor scale

7-34 Acoustic Scale - (**d**) Melodic minor scale

7-32 Hm - Harmonic minor scale (**a**)

7-32b HM - Harmonic major scale (**C**)

2. FUNCTIONAL HARMONY

In the historical process of tonality expansion, functions have been added and the harmony has been gradually encompassing the chromaticism. Secondary dominant function chords, borrowed modal chords, chords generated by chromatic mediants, reharmonizations based on fixed formal schemes, similar structure chords (parallelism), symmetrical chords (diminished and augmented) with large modulatory possibility, chromatic approach chords and passing chords enlarged the harmonic possibilities.

From the set theory analysis, I have noticed that all the harmonic structures that do not contain three consecutive chromatic notes (3-1 trichord) belong to a finite system of scales. In fact, all four-note chords belong to 4 basic scales of seven notes (7-35, diatonic, 7-34, acoustic or melodic minor and 7-32, major and minor harmonic scales) and two more auxiliary scales (8 -28, octatonic scale and 6-35, whole tone scale).

The table in the example 2a shows all four-note sets and the scales that contain them.

In table 2a, we see that most four-note sets are subsets of only two scales: 7-35 (diatonic scale) and 7-32 (harmonic minor scale or the diatonic scale with the fifth degree altered upwards).

2a

Forte	PF(a)	IF(b)	
4-1:	(0,1,2,3)		*Superset of 3-1*
4-2:	(0,1,2,4)	[0,2,3,4]	*Superset of 3-1*
4-3:	(0,1,3,4)		7-32a,7-32b, 7-34, 8-28
4-4:	(0,1,2,5)	[0,3,4,5]	*Superset of 3-1*
4-5:	(0,1,2,6)	[0,4,5,6]	*Superset of 3-1*
4-6:	(0,1,2,7)		*Superset of 3-1*
4-7:	(0,1,4,5)		7-32a, 732b
4-8:	(0,1,5,6)		**7-35**, 7-32a, 7-32b
4-9:	(0,1,6,7) (6)		8-28
4-10:	(0,2,3,5)		**7-35**, 7-32a, 7-32b, 7-34, 8-28
4-11:	(0,1,3,5)	[0,2,4,5]	**7-35**, 7-32a, 7-32b, 7-34
4-12:	(0,2,3,6)	[0,3,4,6]	7-32a, 7-32b, 7-34, 8-28
4-13:	(0,1,3,6)	[0,3,5,6]	**7-35**, 7-32a, 7-32b, 7-34, 8-28
4-14:	(0,2,3,7)	[0,4,5,7]	**7-35**, 7-32a, 7-32b, 7-34
4-Z15:	(0,1,4,6)	[0,2,5,6]	(a) 7-32a, 7-34, 8-28 (b) 7-32b, 7-34, 8-28
4-Z29:	(0,1,3,7)	[0,4,6,7]	(a) **7-35**, 7-34, 7-32b, 8-28 (b) **7-35**, 7-34, 7-32a, 8-28
4-16:	(0,1,5,7)	[0,2,6,7]	**7-35**, 7-32a, 7-32b, 7-34
4-17:	(0,3,4,7)		7-32a, 7-32b, 8-28
4-18:	(0,1,4,7)	[0,3,6,7]	7-32a, 7-32b, 8-28
4-19:	(0,1,4,8) m7M	[0,3,4,8]	7-32a, 7-32b, 7-34
4-20:	(0,1,5,8) 7M		**7-35**, 7-32a, 7-32b
4-21:	(0,2,4,6)		**7-35**, 7-34, 6-35
4-22:	(0,2,4,7)	[0,3,5,7]	**7-35**, 7-32b, 7-34
4-23:	(0,2,5,7) Q4		**7-35**, 7-32a, 7-32b, 7-34
4-24:	(0,2,4,8) 7(#5)		7-32a, 7-32b, 7-34, 6-35
4-25:	(0,2,6,8) Fr6 (6)		7-34, 8-28, 6-35
4-26:	(0,3,5,8) m7, 6		**7-35**, 7-32a, 7-32b, 7-34, 8-28
4-27:	(0,2,5,8) ø	[0,3,6,8] 7	**7-35**, 7-32a, 7-32b, 7-34, 8-28
4-28:	(0,3,6,9) ° (3)		7-32a, 7-32b, 8-28

Thus, a single tonal center can incorporate all the necessary harmonic structures.

The harmonic structure itself already points to the scale at which it is contained. Chords and scales can be considered both sides of a same coin.

In both the compositional practice and in improvisation, we often use different scales for each chord that occurs in harmonic progression, especially when the movement between the chords can not be identified with a single tonal center. Study the example of SubV.

The example 2b shows:

a) the analysis of SubV, considering this function as a chromatic enlargement of the tonal center [C:];
b) the analysis we propose here, subsuming the Db7(9) chord to the tonal center [Gb:];
c) the second analysis is more useful because it indicates the most appropriate scale for improvising on each chord, as we see in the example;
d) in the case of Db7(9,#11) below, we may use the [Gb:] scale, changing the 'Gb note for 'G note, thus generating the lydian b7 mode of Db (Ab melodic minor scale).

At the end of Chapter 7, we will present the analysis of various current situations, using our system of tonal organization.

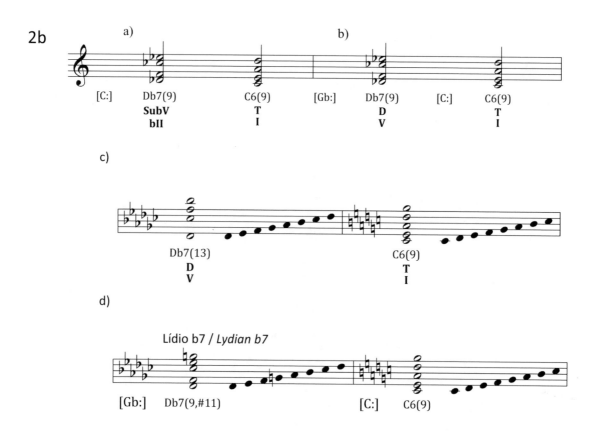

2.1 FUNCTIONAL NOTATION

In order to use functional notation, we need to organize the harmonic content of the scales of our tonal system into three functional axes: the tonic axis, the dominant axis and the subdominant axis.

Although we can use chords of all types (discussed later) in all three functions, we must consider that the functionality concept started from harmony based on chord stacks with expanded triads and seventh chords, i.e. chords resulting from the superimposition of sucessive thirds (9th, 11th and 13th added to the traditional seventh chord).

2.2 SUPERIMPOSITION OF THIRDS CHORD MODEL

Table 2.2 shows:

a) the superimposition (stacking) of thirds chord model starting at any root note;
b) a scale organized sequentially. In this case, the fourth degree of the diatonic scale, called Lydian mode that goes from 'F note to the'F octave higher note in [C:];
c) the Lydian mode of the previous example, organized according to the superimposition (stack) of thirds chord model;
d) the entanglement of three-note and four-note chords juxtaposed in the chord stack. In three-note chords, the last two notes of the previous chord are the first two notes of the next chord. There are two common notes between two diatonic triads separated by thirds. In four-note chords, the last three notes of the previous chord are the first three notes of the next chord. There are three common notes between two diatonic seventh chords separated by thirds.

2.2   STACK OF THIRDS CHORD MODEL

a) Stack of Thirds

| T | 3 | 5 | 7 | (9 | 11 | 13) |

b) Scale

F	G	A	B	C	D	E	F
T	2M	3M	4A	5J	6M	7M	

c) Lydian Mode Stack of Thirds

F	A	C	E	(G	B	D)	F	
T	3M	5J	7M	(9M	11A	13M)	T	F7M(9,#11,13)[*]

---

*In Standard American songbooks, the chord F7M appears
  as Fmaj7 or sometimes as FΔ.

d) Common tones between chords

F	A	C	E	G	B	D				F6/ 7M (9,#11)
F	A	C								F
	A	C	E							Am
		C	E	G						C
			E	G	B					Em
				G	B	D				G
					B	D	F			Bdim
						D	F	A		Dm

F	A	C	E	G	B	D				F6/ 7M (9,#11)
F	A	C	E							F7M
	A	C	E	G						Am7
		C	E	G	B					C7M
			E	G	B	D				Em7
				G	B	D	F			G7
					B	D	F	A		Bm7b5
						D	F	A	C	Dm7

In the chord stack model shown in a), the intervals are named as "generic intervals", that is, 3 may be a major third (3M) or a minor third (3m); 5 may be a perfect fifth (5J), diminished (5D) or augmented (5A), depending on the scale degree we start (mode). The concept of "generic intervals"(discussed later in Chapter 4) will also be used when discussing the chord typology and voicings.

From this chord stack model, we can use all notes of the scale on a single chord. In the example c) we use all the notes of the scale and it is only necessary to go up to the 13 (thirteenth), because a third added to 13 equals T (root note, starting point). We can summarize the content of this chord stack in one chord only: F7M (9, #11, 13). As the 6M is commonly added to major and minor chord triads, we will use it in the position of the 13M. Thus, the chord synthesis of IV mode (Lydian) in [C:] will be: F6 / 7M (9, #11).

2.3 TONAL SYSTEM - AXES

The concept that chords separated by thirds have common notes allows axes to include chords that have a similar functional effect. There are three basic stations, also called regions or functional axes. In Chapter 7 we will explore the cadence movements through the tonal cycle.

T (TONIC AXIS), I degree, represented in [C:] by the chords C, C6 or C7M. As tonal function, it is characterized by rest, feeling of completion, "feeling of being home," stability, low expectation, simplicity. (END NOTE 4)

S (SUBDOMINANT AXIS), IV degree, represented in [C:] by the chords, F, F6 or F7M. As tonal function, it is characterized by preceding the preparation, by movement away from rest, exploration, argumentation, uncertainty, increasing complexity.

D (DOMINANT AXIS), V degree, represented in [C:] by the chord G7. As tonal function, it is characterized by tension, conflict, high expectation, complexity.

2.3.1 TONAL CYCLE / CHORD PROGRESSION

The idea of "Rest - Movement - Tension - Rest" can be expressed in chords as "C - F - G - C "; in degrees as " I - IV - V – I" and finally in functions as "T - S - D - T ". There are three different ways of expressing the progression: according to the chords used (chord symbols), according to the degrees used (degree convention), and according to the functions of tonal perspective (functional notation). (END NOTE 5)

From the notion of tones in common, note the table (ex. 2.3.1a).

In major tonality, the diatonic chord that is one third below the I degree chord (tonic axis chord), i.e. the chord located in the VI degree, will have the tonic major relative function, named **Tr**. The abbreviation **Tr** in this case means the minor chord (lower case letter r) related to the Tonic major chord (capital letter T), and refers to the chord Am7. The abbreviation **Ta** means the chord that is one third above the Tonic chord, i.e. the chord Em7, and will be called the tonic major antirelative. (END NOTE 6)

Note the strong relationship that the chord C6 ('C, 'E, 'G, 'A) has with the chord Am7 ('A, ' C, 'E, 'G), since they have exactly the same tones, which strengthens the relationship between T and **Tr**. (Ex. 2.3.1b)

2.3   TONAL SYSTEM - AXES

2.3.1a

T		
VI	I	III
Tr	T	Ta
Am7	C7M	Em7
A		
C	C	
E	E	E
G	G	G
	B	B
		D

2.3.1b

I	VI
T	Tr
C6	Am7
C	C
E	E
G	G
A	A

From this same idea, we can build the subdominant axis and the dominant axis similarly, based on the common tones between the chords arranged in thirds. (ex. 2.3.1c).

2.3.1c

S	
II	IV
Sr	S
Dm7	F7M
D	
F	F
A	A
C	C
	E

D	
V	VII
D	Đ9
G7	Bø
G	
B	B
D	D
F	F
	A

Comments: It is also possible to think of Am7 as **Sa** (subdominant major antirelative), but its strongest function in [C:] is as **Tr** (tonic major relative). Similarly, it is possible to think of Em7 as a **Dr** (dominant major relative), but the characteristic trait of the dominant function is to contain simultaneously the notes 'B and 'F, creating the tritone interval, which is not present in Em7 chord.

Below, we show the functional axes in a more comprehensively way, including the variations resulting from the scales superimposition mentioned above: 7-34 (acoustic or melodic minor, generated by the substitution of the 'C for the 'C# note) and 7-32b (harmonic major generated by the substitution of the 'Ab for the 'A note).

2.4 MAJOR TONALITY– FUNCTIONAL AXES

2.4.1 TONIC AXIS IN [C:]

Note: The chord F#m7b5, despite being out of the scale superimposition system, may be used as a relative function of the tonic major with the sixth in the bass, that is, **Tr/6** (Am6=F#m7b5). The same tone 'F# can be used to create a Lydian tonic in chord C7M(#11), represented by **Tlyd**. These two chords relate more to the tonal center [G:] than to the tonal center [C:] and for this reason they are in parentheses. These functions suggest the expansion and the inter-relationship between the tonal centers, specially among those centers which are neighbors, as we can notice with [C:] and [G:].

2.4.1   TONIC AXIS in [C:]

[C:]	T			
	(#IV) ant	VI	I	III
	(Tr/6)	Tr	T	Ta
	(F#ø)	Am7	C7M	Em7

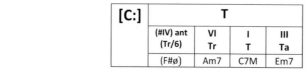

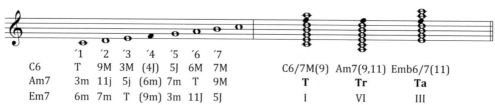

	'1	'2	'3	'4	'5	'6	'7			
C6	T	9M	3M	(4J)	5J	6M	7M	C6/7M(9)	Am7(9,11)	Emb6/7(11)
Am7	3m	11j	5j	(6m)	7m	T	9M	**T**	**Tr**	**Ta**
Em7	6m	7m	T	(9m)	3m	11J	5J	I	VI	III

T - Tonic Major

Tr - Tonic Major relative (Parallel)

Ta - Tonic Major antirrelative (Counter Parallel)

D - Dominant major. In the diatonic scale (7-35) over this degree we have the G7,4 (9,13) chord or G7sus4 (dominant chord with a suspended fourth), emphasizing the fourth instead of the third, in addition to the G7(9,13) with the fourth acting as a passing tone.

From the acoustic scale (7-34), we have the G7 (9, #11,13) chord without avoided tones. Consider the relationship that exists between degrees V and bII, respectively **D** and **Dalt**.

Note: This chord, in a blues context, may be used as tonic blues, represented by **Tblues**, featuring rest and non - stress feeling, contrary to the tense character of the dominant axis.

Đ9 - Dominant with the ninth (omitted root). From the acoustic scale (7-34), we have Bø (9,11, b13), without avoided tones.

Dalt - The C#7 (alt) chord comes from the acoustic scale generated by the subtitution of 'C for the 'C# note (D melodic minor, 7-34). Its functional chord symbol is **Dalt** (altered dominant). This degree provides a C#7 (T, 3M and 7m) chord with all alterations of the ninth and fifth (b9, #9, b5, #5) that are commonly summarized as (alt.). There are no avoided tones. The perfect fifth is not present.

The Sub V chord – Usually, the **SubV** is a dominant seventh chord built on the bII degree and it may contain the (9, #11, 13) tensions. Then, in a song in the [C:] tonality, the **SubV** is the Db7(9, #11, 13) chord. However, we will analyze the SubV as a chord of the V degree of a tone, so Db7 will be understood as belonging to [Gb:]. See the explanation in the beginning of the chapter (ex. 2b).

2.4.2   DOMINANT AXIS in [C:]

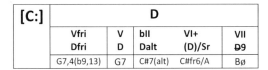

[C:]	D				
Vfri	**V**	**bII**	**VI+**	**VII**	
Dfri	**D**	**Dalt**	**(D)/Sr**	**Đ9**	
G7,4(b9,13)	G7	C#7(alt)	C#fr6/A	Bø	

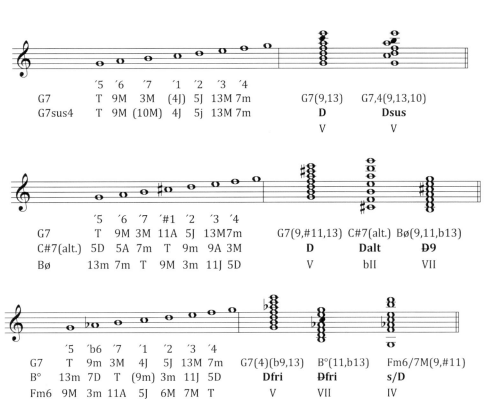

In the example 2.4.2a:
a) the traditional analysis of SubV, subsuming this function as an enlargement of the tonal center [C:];
b) the analysis we propose here, subsuming the Db7(9, #11) chord to the tonal center [Gb:].

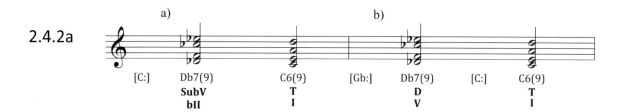

DFri - Phrygian dominant major – this function comes from the major harmonic scale and it corresponds to dfri (Phrygian dominant minor) that we will discuss in the minor tonal center. The harmonic major scale (7-32b) also has a subdominant minor chord, which will be incorporated in our center in [C:]. This subdominant minor chord with the bass in the dominant generates the **Dfri** sound.

(D)/Sr - The French sixth chord (Fr6) C#7(b5), with the bass note in tone 'A, creates a A7 (#5,9) chord that works as dominant of the subdominant relative (Dm7) or **(D)/Sr**. Being a secondary dominant, i.e. a dominant of a degree that is not the tonic, we put the D in parentheses. The degree convention will be VI+, that is, the sixth degree exceptionally major, since this degree is usually minor: **Tr**, Am7 in [C:]. The "+" symbol also indicates that in this degree (VI+) we can build an augmented triad (Forte 3-12), a symmetrical chord that may have a dominant function, that is, F/A/C#(#5). The chord Fr6 (sixth French, Forte number 4-25) has limited transpositions (6). Thus, C#7(b5) = G7 (b5), and both prepare for T and to **Sr**, as well. (Ex 2.4.2b)

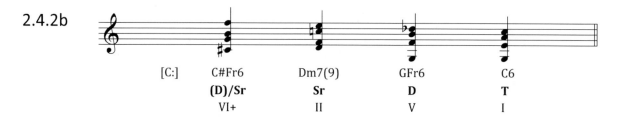

2.4.2.1 TRITONE (LEADING TONES)

The tones 'F ('4) and 'B ('7) have, respectively, the roles of superior and inferior leading tones. The chords of the dominant axis (**D** and **Dalt** functions) have these two tones, forming what we call leading tone in two voices (tritone).

Note that [C:] and [Gb:] tonalities have exactly the same tritone. For this reason, these two tones are connected (though in the circle of fifths they occupy distant positions), corresponding to what is called "antipode," a term meaning two diametrically opposite points on a sphere. In the circle of fifths, the tonal center [Gb:] is the farthest possible from the tonal center [C:]. See also 7.9.2.

2.4.2.1 TRITONE (LEADING TONE)

In the subdominant axis of the tonal center [a:] we have two functions:

S - subdominant major, F7M chord;

Sr – minor relative of subdominant major, Dm7 chord;

s/3 – subdominant minor of the tonal center [C:]. From the change of tone 'A to 'Ab, we have the harmonic major scale, which will work in [C:] analogously to the harmonic minor scale in [a:]. Thus, in [C:] we have the possibility of obtaining a kind of minor subdominant.

Between the parentheses, we show the F#m7b5 chord, built on the #IV degree that may have subdominant function in some contexts. However it will not be considered as part of the [C:] center, but rather borrowed from the [G:] center.

The chords found in the subdominant axis may also take a tonic function in certain contexts because of their stable character:

a) for example, a song in [C:] may end with a C7M(#11);

b) in the context of chord sequences out of the tonal cycle, especially for long duration chords in modal harmony, 7M(#11) chords are commonly used and we will call them **Tlyd** or **Lydian Tonic**.

In tonalities or cadences ending in minor chords it is common to use chords such as m7(9,11,13), m6(9) or m6/7M (9). Therefore:

a) a song in [d:] ending with a Dm7(13) chord indicates a chord derived from the Dorian mode that we will call **Tdor**, or **Dorian Tonic**.

b) in the context of chord sequences out of the tonal cycle, especially for long duration chords in modal harmony, it is common to use m7(9,11,13)chords that we will call **Tdor** or **Dorian Tonic**.

c) the m6/7M (9,11) "minor tonic chord" can be built from the Dorian mode with the 7M, thus a melodic minor scale. We will call this function **Tmel**.

2.4.3 SUBDOMINANT AXIS in [C:]

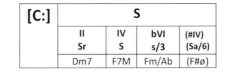

[C:]	S			
	II	IV	bVI	(#IV)
	Sr	S	s/3	(Sa/6)
	Dm7	F7M	Fm/Ab	(F#ø)

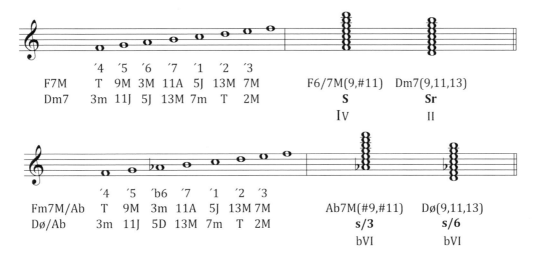

Next, we will build a similar model over the minor tonality.

In the minor tonal center, the functions are represented by lower case letters. Similar to the major tonal center, we have three basic functions:

t (tonic minor), i degree, represented in [a:] by the chords Am or Am7
s (subdominant minor), iv degree, represented in [a:] by the chords Dm or Dm7
d (dominant minor), v degree, represented in [a:] by the chord Em7
d+ (dominant major of a minor tonality), v+ degree, represented in [a:] by the chord E7

As we have seen before, the minor scale is polyscalar, i.e., in the minor tonal center we think of different forms of the minor scale. The harmonic minor scale in [a:] generates the note 'G# to serve as a leading tone ascending to the tonic of a minor chord, the note 'A. This way, it is possible to obtain an E7 chord on the v+ degree of the minor scale [a:].

In the example 2.5 we have:

a) the chord E7(b9) with the leading tone 'G# resolving in 'A, and 'D resolving in 'C. This resolution is similar to that in the major tonal center, where the tritone 'B –'F, present in the G7 chord, resolves in the C chord;

b) the E7(b9) chord also containing the leading tone 'B, which resolves in the tone 'C, being an example of leading tone in three voices.

2.5   MINOR TONALITY - FUNCTIONAL AXES

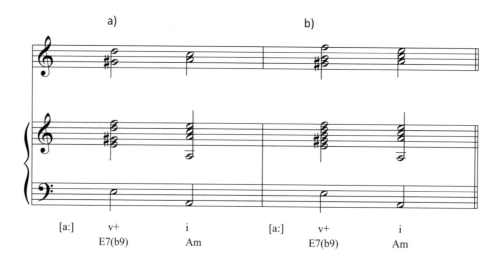

To differ between degree and functional chord symbol, we use different symbols according to the chord used in the fifth degree. For dominant minor, that is Em7 in [a:], we use the v degree symbol and d functional symbol (dominant minor). When the dominant is major, that is E7 in [a:], we use v+ degree symbol and d+ (dominant major of minor tonality).

Note that in the minor tonal center, the positions are reversed in comparison to the major tonal center. In the minor tonality, the chord that is one third above the chord of i degree (main chord of the tonic minor axis), that is the chord located in biii degree, will be called the tonic major relative and symbolized by **tR**. The abbreviation **tR** in this case means the major chord (capital R) that is related to the tonic minor chord (lower case t), i.e., the C7M chord. In the natural minor scale (and also in the harmonic scale), the chord that is one third below the i degree (Am7) is F7M, which has no tonic function. In accordance with the traditional form of the melodic minor scale of [a:] (which contains the tone 'F#'), we will use the chord (F#m7b5) as **t/6**, that is the tonic minor chord with the sixth in the bass (F#m7b5=Am6). The use of parentheses indicates that it is out the main core of the scales. This function is usually called tonic minor chord, in this case a Am6/7M (9,11). The function of the tonic minor chord is represented by **tmel**. In our analysis, the tonic minor chord Am6/7M quoted above will be considered as originating from a II degree in [G:] tonality, i.e. a chord from the subdominant axis used as tonic (see item 2.4.3).

From the harmonic minor scale, where we have the note 'G# in place of the tone 'G, the chords Am7M and C7M(#5) may function as the tonic minor (**t**) and tonic minor relative (**tR**), respectively. Note that these chords contain an augmented triad, a structure of limited transpositions (4), Forte number 3-12 (0,4,8).

2.5.1 TONIC AXIS in [a:]

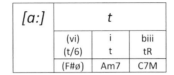

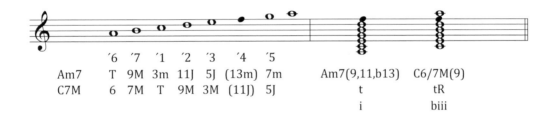

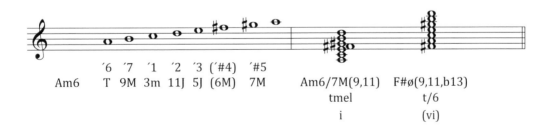

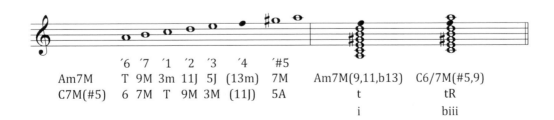

Due to the polyscalar nature of the minor scale and to the idea of scale superimposition that we refer to, the dominant axis of the minor tonal center involves four functions:

d - dominant minor, chord Em7, based on the natural form of the minor scale

dfri - Phrygian dominant, generating the Dm/E chord ('A natural minor) or Dm7M/E (based on the acoustic scale, 7-34), which can also be written as E7, 4(b9,13)

d+ - dominant major of the minor scale, generating the E7(b9,b13) chord from the harmonic minor scale*

Đb9 - diminished chord rooted on the seventh degree, traditionally regarded as a dominant chord with the seventh and ninth (omitted root), e.g. G#°= E7(b9) without the root 'E

(*) We use the "+" sign indicating:

1) the presence of a major chord on the dominant minor, but we have kept the lower case "**d**" to indicate that it is the dominant in the [a:] minor tonal center

2) in this degree (v degree) we can build an augmented triad G#/C/E (#5), Forte 3-12 (048), a symmetrical chord of limited transpositions (4) which also acts as dominant. So on the tone 'G# (vii+ degree) we can build a diminished chord (4-28) and an augmented chord (3-12). On the tone 'F (degree bvi) is still possible to build both F° (4-28) and F(#5) chords (3-12).

2.5.2   DOMINANT AXIS in [a:]

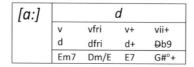

[a:]		d		
	v	vfri	v+	vii+
	d	dfri	d+	Đb9
	Em7	Dm/E	E7	G#°+

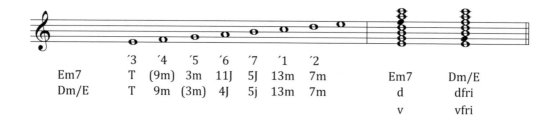

	'3	'4	'5	'6	'7	'1	'2			
Em7	T	(9m)	3m	11J	5J	13m	7m		Em7	Dm/E
Dm/E	T	9m	(3m)	4J	5j	13m	7m		d	dfri
									v	vfri

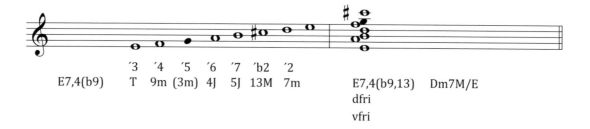

	'3	'4	'5	'6	'7	'b2	'2			
E7,4(b9)	T	9m	(3m)	4J	5J	13M	7m		E7,4(b9,13)	Dm7M/E
									dfri	
									vfri	

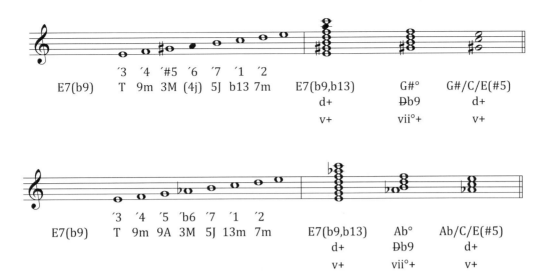

			'3	'4	'#5	'6	'7	'1	'2			
E7(b9)			T	9m	3M	(4j)	5J	b13	7m	E7(b9,b13)	G#°	G#/C/E(#5)
										d+	Db9	d+
										v+	vii°+	v+

			'3	'4	'5	'b6	'7	'1	'2			
E7(b9)			T	9m	9A	3M	5J	13m	7m	E7(b9,b13)	Ab°	Ab/C/E(#5)
										d+	Db9	d+
										v+	vii°+	v+

From the harmonic major scale, we have an interesting variation of the dominant axis that can be thought of as an altered scale with the 5J (perfect fifth). See the last scale of the ex. 2.5.2.

2.5.3 SUBDOMINANT AXIS IN [a:]

In the subdominant axis of the tonal center [a:] we have four functions:

s - subdominant minor, Dm7 chord
sR – major relative of subdominant minor, F7M chord
s/6 - subdominant minor with the sixth in the bass, Bm7b5 = Dm6
s6/4 - subdominant minor with added sixth and the fourth in the bass. The G7 chord can be thought as a Dm6(11).

2.5.3   SUBDOMINANT AXIS in [a:]

[a:]	s			
	bvii	ii	iv	bvi
	s6/4	s/6	s	sR
	G7	Bø	Dm7	F7M

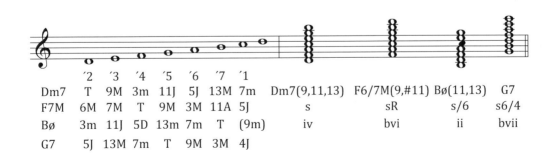

		'2	'3	'4	'5	'6	'7	'1				
Dm7		T	9M	3m	11J	5J	13M	7m	Dm7(9,11,13)	F6/7M(9,#11)	Bø(11,13)	G7
F7M		6M	7M	T	9M	3M	11A	5J	s	sR	s/6	s6/4
Bø		3m	11J	5D	13m	7m	T	(9m)	iv	bvi	ii	bvii
G7		5J	13M	7m	T	9M	3M	4J				

2.6 SYMMETRICAL AXES

2.6.1 OCTATONIC DOMINANT AXIS

From the octatonic scale (8-28) or Messiaen mode number 2, which has limited transpositions (3), we can build four dominant chords that can also contain the extensions (b9, #9, #11,13), as we see in 2.6.1.

The **Doct** function (octatonic dominant) corresponds precisely to the degrees of the dominant axes previously presented, except for degree (bii, ´Bb) which is not present in our scale superimposition system. The (bii) degree is in parentheses because the tone ´Bb is not part of the center [C:] or [a:] in the scale superimposition system.

2.6.1   Octatonic Dominant Axis

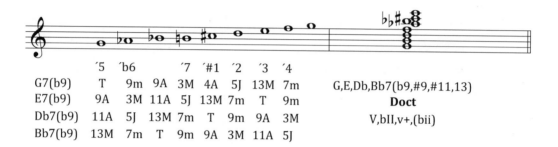

	´5	´b6	´7	´#1	´2	´3	´4	
G7(b9)	T	9m	9A	3M	4A	5J	13M	7m
E7(b9)	9A	3M	11A	5J	13M	7m	T	9m
Db7(b9)	11A	5J	13M	7m	T	9m	9A	3M
Bb7(b9)	13M	7m	T	9m	9A	3M	11A	5J

G,E,Db,Bb7(b9,#9,#11,13)

Doct

V,bII,v+,(bii)

2.6.2 OCTATONIC DIMINISHED AXIS

From the same octatonic scale, we can build four diminished chords, as shown in 2.6.2, forming the function **Ddim** that can be applied on the degrees that contain diminished chords, i.e., the degrees VII in [C:] and vii in [a:].

2.6.2   Octatonic Diminished Axis

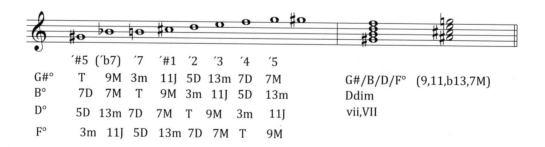

	´#5	(´b7)	´7	´#1	´2	´3	´4	´5	
G#°	T	9M	3m	11J	5D	13m	7D	7M
B°	7D	7M	T	9M	3m	11J	5D	13m
D°	5D	13m	7D	7M	T	9M	3m	11J
F°	3m	11J	5D	13m	7D	7M	T	9M

G#/B/D/F° (9,11,b13,7M)

Ddim

vii,VII

Note that the **Doct** and **Ddim** axes, due to their symmetrical nature, may be part of four distinct tonal centers: [C:] [a:], [A:] [f#:], [Gb:] [eb:] and [Eb] [c:].

From the whole tone scale (6-35) or Messiaen mode number 1, which has limited transpositions (2), we can build six dominant chords that can also contain the extensions (#5,9,#11) as shown in 2.6.3.

The **DWT** (dominant whole-tone) function occurs where there are dominant chords with 5A, that is, on the degrees V, bII and VI+. Moreover, in another possible transposition for this scale, we can apply it on the v+ degree (on the dominant of the minor tonality).

2.6.3   Whole-Tone Dominante Axis

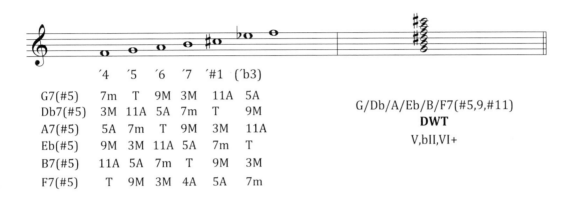

	′4	′5	′6	′7	′#1	(′b3)
G7(#5)	7m	T	9M	3M	11A	5A
Db7(#5)	3M	11A	5A	7m	T	9M
A7(#5)	5A	7m	T	9M	3M	11A
Eb(#5)	9M	3M	11A	5A	7m	T
B7(#5)	11A	5A	7m	T	9M	3M
F7(#5)	T	9M	3M	4A	5A	7m

G/Db/A/Eb/B/F7(#5,9,#11)
DWT
V,bII,VI+

Note that the **Doct** may be part of six distinct tonal centers: [C:] [a:], [Gb:] [eb:], [D:] [b:], [Ab:] [f:], [E:] [c#:] and [Bb:] [g:].

2.7   USUAL CHORD SYMBOLS RELATED TO HARMONIC FUNCTION

			Symbols	Chord	Usual Symbols
bVI°+	s/3	Fm/Ab		Ab7M(#9,#11)	
IV bvi	S sR	F7M	☆ △3 ⬤5 ⬛6 ⬛7M ⬡9 ⬛#11	F6/7M(9,#11)	F, F6, F7M, F7M(9), F7M(#11)*
ii iv	Sr s	Dm7	☆ℝ m ⬤5 ⬛7 ⬡9 ⬡11 ⬛13	Dm6/7(9,11)	Dm, Dm6, Dm7, Dm7(9), Dm7(13).
II	Sr	Dm7	☆ℝ m ⬤5 ⬛6 ⬛7M ⬡9 ⬡11	Dm6/7M (9,11)**	Dm7M, Dm7M(9),Dm6(7M).
VII ii	Đ9 s/6	Bø	☆ℝ m ⬛b5 ⬛7 ⬡9 ⬡11 ▲b13	Bø (9,11,b13)	Bm7(b5), Bø(9), Bø(11)
VI+	Đ/Sr	Db7(alt)-C#fr6/A-	☆ℝ △3 ▲#5 ⬛7 ⬡9 ⬛#11	A7#5 (9,#11)	A7(#5), A7(#11), A7#5(9).
bII	Dalt	Db7(alt)-C#fr6/A-	☆ △3 ⬛b5 ▲#5 ⬛7 ⬡b9 ⬜#9	Db7(alt)	Db7 (b9,#9,b5,#5)
V bvii	D s6/4-	G7	☆ △3 ⬤5 ⬛7 ⬡9 ⬜#11 ⬛13	G7(9,#11,13)	G7, G7(#11), G7(9,#11), G7(#11,13)
		G7	☆ sus4 ⬤5 ⬛7 ⬡9 △10 ⬛13	G7(4)(9,13)	G7,G7(9,13), G7sus4, F/G, F7M/G
		G7	☆ △3 ⬤5 ⬛7 ⬡b9 ⬜#9 ⬜#11 ⬛13	G7(b9,#9,#11,13)	G7, G7(b9), G7(b9,13)
Vfri	Dfri	Fm/G-		G7(4) (b9,13)	
vii°+	Đb9	G#°+	☆ m ⬛b5 ⬛7° ⬡9 ⬡11 ▲b13 ⬤7M	G#°(9,11,b13,7M)	G#/B/D/F ° G#°(b13)
v+	d+	E7		E7(b9,b13)	E7, E7(b9), E7(b9,13)
v- vfri-	d- dfri-	Dm/E-	☆ℝ sus4 ⬤5 ⬛7 ⬡b9 ⬜#9 ⬛13	E7(4) (b9,13)	E7sus4(b9,13)
		Dm/E-	☆ℝ sus4 ⬤5 ⬛7 ⬡b9 ⬜#9 ▲b13	Dm/E , F/E	E7sus4, Dm/E, F/E
III	Ta	Em7-			Em7, Em7(#5), [E7(#9)]
biii	tR	C			C, C6, C6(9), C7M, C7M(9), C7M(#5)
VI i I	Tr t T	Am7			Am, Am7, Am7(9), Am7M
[C:]					
[a:]					

---

*   Fmaj7 or FΔ in some fakebooks.

**   (♭) D-maj7 or D-Δ in some fakebooks.

2.8 SCALE / FUNCTION RELATIONSHIP

Degree reference (left header):

[C:]	I	bII	II	III	IV	V	#V	VI	VII
[a:]	biii	v	iv	bvi	v	vii	i	ii	
deg	'1		'2	'3	'4	'5	'6	'7	

Scale / Function matrix:

Scale	Fn [C:]	Fn [a:]	Other fn	Chord	VII	VI	#V	V	IV	III	II	bII	I (tensions)	Set-class
Aeolian	VI	i	Tr · t · T	Am7	B	A		G	F	E	D		C	
Ionian	I	t	t · T · tR	C	B	A		G	F	E	D		**C**	7-35
Phrygian	III	d	Ta · d	Em7	B	A		G	F	E	D	C	C	
Phrygian 6M	vfri	dfri		Dm/E	B	A		G	F	E	D	C#	7(4) (b9,13)	7-34
Phrygian Major	v+	d+		E7	B	A	G#		F	E	D	C	(b9,b13)	7-32a
Diminished	vii°+	Ðb9	OCTA*	G#°+	B	(A#)	G#	G	F	E	D	C#	°(9,11 b13 7M)	8-28
Mixolydian 9m	Vfri	Dfri		Fm/G	B	Ab		**G**	F	E	D	C	7(4) (b9,13)	7-32b
Mixolydian	V	D	Tblues	G7	B	A		**G**	F	E	D	C	7(4) (9,13)	7-35
Dom Dim	(D)		OCTA	G7	B	Ab	(A#)	**G**	F	E	D	C#	(b9,#9 #11,13)	8-28
Lydian b7	bvii	s6/4	T/S blues		B	A		G	F	E	D	C#	(9,#11,13)	7-34
Altered	bII	Dalt		Db7(alt)	B	A		G		E	D	C#	7(b9,#9 b5,#5)	7-34
Whole-Tone	VI+	Ð/Sr	DWT	C#+6/A	B	A		G	(Eb)			C#	7(#5, 9,#11)	6-35
Locrian 9M	VII	Ð9 · ii · s/6		Bø	**B**	A		G	F	E	D	C#		7-34
Melodic Minor	II	Sr	Tmel	Dm	B	A		G	F	E	**D**	C#	m6/7M (9,11) / m7(9,11,13)	7-34
Dorian	iv	s	Tdor	Dm	B	A		G	F	E	**D**	C		7-35
Lydian	IV	S	TLyd	F7M	B	A		G	**F**	E	D	C	(9,#11,13)	7-35
Lydian Diminished	bvi	sR · bVI°+ · s/3		Fm/Ab	B	Ab		G	F	E	D	C		7-32b

* In the vii° degree the 7-32a scale (harmonic minor) can also be used: 'G# 'A 'B 'C 'D 'E 'F.

3. CARDINALITY 3 - CHORDS TYPOLOGY

HARMONIC CONTENT OF SCALE 7-35 (DIATONIC)

The diatonic scale (7-35) has the property of maintaining similar interval classes in specific "families", corresponding to what we called before a "diatonic step" (chapter 1). For example, the family of thirds contains a major and a minor third, the family of the fourths contains the perfect and augmented fourth and so on. Each family has two sizes of intervals. (END NOTE 7)

This property, when applied to chords of three or more notes, enables us to separate the chords into specific groups (typologies).

As chord typology, we understand the organization of the harmonic content according to the forms of building (chords built by chord stacks of thirds, fourths, seconds, etc.).

3.1 "A" TYPOLOGY - TRIADS (please refer to page 48)

In typology "A" of three-note chords, all the chords on all degrees are built according to the superimposition of two thirds, i.e., they are all traditional triads.

Note that the Forte numbers are not repeated in all chords, only in those that are different and appear in each typology.

3.2 "B" TYPOLOGY – QUARTAL CHORDS

The same occurs with the "B" typology: all chords are superimposition of fourths.

The chord symbol **Q3** means two perfect fourths superimposed; **TQ** means superimposing a tritone and a perfect fourth and **QT** means superimposing a perfect fourth and a tritone.

3.3 "C" TYPOLOGY – SEVENTH WITHOUT THE FIFTH CHORDS

These chords are frequently used as framework or "shell voicings" for building seventh chords. Pianists use this type of chord (with the basic sounds of T, 3 and 7) in the left hand, supplementing the other ornamental tension (9,11,13) in the right hand or simply improvising a melodic line. (END NOTE 8)

The **C7M(¬5)** chord symbol means C7M with the fifth omitted.

The **D^m7** chord symbol means the D tone with the minor third and seventh added.

The **GIt** chord symbol means Italian sixth chord (T ,3M and 7m) or simply the most basic framework of the dominant chord.

3.4 "D" TYPOLOGY – SEVENTH WITHOUT THE THIRD CHORDS

The chord symbol **B^7(b5)** indicates the root with the addition (^) of the seventh and fifth (in parentheses). This chord is used as a basic framework of the m7(b5) chord.

3.5 "E" TYPOLOGY - CLUSTERS (THREE NOTE SEGMENTS)

Chords like **D^7(9)** can be viewed as the root, with the addition (^) of the seventh and ninth, or simply as clusters, segments of three consecutive notes (7, T, 9).

3.6   Card 3 - Tipology

3.6.1   7-35 Diatonic Scale

Card 3		
A	Triads	
B	Quartal Chords	Q3 QT , TQ
C	Seventh (no 5th)	7(¬5)
D	Seventh (no 3rd)	7(¬3)
E	Cluster 3 note Segments T 7 (9)	^7(9)

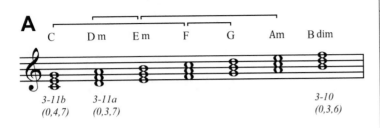

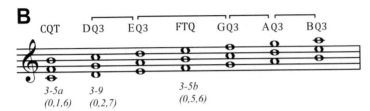

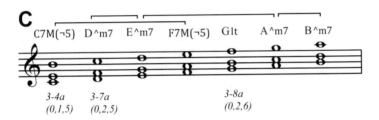

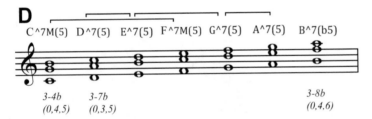

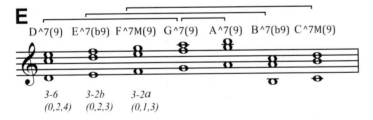

COMBINATORIAL HARMONY - BY JULIO HERRLEIN - MEL BAY

3.6.2　　7-32a Harmonic Minor Scale

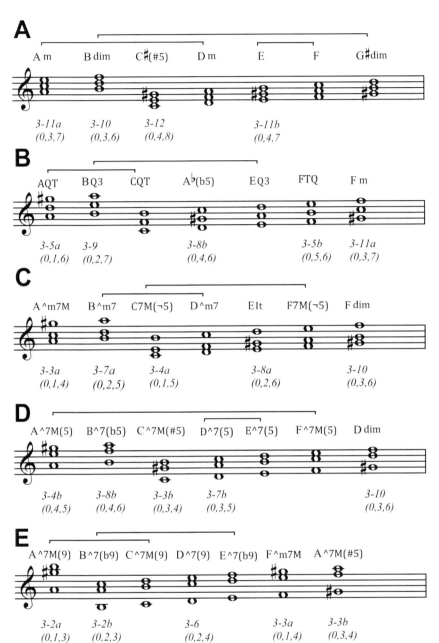

Card 3		
A	Triads	
B	Quartal Chords	Q3 QT , TQ
C	Seventh (no 5th)	7(¬5)
D	Seventh (no 3rd)	7(¬3)
E	Cluster 3 note Segments T 7 (9)	^7(9)

3.6.3   7-34 Melodic Minor Scale

Card 3		
A	Triads	
B	Quartal Chords	Q3 QT , TQ
C	Seventh (no 5th)	7(¬5)
D	Seventh (no 3rd)	7(¬3)
E	Cluster 3 note Segments T 7 (9)	^7(9)

A

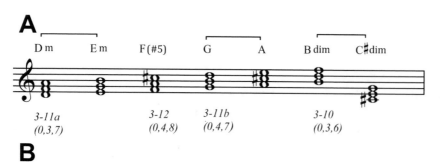

B

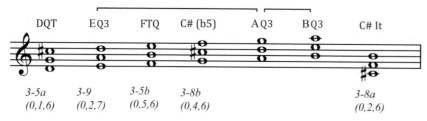

C

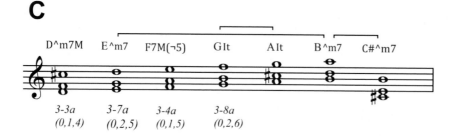

D

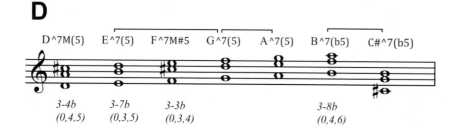

E

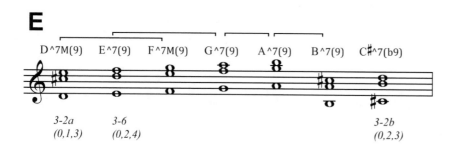

3.6.4   7-32b Harmonic Major Scale

Card 3		
A	Triads	
B	Quartal Chords	Q3 QT , TQ
C	Seventh (no 5th)	7(¬5)
D	Seventh (no 3rd)	7(¬3)
E	Cluster 3 note Segments T 7 (9)	^7(9)

A

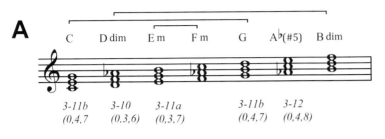

C   Ddim   Em   Fm   G   Ab(#5)   Bdim

3-11b   3-10   3-11a   3-11b   3-12
(0,4,7)   (0,3,6)   (0,3,7)   (0,4,7)   (0,4,8)

B

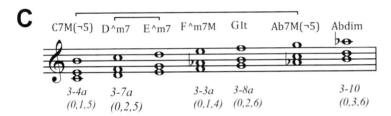

CQT   DQ3   EIt   FTQ   GQ3   AbTQ   E

3-5a   3-9   3-8a   3-5b   3-11b
(0,1,6)   (0,2,7)   (0,2,6)   (0,5,6)   (0,4,7)

C

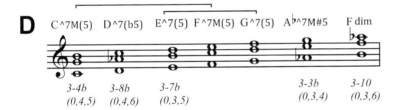

C7M(¬5)   D^m7   E^m7   F^m7M   GIt   Ab7M(¬5)   Abdim

3-4a   3-7a   3-3a   3-8a   3-10
(0,1,5)   (0,2,5)   (0,1,4)   (0,2,6)   (0,3,6)

D

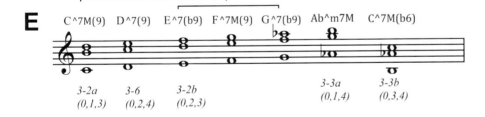

C^7M(5)   D^7(b5)   E^7(5)   F^7M(5)   G^7(5)   Ab^7M#5   Fdim

3-4b   3-8b   3-7b   3-3b   3-10
(0,4,5)   (0,4,6)   (0,3,5)   (0,3,4)   (0,3,6)

E

C^7M(9)   D^7(9)   E^7(b9)   F^7M(9)   G^7(b9)   Ab^m7M   C^7M(b6)

3-2a   3-6   3-2b   3-3a   3-3b
(0,1,3)   (0,2,4)   (0,2,3)   (0,1,4)   (0,3,4)

3.6.5 8-28 Octatonic Scale
Messiaen 2

Card 3		
A	Triads	
B	Quartal Chords	Q3 QT , TQ
C	Seventh (no 5th)	7(¬5)
D	Seventh (no 3rd)	7(¬3)
E	Cluster 3 note Segments T 7 (9)	^7(9)

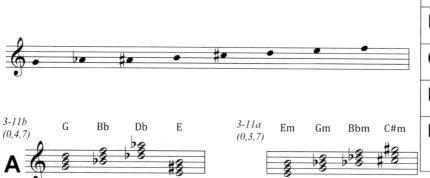

3-11b (0,4,7) G Bb Db E **A**
3-11a (0,3,7) Em Gm Bbm C#m

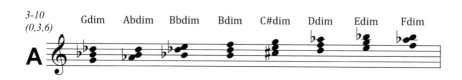

3-10 (0,3,6) Gdim Abdim Bbdim Bdim C#dim Ddim Edim Fdim **A**

3-5a (0,1,6) AbQT BQT DQT FQT **B**

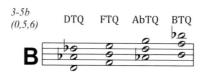

3-5b (0,5,6) DTQ FTQ AbTQ BTQ **B**

3-7a (0,2,5) Bb^m7 C#^m7 E^m7 G^m7 **C**

3-7b (0,3,5) C#^7(5) E^7(5) G^7(5) Bb^7(5) **D**

3-8a (0,2,6) GIt BbIt DbIt EIt **C**

3-8b (0,4,6) B^7(b5) D^7(b5) F^7(b5) Ab^7(b5) **D**

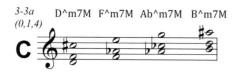

3-3a (0,1,4) D^m7M F^m7M Ab^m7M B^m7M **C**

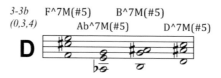

3-3b (0,3,4) F^7M(#5) B^7M(#5) Ab^7M(#5) D^7M(#5) **D**

3-2a (0,1,3) Ab^7M(9) B^7M(9) D^7M(9) F^7M(9) **E**

3-2b (0,2,3) Bb^7(b9) Db^7(b9) E7(b9) G7(b9) **E**

COMBINATORIAL HARMONY - BY JULIO HERRLEIN - MEL BAY

9-12 Nonatonic Scale
Messiaen 3

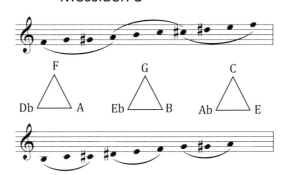

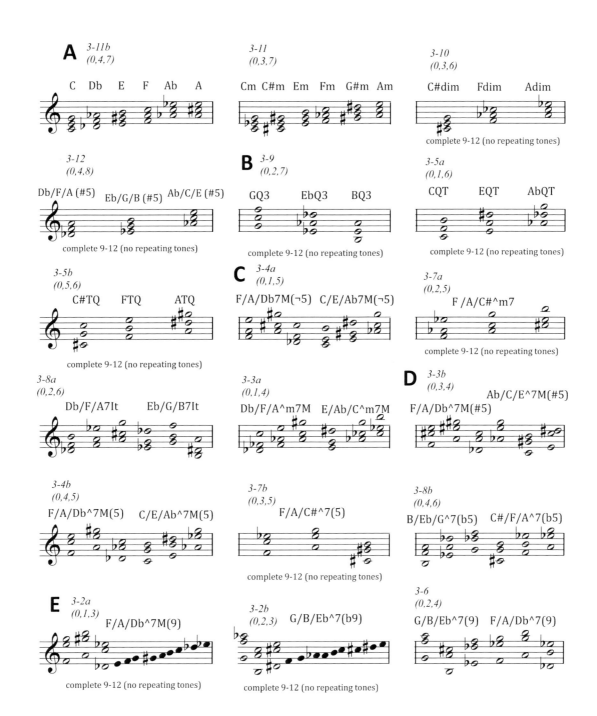

3.6.7   Auxiliary Scales Typologies

6-35 Whole-Tone Scale
Messiaen 1

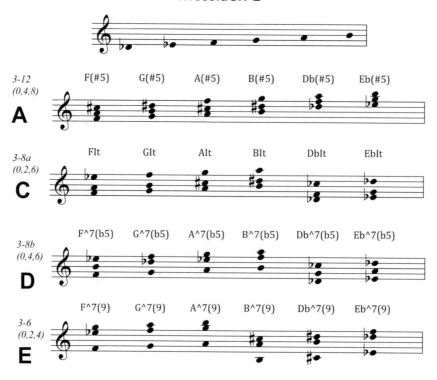

6-20 Augmented Scale
(Subset of Messiaen 3)

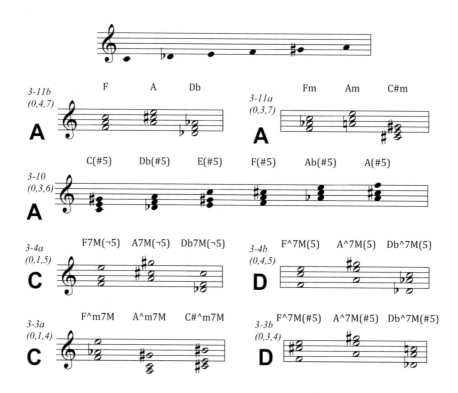

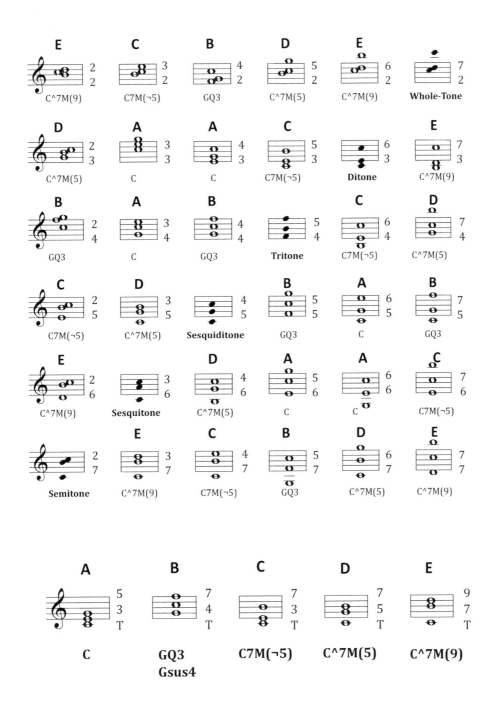

* About "Generic intervals" , please refer to chapter 4, on 4.7 "Theory of Generic Intervals".

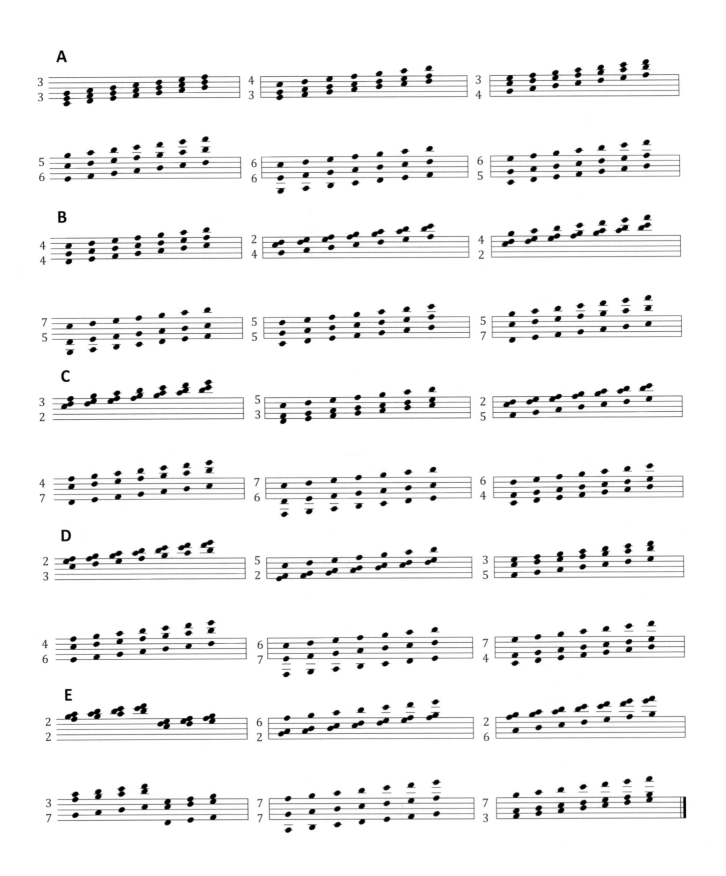

COMBINATORIAL HARMONY - BY JULIO HERRLEIN - MEL BAY

3.6.10   Trichords - Steps Through Symmetrical Scales

Trichords - Steps Through 8-28 Octatonic Scale Steps

Trichords - Steps Through 9-12 Nonatonic Scale Steps

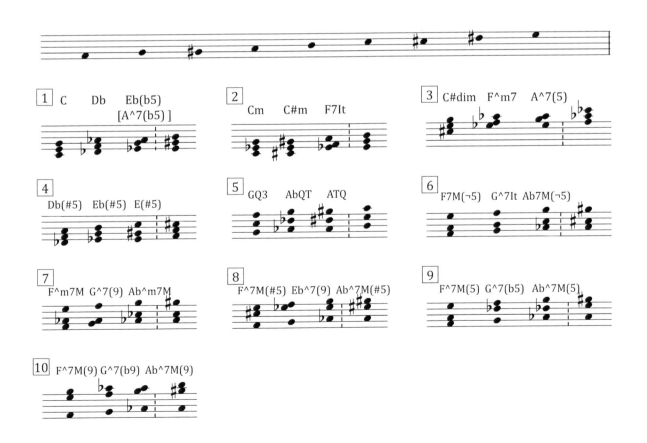

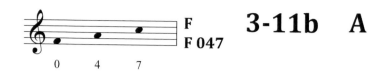

F
F 047

3-11b   A

0   4   7

3.7 THREE-NOTE CHORDS

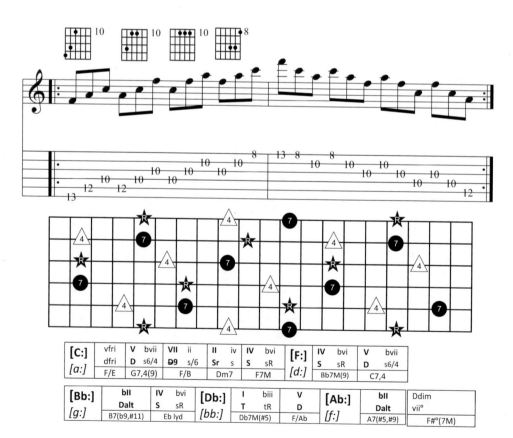

[C:]	vfri	**V**	bvii	**VII**	ii	**II**	iv	**IV**	bvi	**[F:]**	**IV**	bvi	**V**	bvii
[a:]	dfri	**D**	s6/4	**D9**	s/6	**Sr**	s	**S**	sR	**[d:]**	**S**	sR	**D**	s6/4
	F/E	G7,4(9)		F/B		Dm7		F7M			Bb7M(9)		C7,4	

[Bb:]		**bII**		**IV**	bvi	**[Db:]**	**I**	biii	**V**		**[Ab:]**		**bII**		Ddim
[g:]		**Dalt**		**S**	sR	**[bb:]**	**T**	tR	**D**		**[f:]**		**Dalt**		vii°
		B7(b9,#11)		Eb lyd			Db7M(#5)		F/Ab				A7(#5,#9)		F#°(7M)

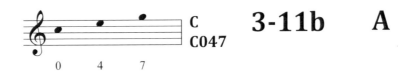

C
C047

3-11b   **A**

Open position

[G:]	vfri	V	bvii	VII	ii	II	iv	IV	bvi	**[C:]**	IV	bvi	V	bvii
	dfri	D	s6/4	~~D9~~	s/6	Sr	s	S	sR		S	sR	D	s6/4
[e:]	C/B	D7,4(9)		C/F#		Am7		C7M		**[a:]**	F7M(9)		G7,4	

[F:]		bII		IV	bvi	**[Ab:]**	I	biii	V		**[Eb:]**		bII		Ddim
		Dalt		S	sR		T	tR	D				Dalt		vii°
[d:]		F#7(b9,#11)		Ab (#5)		**[f:]**	Ab7M(#5)		C/Eb		**[c:]**		E7(#5,#9)		C#°(7M)

Track 03

3-11a A

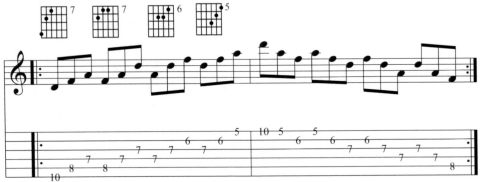

3.7 THREE-NOTE CHORDS

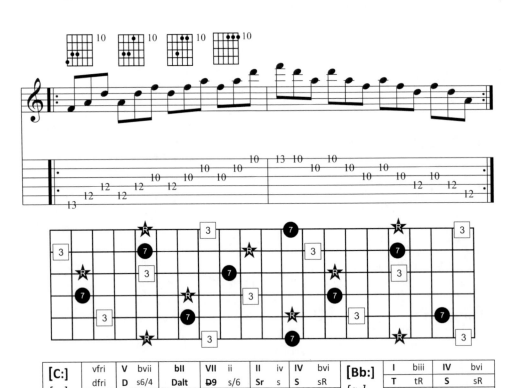

[C:]	vfri	**V**	bvii	**bII**	**VII**	ii	**II**	iv	**IV**	bvi	**[Bb:]**	**I**	biii	**IV**	bvi
	dfri	**D**	s6/4	**Dalt**	**D9**	s/6	**Sr**	s	**S**	sR		**T**	tR	**S**	sR
[a:]	Dm/E	G7,4		Db7(alt)	Bø		Dm7		F6		**[g:]**	Bb7M		Eb7M(9,#11)	

Docta	Ddim
V (bVII, III)	vii°
F/Ab/D 7	F#°(b13,7M)

COMBINATORIAL HARMONY - BY JULIO HERRLEIN - MEL BAY

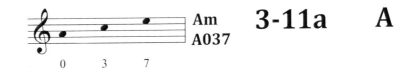

Am
A037

3-11a   A

0   3   7

Open position

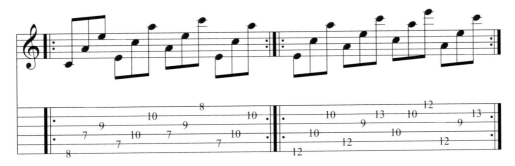

3.7 THREE-NOTE CHORDS

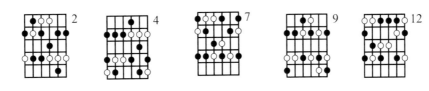

[G:]	vfri	**V**	bvii	**bII**	**VII**	ii	**II**	iv	**IV**	bvii	**[F:]**	**I**	biii	**IV**	bvi
	dfri	**D**	s6/4	**Dalt**	~~D9~~	s/6	**Sr**	s	**S**	sR	**[d:]**	**T**	tR	**S**	sR
[e:]	Am/B	D7,4		Ab7(alt)	F#ø		Am7		C6			F7M		Bb7M(9,#11)	

Docta	Ddim
V (bVII, III)	vii°
C/Eb/A 7	C#°(b13,7M)

Bdim
B 036

3-10   A

3.7 THREE-NOTE CHORDS

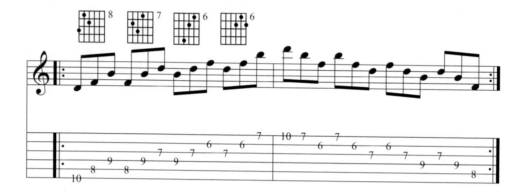

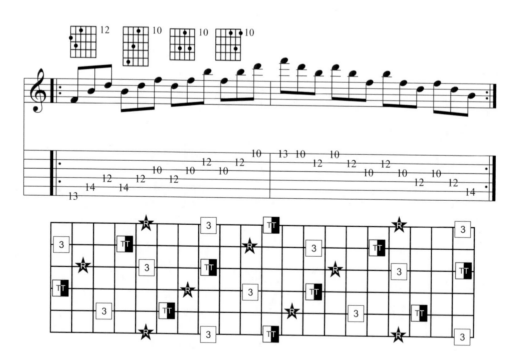

[C:]	vfri	vii°	**V** bvii	**bII**	**VII** ii
	dfri	~~Db9~~	**D** s6/4	**Dalt**	~~D9~~ s/6
[a:]	Dm/E	G#°	G7(13)	Db7(b9)	Bø

Docta	Ddim
V (bVII, bII, III)	vii°
bvii (bii, iii, v)	
G/Bb/Db/E 7	B / D/ F/ G#°

Bdim
B036 **3-10** **A**

Open position

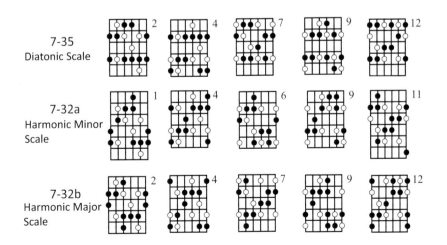

7-35
Diatonic Scale

7-32a
Harmonic Minor
Scale

7-32b
Harmonic Major
Scale

F(#5)
F/A/C# 048

3-12 A

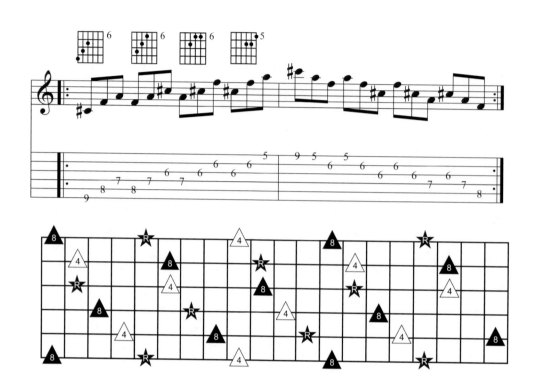

3.7 THREE-NOTE CHORDS

[C:]	[E:]	[Ab:]	vfri	V	bvii	bII	VI+	VII	ii	II	iv	IV	bvi
[a:]	[c#:]	[f:]	dfri	D	s6/4	**Dalt**	~~D~~/Sr	~~D9~~	s/6	**Sr**	s	**S**	sR
			E/G#/C sus4(b9,13)	G/B/Eb7 (9,#11)		Db/F/A 7(alt)	C#fr6/A Ffr6/C# Afr6/F	B/D#/G ø(9)		D/F#/Bb m7M		F/A/Db (#5)	

[Db:]	[F:]	[A:]	v+	Vfri	bVI°+
[bb]	[d:]	[f#:]	d+	**Dfri**	s/3
			F/A/C# 7(#5)	Ab/C/E sus4(b9,13)	Gb/Bb/D m7M

F(#5)
F/A/C# 048

3-12 A

0   4   8

Open position

7-34
Melodic Minor Scale

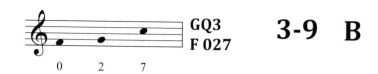

GQ3
F 027

3-9 B

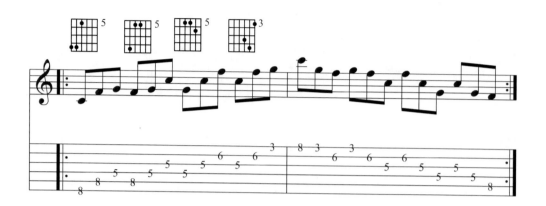

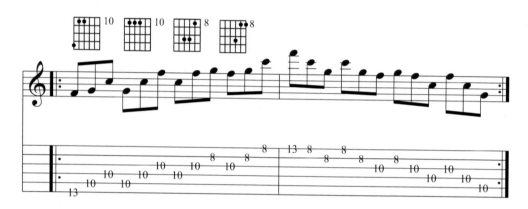

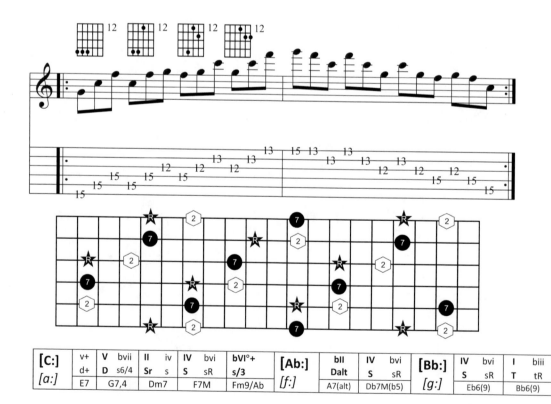

[C:]	v+	V	bvii	II	iv	IV	bvi	bVI°+	[Ab:]	bII	IV	bvi	[Bb:]	IV	bvi	I	biii
[a:]	d+	D	s6/4	Sr	s	S	sR	s/3	[f:]	Dalt	S	sR	[g:]	S	sR	T	tR
	E7	G7,4		Dm7		F7M		Fm9/Ab		A7(alt)	Db7M(b5)			Eb6(9)		Bb6(9)	

GQ3
F 027

3-9 B

Open position

3.7 THREE-NOTE CHORDS

Track 11

CQT
B016

0 1 6

3-5a B

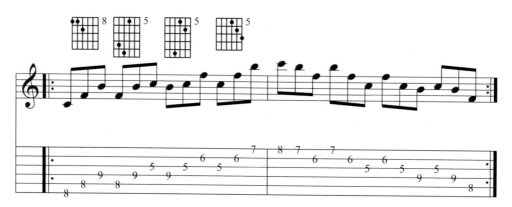

3.7 THREE-NOTE CHORDS

[C:]	v+	V	bvii	II	iv	IV	bvi
[a:]	d+	D	s6/4	Sr	s	S	sR
	E7	G7(11)		Dm7(13)		F(#11)	

	Ddim		Docta
	vii° / Cm,Ebm,Gbm,Bbm		V v
	B°(b9-m) / D°(7m-R) / F°(b13-7d)/G#°(b11-5d)		B / D / F / G# 7

68   COMBINATORIAL HARMONY - BY JULIO HERRLEIN - MEL BAY

CQT
B 016

3-5a B

0   1   6

Open position

 2   4   7   9   12

FTQ
B 056

3-5b   B

3.7 THREE-NOTE CHORDS

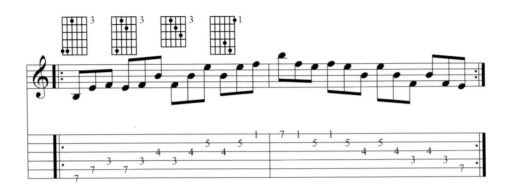

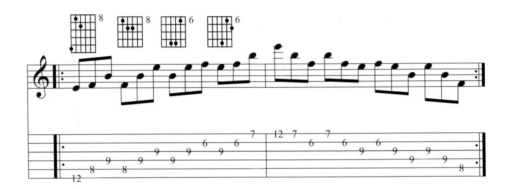

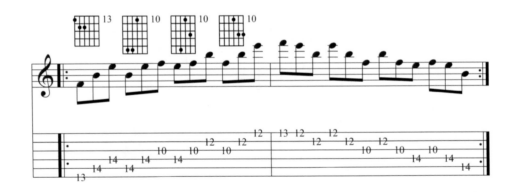

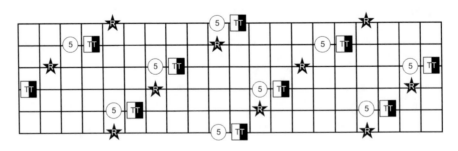

[C:]	vfri	v+	vii°	V	bvii	bII		VII	ii	II	iv	IV	bvi
	dfri	d+	~~Db9~~	D	s6/4	Dalt		~~D9~~	s/6	Sr	s	S	sR
[a:]		E7	G#°(b13)		G7(13)	Db7(#9)		Bø		Dm6(9)		F7M(#11)	

Dm/E

FTQ
B 056

3-5b B

Open position

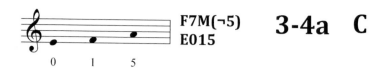

F7M(¬5)
E015

3-4a   C

3.7 THREE-NOTE CHORDS

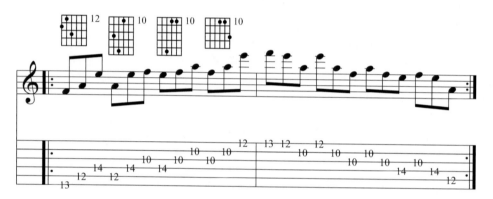

[C:]	vfri	**V**	bvii	**bII**	**VII**	ii	**II**	iv	**IV**	bvi	**[F:]**	**IV**	bvi
	dfri	**D**	s6/4	**Dalt**	~~**D9**~~	s/6	**Sr**	s	**S**	sR		**S**	sR
[a:]	Dm/E	G7		Db7(alt)	Bø		Dm7		F7M		**[d:]**	Bb7M(#11)	

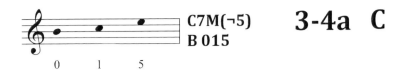

C7M(¬5)
B 015

3-4a C

Open position

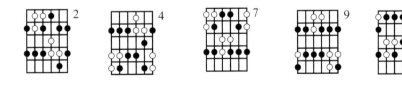

[G:] [e:]	vfri	V	bvii	bII	VII	ii	II	iv	IV	bvi	[C:] [a:]	IV	bvi
	dfri	D	s6/4	Dalt	D9	s/6	Sr	s	S	sR		S	sR
	Am/B	D7		Ab7(alt)	F#ø		Am7		C7M			F7M(#11)	

D^m7
C025

3-7a   **C**

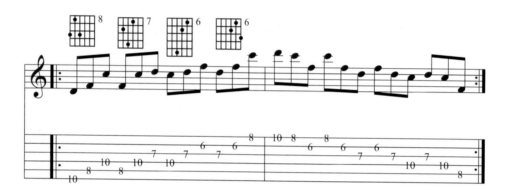

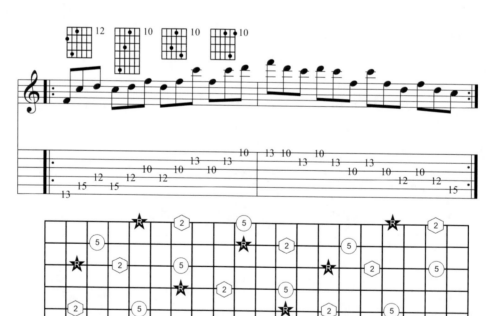

[C:]	v+	**V**	bvii	**II**	iv	**IV**	bvi	**bVI°+**	**[F:]**	**IV**	bvi	**[Bb]**	**IV**	bvi
	d+	**D**	s6/4	**Sr**	s	**S**	sR	**s/3**		**S**	sR		**S**	sR
[a:]	E7		G7,4		Dm7(9)		F7M	Fm/Ab	[d:]		Bb(add9)	[g:]		Eb6/7M(9)

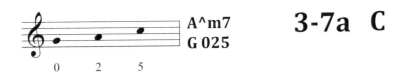

A^m7
G 025

3-7a C

Open position

[G:]	v+	**V**	bvii	**II**	iv	**IV**	bvi	**bVI°+**	**[C:]**	**IV**	bvi	**[Eb]**	**IV**	bvi
	d+	**D**	s6/4	**Sr**	s	**S**	sR	s/3	**[a:]**	**S**	sR	**[c:]**	**S**	sR
[e:]	B7	D7,4		Am7(9)		C7M		Cm/Eb		F(add9)			Bb6/7M(9)	

3-8a C

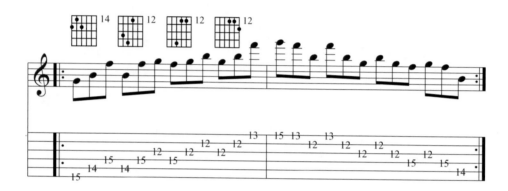

[C:]	v+	vii°	**V**	bvii	**bII**	**IV**	bvi
	d+	D̶b̶9	**D**	s6/4	**Dalt**	**S**	sR
[a:]	E7	G#°(7M)	G7		DbFr6	F9(#11)	

DHex
V (IV, bIII, bII, VII, VI)
G /F /Eb /Db /B /A 7

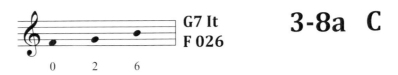

3-8a C

Open position

D^m7M
C#014

3-3a **C**

0   1   4

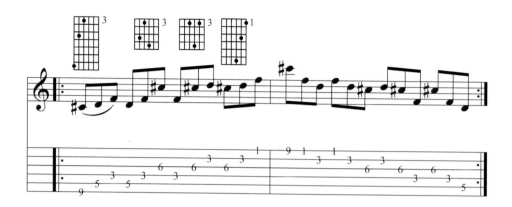

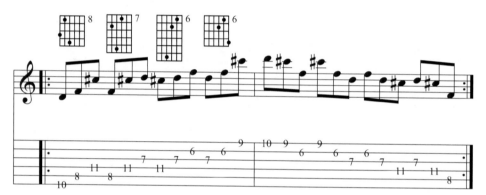

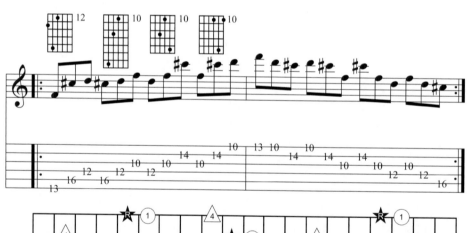

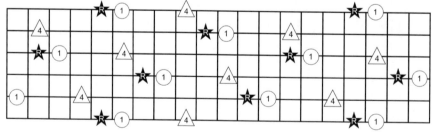

[C:]	vfri	v+	vii°+	V	bvii	bII		VII	ii		II	iv
[a:]	dfri	d+	Db9	D	s6/4	Dalt		D9	s/6		Sr	s
	Dm/E	E7	G#°+	G7		Db7(alt)		Bø			Dm7M	

Docta	Ddim
V (bVII, bII, III)	vii°
bvii (bii, iii, v)	
G/Bb/Db/E 7	B / D / F/ G#°

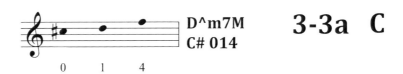

D^m7M
C# 014

3-3a C

0   1   4

Open position

F^7M(#5) **3-3b** **D**
C#034

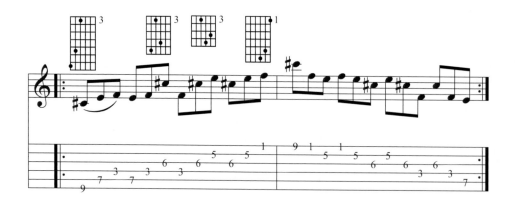

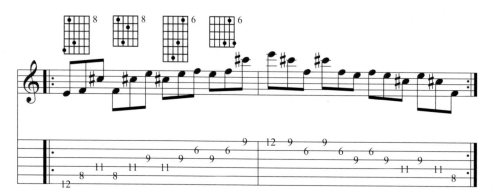

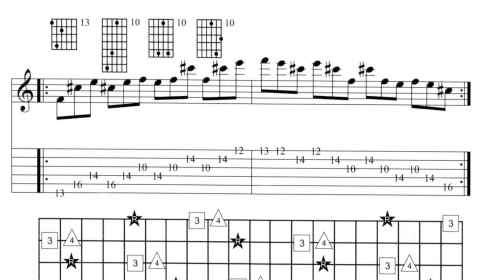

[C:]	vfri	v+	vii°+	V	bvii	bII		VII	ii	II	iv	IV	bvi	Docta	Ddim
[a:]	dfri	d+	~~Db9~~	D	s6/4	Dalt		~~D9~~	s/6	Sr	s	S	sR	V (bVII, bII, III)	vii°
	Dm/E	E7	G#°+	G7		Db7(alt)		Bø		Dm7M		F7M(#5)		bvii (bii, iii, v)	
														G/Bb/Db/E 7	B / D/ F/ G#°

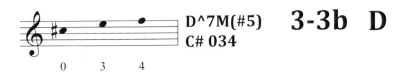

D^7M(#5) **3-3b D**
C# 034

Open position

Track 18

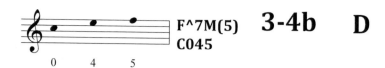
F^7M(5) **3-4b** **D**
C045

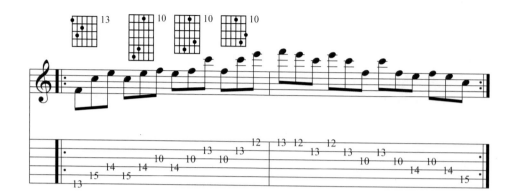

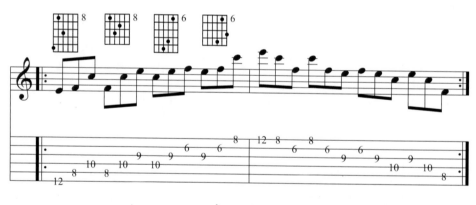

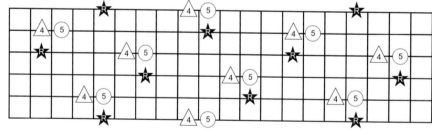

[C:] [a:]	v+ d+ E7	V D G7	bvii s6/4	II Sr Dm7	iv s	IV S F7M	bvi sR	bVI°+ s/3 Fm/Ab	[F:] [d:]	IV S Bb(#11)	bvi sR	[Ab] [f:]	IV S Db7M(#9)	bvi sR

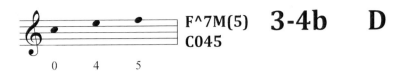

F^7M(5) **3-4b** **D**
C045

Open position

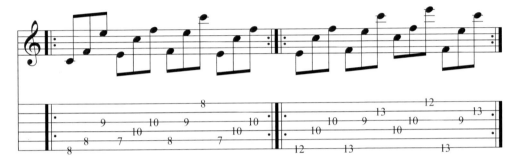

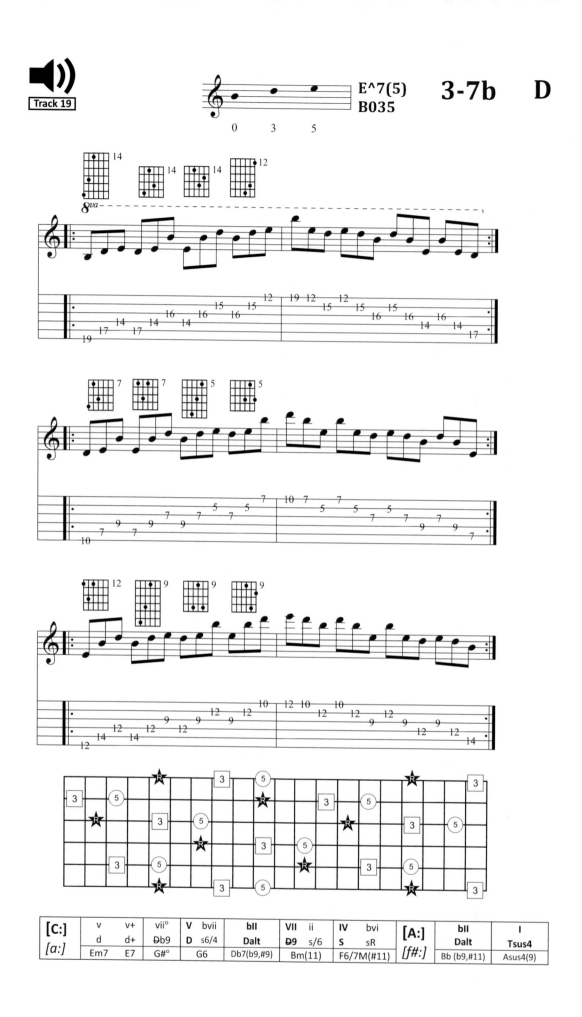

Track 19

E^7(5)
B035

3-7b   **D**

[C:]	v	v+	vii°	V	bvii	bII	VII	ii	IV	bvi	[A:]	bII	I
	d	d+	~~Db9~~	D	s6/4	**Dalt**	~~D9~~	s/6	S	sR		**Dalt**	**Tsus4**
[a:]	Em7	E7	G#°	G6		Db7(b9,#9)	Bm(11)		F6/7M(#11)		[f#:]	Bb (b9,#11)	Asus4(9)

$D^{\wedge}7(5)$ **3-7b** **D**
A 035

Open position

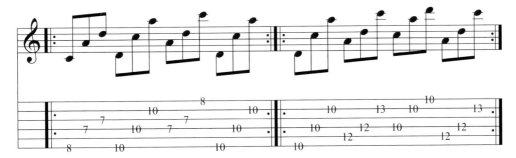

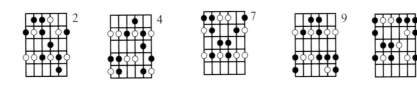

[G:]	v	v+	vii°	V	bvii	bII	VII	ii	IV	bvi	[E:]	bII	I
	d	d+	D♭9	D	s6/4	Dalt	D9	s/6	S	sR		Dalt	Tsus4
[e:]	Bm7	B7	D#°	D6		Ab7(b9,#9)	F#m(11)		C6/7M(#11)		[c#:]	F (b9,#11)	Esus4(9)

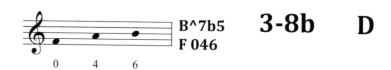

B^7b5
F 046

3-8b   **D**

3.7 THREE-NOTE CHORDS

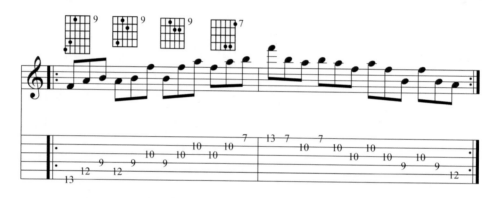

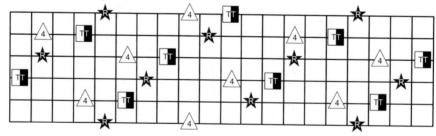

[C:]	vfri	**V**	bvii	**bII**		**VI+**	**VII**	ii	**II**	iv	**IV**	bvi	[Bb:]		**bII**
[a:]	dfri	**D**	s6/4	**Dalt**		**D̶/Sr**	**D̶9**	s/6	**Sr**	s	**S**	sR	[d:]		**Dalt**
	Dm/E	G7		Db7(alt)	C#fr6/A		Bø		Dm6		F(#11)				B 7(alt)

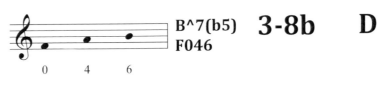

B^7(b5) **3-8b** **D**
F046

0   4   6

Open position

3.7 THREE-NOTE CHORDS

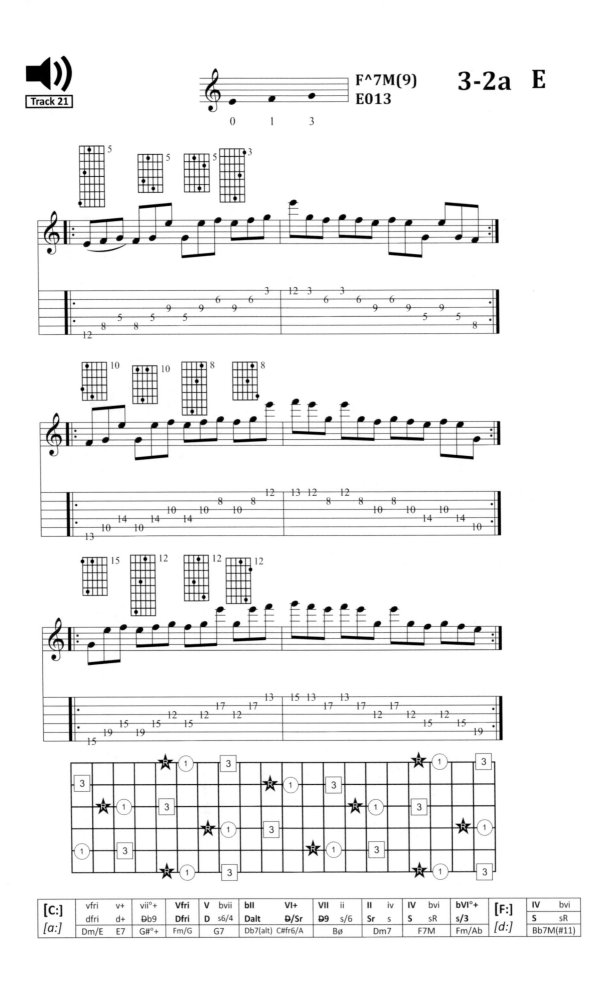

Track 21

F^7M(9)
E013

0   1   3

3-2a   E

[C:]	vfri	v+	vii°+	**Vfri**	V	bvii	**bII**	**VI+**	**VII**	ii	**II**	iv	**IV**	bvi	**bVI°+**	[F:]	**IV**	bvi
[a:]	dfri	d+	~~Db9~~	**Dfri**	D	s6/4	**Dalt**	**D̶/Sr**	**D̶9**	s/6	**Sr**	s	**S**	sR	**s/3**	[d:]	**S**	sR
	Dm/E	E7	G#°+	Fm/G	G7		Db7(alt)	C#fr6/A	Bø		Dm7		F7M		Fm/Ab		Bb7M(#11)	

C^7M(9) **3-2a** **E**
B 013

Open position

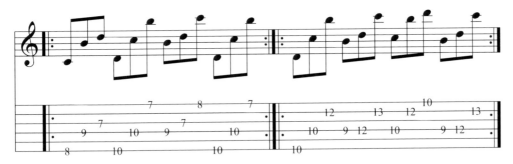

[G:]	vfri	v+	vii°+	**Vfri**	**V**	bvii	**bII**	**VI+**	**VII**	ii	**II**	iv	**IV**	bvi	**bVI°+**	**[C:]**	**IV**	bvi
	dfri	d+	~~Db9~~	**Dfri**	D	s6/4	**Dalt**	**~~D~~/Sr**	**~~D~~9**	s/6	**Sr**	s	**S**	sR	**s/3**	**[a:]**	**S**	sR
[d:]	Am/B	B7	D#°+	Cm/D		D7	Ab7(alt)	G#fr6/A		F#ø	Am7		C7M		Cm/Eb			F7M(#11)

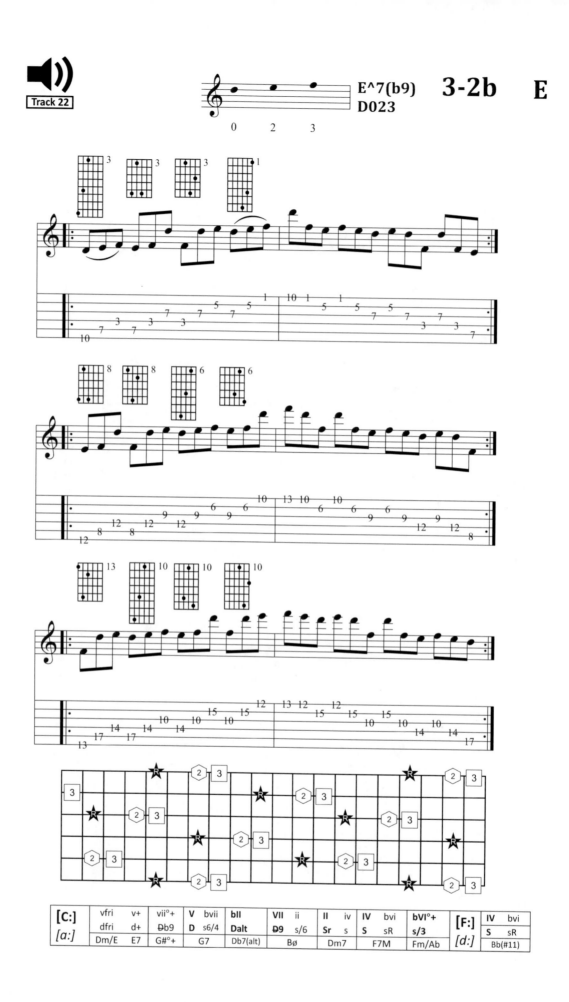

E^7(b9)
D023
3-2b
E

[C:]	vfri	v+	vii°+	V	bvii	bII		VII	ii	II	iv	IV	bvi	bVI°+	[F:]	IV	bvi
	dfri	d+	~~Db9~~	D	s6/4	Dalt		~~D9~~	s/6	Sr	s	S	sR	s/3		S	sR
[a:]	Dm/E	E7	G#°+	G7		Db7(alt)		Bø		Dm7		F7M		Fm/Ab	[d:]	Bb(#11)	

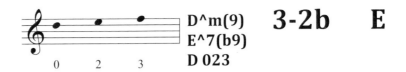

D^m(9)
E^7(b9)   **3-2b**   **E**
D 023

Open position

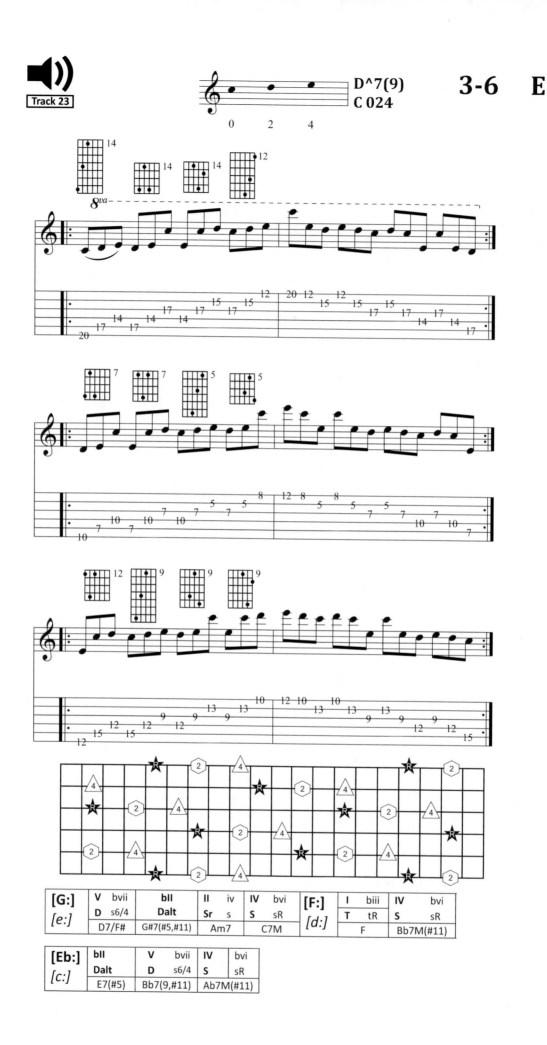

Track 23

D^7(9)
C 024

3-6   E

[G:]	V	bvii	bII		II	iv	IV	bvi
[e:]	**D**	s6/4	**Dalt**		**Sr**	s	**S**	sR
	D7/F#		G#7(#5,#11)		Am7		C7M	

[F:]	I	biii	IV	bvi
[d:]	**T**	tR	**S**	sR
	F		Bb7M(#11)	

[Eb:]	bII		V	bvii	IV	bvi
[c:]	**Dalt**		**D**	s6/4	**S**	sR
	E7(#5)		Bb7(9,#11)		Ab7M(#11)	

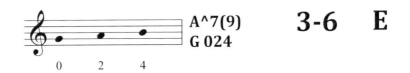

A^7(9)
G 024

3-6 **E**

Open position

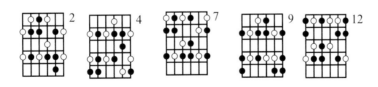

[D:]	V	bvii	bII		II	iv	IV	bvi	[C:]	I	biii	IV		bvi	[Bb:]	bII		V	bvi	IV		bvi
[b:]	D	s6/4	**Dalt**		**Sr**	s	S	sR	[a:]	**T**	tR	S		sR	[g:]	**Dalt**		D	s6/4	S		sR
	A7/C#		C#7(#5,#11)		Em7		G7M			C		F7M(#11)				B7(#5)		F7(9,#11)		Eb7M(#5)	

4. CARDINALITY 4
FOUR-NOTE CHORDS OF THE DIATONIC SCALE

The four-note chords follow a typology similar to the that of the three-note chords.

4.1 "A" TYPOLOGY – SEVENTH CHORDS (please refer to page 106)

These chords are built by the superimposition (stacking) of three thirds on a root. They are the traditional seventh chords.

4.2 "B" TYPOLOGY - QUARTAL CHORDS

These chords are built by the superimposition of three fourths on a root.

When the superimposition is only with perfects fourths, we use the symbol **Q4**.

We have chosen a chord symbol system that mentions the seventh chords ("A" typology), which are usually learned first and by which the other chord typologies ("B","C","D" and "E") may be derived through comparison. It also makes learning the instrument easier, because after learning the voicings for the seventh chords, we can turn some of its tones in order to obtain chords of other typologies.

Thus, the first chord of quartal typology (see the typologies in 4.9) can be understood as a C7M chord. However, it has the fourth instead of the fifth, and for this reason, we will use the chord symbol C7M(4-5). This chord can also be understood as a chord F7M with #11 instead of the major third (sounding like the Lydian mode). All quartal chords can be seen as: a) seventh chords with the fourth instead of the third (**4-3**), in the chord symbols placed over the notes and b) seventh chords with the fourth instead of the fifth (**4-5**) or (**11-5**) in the chord symbols placed under the notes. (please refer to page 106, type "B" quartal chords)

The fifth chord in this category (Forte 4-16b) can be understood as a chord with a major third and perfect fourth simultaneously, built on the root G. This kind of chord sounds fine when the third is placed above the fourth, forming a major seventh interval, and not the opposite, as when a minor ninth interval is formed. However, depending on the musical language chosen, the second combination can be equally interesting.

4.3 "C" TYPOLOGY – TRIADS WITH AN ADDED NINTH OR IN THE BASS (SUS)

In this typology we talk about triads with the added ninth, that is, chords where the ninth is added to a triad without the seventh. If the ninth is placed in the bass instead of placed on the root, we have a 7sus4(9) chord, i.e., a suspended chord (with the fourth instead of the third) without the fifth and with an added ninth. It is a common practice to omit the fifth in the seventh chords that contain any tension above the octave (like 9, 11 or 13), putting the characteristic tension in its place, keeping the four-part writing.

We may think of the chords of the "C" typology: a) seventh chords with the sixth instead of the fifth (**6-5**); b) triads with the added ninth C(add9); c) triads with the ninth in the bass, that is, 7sus4 (9) chords.

At this point it is evident that a same sound set can have more than one function: the 7sus4(9) chord usually has a dominant function (tension), whereas the added ninth chord has a harmonic function of stability and rest.

The 4-z29 or Em/F chord can be understood as a G7(13) chord.

4.4 "D" TYPOLOGY – TRIADS WITH AN ADDED FOURTH IN THE BASS

These chords can be understood as: a) triads with the fourth in the bass; b) seventh and ninth chords (cardinality 5) with the third omitted and; c) seventh chords with the ninth in the position of third (**9-3**).

These chords can be understood as a chord where the fifth was omitted in favor of the ninth (typically used in acoustic and electric guitar). They also form four-note segments in the scale, from the seventh of the chords, i.e., C7M (9-5) is the segment between the notes 'B, 'C, 'D,' E. These chords are usually written as 7M (9). Experienced musicians naturally omit the fifth in favor of the ninth, but our purpose is to investigate how each typology is built. We can understand this typology as seventh chords with two alterations (9-3) and (6-5), i.e., the ninth in the position of the third and the sixth in the position of the fifth. This is not practical or usual, but it helps to understand the transformation of one typology into another and also how we can, through chord transformation, gradually change one kind of chord into another.

So far we have all three-note and four-note harmonic entities that are possible within the diatonic scale. Any of the chords mentioned can be reduced to one of these typologies.

4.6 VOICING THEORY

Voicing is the way of distributing a single chord (or sound sets).

Closed position is a position in which the chord is restricted to one octave.

In the following examples, we will always use the chord 4-20 (C7M, 'C, 'E, 'G, 'B notes):

a) the voices are always counted from top to bottom, the highest note (top note, voice number 1) to the lowest note (bass or voice number 4);

b) the chord's inversions do not affect the voice counting. We note that the seventh chord inversions involve second intervals;

c) note the arrangement of these chords on the guitar fretboard.

4.6   VOICING THEORY

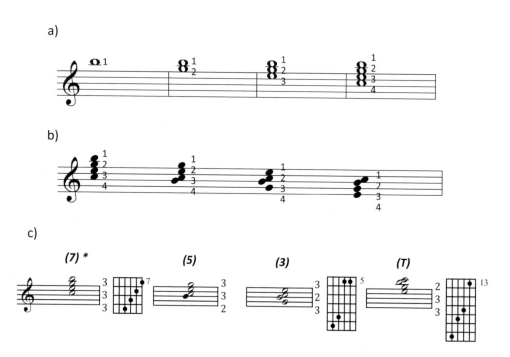

4.6.1 CLOSED POSITION CHORDS

On the guitar, it is easier to play chords based on the superimposition of fourths, thirds and even fifths. However, when an interval of a second is part of the "voicing" (chosen chord position) the execution becomes more complicated, even for those with big hands . On the piano, unlike the guitar, these chords in the closed position are the easiest to play.

To enable the execution, we can rearrange the chords in more open positions more appropriate for guitarists. This solution is used not only because of the mechanical layout of the guitar, but because it provides a technique of distributing the chord voices in a general form. This technique is also useful in the elaboration of an arrangement for string sections, horn sections, etc.

4.6.2 OPEN POSITION CHORDS

4.6.2.1 DROP 2 VOICING

The Drop 2 voicing is the most common open position and it consists of dropping the second voice of the closed position one octave below. Note that the counting of voices remains from the top to bottom.

4.6.2.1   DROP 2 VOICINGS

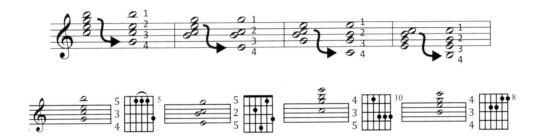

4.6.2.2 DROP 3 VOICING

The Drop 3 voicing is a widely used open position and it consists of dropping the third voice of the closed position one octave below. Note that the counting of voices remains from the top to bottom.

4.6.2.2   DROP 3 VOICINGS

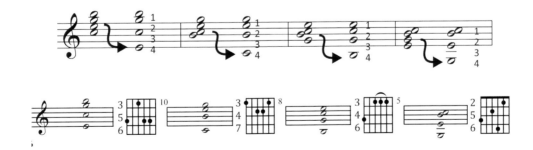

4.6.2.3 STRING TRANSFERENCE

In the pages of four-note chords, the numbers on the left at the beginning of each line refer to the string groups. The same voicing can be performed in different string groups. For this reason, the nearly 800 four-note chords voicings are multiplied, showing the complexity of the acoustic and electric guitar.

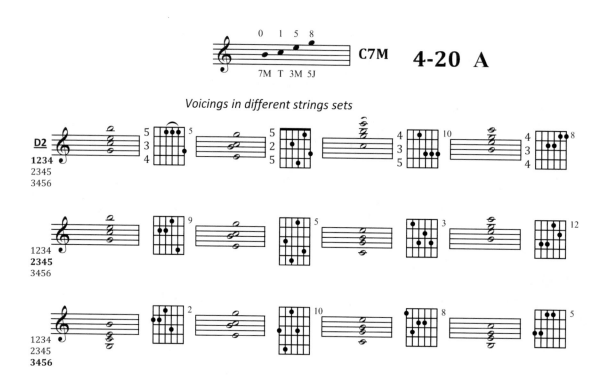

4.6.2.4 VOICINGS (SUMMARY TABLE)

In the ex. 4.6.2.4, we will show how the four-note chords will be presented in this book. Besides the Drop 2 and Drop 3 voicings, we will present three different voicings: Drop 2+4, Drop 2+3 and Drop DD2+D3 (double Drop 2 with Drop 3, i.e., dropping the second voice two octaves below and the third voice one octave). The voicing DD2+D3 generates ultra-wide voicings that sound great, though can be difficult to play on the guitar.

4.6.2.4   VOICINGS (SUMMARY TABLE)

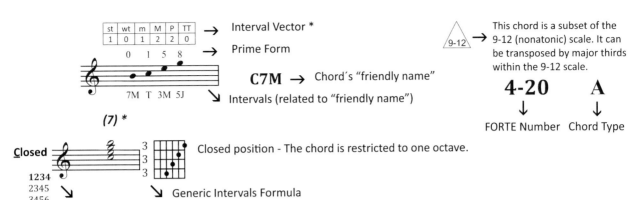

st	wt	m	M	P	TT
1	0	1	2	2	0

→ Interval Vector *

0 1 5 8 → Prime Form

C7M → Chord's "friendly name"

7M T 3M 5J   ↘ Intervals (related to "friendly name")

*(7) ***

This chord is a subset of the 9-12 (nonatonic) scale. It can be transposed by major thirds within the 9-12 scale.

4-20   **A**
↓   ↓
FORTE Number   Chord Type

Closed
1234
2345
3456

3
3
3

Closed position - The chord is restricted to one octave.

↘ String Sets   ↘ Generic Intervals Formula

D2
1234
2345
3456

5
3
4

Drop 2 - Voice 2 dropped one octave below.

D3
1235
2346
1246

3
5
6

Drop 3 - Voice 3 dropped one octave below.

D2+4
1245
2356

5
6
5

Drop 2+4 - Voice 2 and 4 dropped one octave below.

D2+3
1345
2456
1245

7
4
3

Drop 2+3 - Voice 2 and 3 dropped one octave below.

DD2+D3
1246
1346
1356

7
6
6

DD2+D3 - Voice 2 dropped two octaves below and voice 3 dropped one octave below.
DD (Double Drop = two octaves below)

* voice #1 (top)

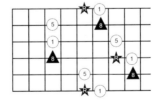

Geometric Location on fretboard.

[G:]	vfri	**V**	bvii	**VII**	ii
	dfri	**D**	s6/4	~~D9~~	s/6
[e:]	Am/B	D7,4(9,13)		F#ø(b9,11)	

Possible harmonic functions for this set.

* Represented by a six-number sequence, the interval vector show how many instances of each interval class is contained in the chord (FORTE, 1973).

st - semitone - 1 ('B-'C)   M - major third - ditone - 2 ('C-'E) and ('G-'B)
wt - whole-tone - 0 instances.   P - Perfect - Sesquiditone - 2 ('C-'G) and ('E-'B)
m - minor third (sesquitone) 1 ('E-'G)   TT - tritone - 0 instances.

4.7 THEORY OF GENERIC INTERVALS

One of the most interesting consequences of the organization of chords by typology is that, due to the similar building method that characterizes each typology, we can recognize a chord from its intervallic constitution.

In Example 4.7:

a) all seventh chords in the closed position and with the seventh as the top voice, i.e., root, third, fifth and seventh, will be built from the superimposition (stacking) of three thirds (3 3 3)

b) all seventh chords in the closed position and with the fifth as the top voice, i.e., the seventh, root, third and fifth, will be built from the superimposition of a second and two thirds (2 3 3)

c) the same chords above (seventh chords with the fifth as the top voice) will always present the intervallic arrangement of fifth, second and fifth (5 2 5) in the Drop 2 voicing.

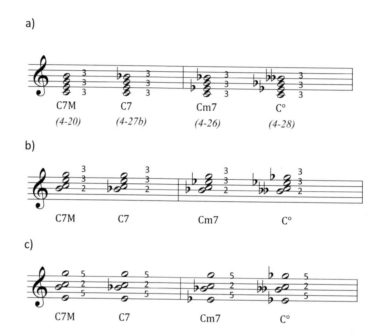

The notion of generic intervals allows a dialogue between theory and instrument. See the example 4-7.b.

Assume you are improvising on your instrument (guitar or piano) and play the chords written in a).

From the intervallic analysis, you can conclude that these chords have the intervallic configuration described in b). We conclude by looking at the table 4.7.1 that the first chord is in Drop 2+4 voicing with the third on the top voice. The second chord is in Drop 3 voicing with the third on the top voice. The third chord is in Drop 2 voicing with the fifth on the top voice. The last chord is in Drop 3 voicing with the seventh on the top voice.

From this, we can deduce the root of each chord and conclude what is described in 4.7.b, Example c).

In d), note how all the chords are quartal (typology B) and are in the intervallic arrangement of the table (in 4-7-1). This occurs with other typologies. Each typology produces unique combinations of generic intervals.

4.7.b

a)

b)

c)

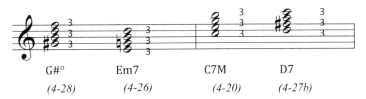

G#°   Em7   C7M   D7

(4-28)   *(4-26)*   *(4-20)*   *(4-27b)*

d)

4.7.1 TABLE OF GENERIC INTERVALS

A *Seventh Chords* **7**   **B** *Quartal Chords* **7(4-3)**   **C** *Triad / II* **7(6-5)**

A

	7	5	3	T
Closed	3	3	3	2
	3	3	2	3
	3	2	3	3
D2	5	5	4	4
	3	2	3	3
	4	5	5	4
D3	3	3	3	2
	5	4	4	5
	6	7	6	6
D2+4	5	5	4	4
	6	6	7	6
	5	4	4	5
D2+3	7	6	6	6
	4	5	5	4
	3	3	2	3
DD2+D3	7	6	6	6
	6	7	6	6
	6	6	7	6

B

	(4-3)	5	7	T
Closed	4	2	3	2
	2	4	2	3
	3	2	4	2
D2	5	5	4	4
	3	2	4	2
	5	4	4	5
D3	4	2	3	2
	4	5	5	4
	6	7	5	7
D2+4	5	5	4	4
	7	5	7	6
	4	5	5	4
D2+3	7	6	7	5
	5	4	4	5
	2	4	2	3
DD2+D3	7	6	7	5
	6	7	5	7
	7	5	7	6

C

	7	(6-5)	3	T
Closed	2	4	3	2
	4	3	2	2
	3	2	2	4
D2	5	6	4	3
	3	2	2	4
	3	5	6	4
D3	2	4	3	2
	6	4	3	5
	6	7	7	5
D2+4	5	6	4	3
	5	6	7	7
	6	4	3	5
D2+3	7	7	5	6
	3	5	6	4
	4	3	2	2
DD2+D3	7	7	5	6
	6	7	7	5
	5	6	7	7

D *Triad / IV* **7(9-3)**   **E** *Cluster T 3 7 (9)* **7(9-3)** **(6-5)** **7(9-5)**
4 note segment

D

	7	5	(9-3)	T
Closed	3	4	2	2
	4	2	2	3
	2	2	3	4
D2	6	5	3	4
	2	2	3	4
	4	6	5	3
D3	3	4	2	2
	5	3	4	6
	7	7	6	5
D2+4	6	5	3	4
	5	7	7	6
	5	3	4	6
D2+3	7	6	5	7
	4	6	5	3
	4	2	2	3
DD2+D3	7	6	5	7
	7	7	6	5
	5	7	7	6

E

| | (6-5) | T | (9-3) | 7 |
	7	(9-5)	3	T
Closed	5	2	2	2
	2	2	2	5
	2	5	2	2
D2	6	3	3	6
	2	5	2	2
	6	3	6	3
D3	5	2	2	2
	3	6	3	6
	7	4	7	7
D2+4	6	3	3	6
	7	7	7	4
	3	6	3	6
D2+3	7	7	4	7
	6	3	6	3
	2	2	2	5
DD2+D3	7	7	4	7
	7	4	7	7
	7	7	7	4

The table shows the intervallic characteristics of chords of different typologies in their different voicings.

4.8 GENERIC INTERVALS FORMULAE

From the arrangement of generic intervals within the typologies, I prepared a table that enables a dialogue between the student and theory. When in doubt about any voicing, the student may consult it to discover the typology of chord, its voicing, and which note is in the top voice.

4.8   Intervals of the voicing - 333 (three superimposed thirds)

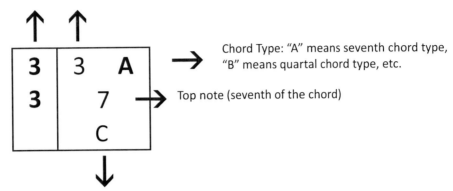

Chord Type: "A" means seventh chord type, "B" means quartal chord type, etc.

Top note (seventh of the chord)

Voicing Type: C means closed voicing, D2 is a drop 2 voicing, etc.

The structure in the example 4.8 represents generically any chord built by three superimposed thirds, exemplified by 4.8a and 4.8b.

4.8.a

4.8.b

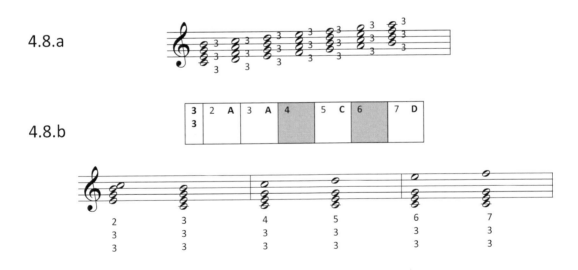

Note the example 4.8b and see in standard notation the representation of the generic intervals. The gray squares correspond to the chords where there are octaves, as in the case of 334 and 336 (where notes are repeated producing three-note chords).

The complete table of this example is in 4.8c is, showing that:

1) the first chord is a type "A" chord (seventh chord, root as the top voice, closed position);

2) the second chord is a type "A" chord (seventh chord, seventh as the top voice, closed position);

3) the third chord is a three-note chord only, with a repeated note (octave);

4) the fourth chord is a type "C" chord (seventh chord with the sixth instead of the fifth), 7 (6-5) (or triad with added ninth) with the seventh as the top voice and in drop 2 position;

5) the fifth chord is a type "D" chord (seventh chord with the sixth instead of the fifth), 7 (9-3) (or triad with added fourth) with the tonic as the top voice and in drop 2+3 position.

When consulting a chord, try to transpose it in order to obtain as minimum accidentals as possible and be careful with the enharmonic intervals (as 4A and 5D), which can confuse the location in the table.

4.8.c

3	2 A	3 A	4	5 C	6	7 D
3	T	7		7		T
	F	F		D2		2+3

2	3	4	5	6	7
3	3	3	3	3	3
3	3	3	3	3	3

4.8.1 FOUR-NOTE CHORDS - GENERIC INTERVALS FORMULAE TABLE

	2	3	4	5	6	7
2 2	2 E (9-3) C	3 C 3 C	4 D 5 C	5 E (6-5) C	6	7
3 2	2 B T C	3 A 5 C	4 C (6-5) C	5	6	7 E T 2+3
4 2	2 B 5 C	3 D 7 C	4	5	6 C T 2+3	7 B 7 2+3
5 2	2 E 7 C	3	4	5 D (9-3) 2+3	6 A 3 2+3	7 B (4-3) 2+3
6 2	2	3	4 E (9-3) 2+3	5 C 3 2+3	6 D 5 2+3	7 E (6-5) 2+3
7 2	2	3	4	5	6	7
2 3	2 D (9-3) C	3 A 3 C	4 B (4-3) C	5	6 E 7 D2	7
3 3	2 A T C	3 A 7 C	4	5 C 7 D2	6	7 D T 2+3
4 3	2 C 7 C	3	4 D T D2	5	6 A T 2+3	7 A 7 2+3
5 3	2	3 E T D2	4	5 B T 2+3	6 A 5 2+3	7 C (6-5) 2+3
6 3	2	3	4	5	6	7
7 3	2	3 E (9-3) 2+4	4 C 3 2+4	5 D 5 2+4	6 E (6-5) 2+4	7
2 4	2 C T C	3 B 7 C	4	5 B 5 D2	6 D 7 D2	7
3 4	2 D T C	3	4 A T D2	5 A 7 D2	6	7 C 7 2+3
4 4	2	3 C T D2	4 B 7 D2	5	6 B 5 2+3	7 D 7 2+3
5 4	2	3	4	5	6	7
6 4	2 E T D3	3	4 B T 2+4	5 A 5 2+4	6 C (6-5) 2+4	7
7 4	2	3 D (9-3) 2+4	4 A 3 2+4	5 B (4-3) 2+4	6	7 E (6-5) DD2

	2	3	4	5	6	7
2 5	2 E T C	3	4 B T D2	5 A 5 D2	6 C (6-5) D2	7
3 5	2	3 D (9-3) D2	4 A 3 D2	5 B (4-3) D2	6	7 E 7 2+3
4 5	2	3	4	5	6	7
5 5	2 C T D3	3 B 7 D3	4	5 B 5 2+4	6 D 7 2+4	7
6 5	2 D T D3	3	4 A T 2+4	5 A 7 2+4	6	7 C 7 DD2
7 5	2	3 C T 2+4	4 B 7 2+4	5	6 B 5 DD2	7 D 7 DD2
2 6	2	3 E (9-3) D2	4 C 3 D2	5 D 5 D2	6 E (6-5) D2	7
3 6	2	3	4	5	6	7
4 6	2 D (9-3) D3	3 A 3 D3	4 B (4-3) D3	5	6 E 7 2+4	7
5 6	2 A T D3	3 A 7 D3	4	5 C 7 2+4	6	7 D T DD2
6 6	2 B 7 D3	3	4 D T 2+4	5	6 A T DD2	7 A 7 DD2
7 6	2	3 E T 2+4	4	5 B T DD2	6 A 5 DD2	7 C (6-5) DD2
2 7	2	3	4	5	6	7
3 7	2 E (9-3) D3	3 C 3 D3	4 D 5 D3	5 E (6-5) D3	6	7
4 7	2 B T D3	3 A 5 D3	4 C (6-5) D3	5	6	7 E T DD2
5 7	2 B 5 D3	3 D 7 D3	4	5	6 C T DD2	7 B 7 DD2
6 7	2 E 7 D3	3	4	5 D (9-3) DD2	6 A 3 DD2	7 B (4-3) DD2
7 7	2	3	4 E (9-3) DD2	5 C 3 DD2	6 D 5 DD2	7 E (6-5) DD2

A	B	C	D	E
7 / 5 / 3 / T	7 / 5 / (4-3) / T	7 / (6-5) / 3 / T	7 / 5 / (9-3) / T	7 / (6-5) / (9-3) / T
F7M	**G7,4**	**G7(13)** [Em/F]	**F7M(9-3)** [C/F]	**Em7(9-3) (6-5)** [Dm7(9)]

4.9 CARD 4 – TYPOLOGY

4.9.1   7-35 Diatonic Scale

Card 4		
A	Seventh Chords	7
B	Quartal Chords	7(4-3) 7(11-5)
C	Triad / II	7(6-5)
D	Triad / IV	7(9-3)
E	Cluster 4 note Segments T 3 7 (9)	7(9-3) (6-5) 7(9-5)

A

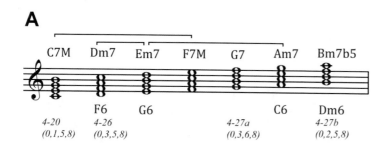

B

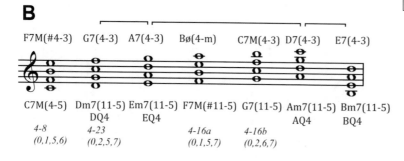

C

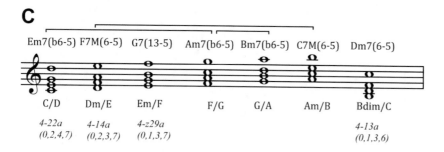

D

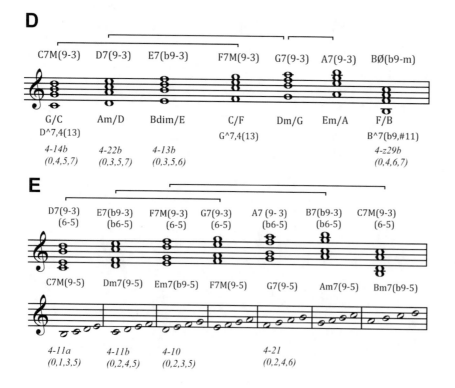

E

COMBINATORIAL HARMONY - BY JULIO HERRLEIN - MEL BAY

4.9.2   7-32a Harmonic Minor Scale

Card 4		
A	Seventh Chords	7
B	Quartal Chords	7(4-3) 7(11-5)
C	Triad / II	7(6-5)
D	Triad / IV	7(9-3)
E	Cluster 4 note Segments T 3 7 (9)	7(9-3) (6-5) 7(9-5)

A

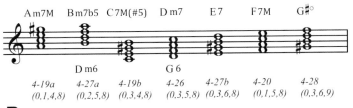

Am7M   Bm7b5   C7M(#5)   D m7   E 7   F 7M   G#°

D m6   G 6

| 4-19a | 4-27a | 4-19b | 4-26 | 4-27b | 4-20 | 4-28 |
| (0,1,4,8) | (0,2,5,8) | (0,3,4,8) | (0,3,5,8) | (0,3,6,8) | (0,1,5,8) | (0,3,6,9) |

B

Fm/B
D7(#4-3)   E7(4-3)   F7M(#4-3)   Fm6   A7M(4-3)   BØ(4-m)   C7M#5(4-3)

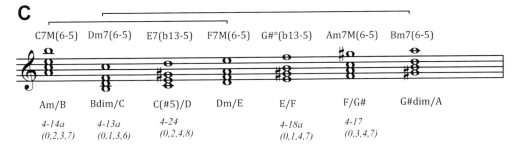

Fdim/C
Am7M(11-5)   Bm7(11-5)   C7M(11-5)   DØ   E7(11-5)   F7M(#11-5)   G#°(3-5)

| 4-z15a | 4-23 | 4-8 | 4-27a | 4-16b | 4-16a | 4-18b |
| (0,2,5,6) | (0,2,5,7) | (0,1,5,6) | (0,2,5,8) | (0,2,6,7) | (0,1,5,7) | (0,3,6,7) |

C

C7M(6-5)   Dm7(6-5)   E7(b13-5)   F7M(6-5)   G#°(b13-5)   Am7M(6-5)   Bm7(6-5)

Am/B   Bdim/C   C(#5)/D   Dm/E   E/F   F/G#   G#dim/A

| 4-14a | 4-13a | 4-24 | | 4-18a | 4-17 | |
| (0,2,3,7) | (0,1,3,6) | (0,2,4,8) | | (0,1,4,7) | (0,3,4,7) | |

D

A7M(9-3)   BØ(b9-m)   C7M#5(9-3)   D7(9-3)   E7(b9-3)   Fm7M   G#°(b9-m)

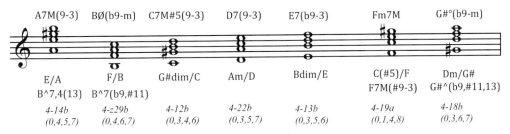

E/A   F/B   G#dim/C   Am/D   Bdim/E   C(#5)/F   Dm/G#
B^7,4(13)   B^7(b9,#11)   F7M(#9-3)   G#^(b9,#11,13)

| 4-14b | 4-z29b | 4-12b | 4-22b | 4-13b | 4-19a | 4-18b |
| (0,4,5,7) | (0,4,6,7) | (0,3,4,6) | (0,3,5,7) | (0,3,5,6) | (0,1,4,8) | (0,3,6,7) |

E

BØ(b9-3)   C7M(9-3)   D7(9-3)   E7(b9-3)   Fm7M(6-5)   G#°(b9-3)   A7M (9 - 3)
(6-5)   (6-5)   (6-5)   (b6-5)   (b6-5)   (b6- 5)

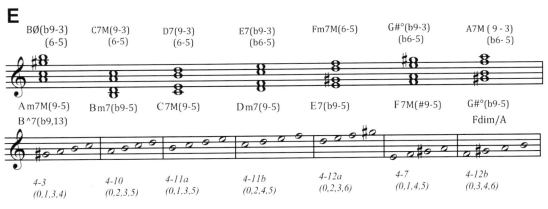

Am7M(9-5)   Bm7(b9-5)   C7M(9-5)   Dm7(9-5)   E7(b9-5)   F7M(#9-5)   G#°(b9-5)
B^7(b9,13)   Fdim/A

| 4-3 | 4-10 | 4-11a | 4-11b | 4-12a | 4-7 | 4-12b |
| (0,1,3,4) | (0,2,3,5) | (0,1,3,5) | (0,2,4,5) | (0,2,3,6) | (0,1,4,5) | (0,3,4,6) |

4.9.3   7-34 Melodic Minor Scale

Card 4		
A	Seventh Chords	7
B	Quartal Chords	7(4-3)
		7(11-5)
C	Triad / II	7(6-5)
D	Triad / IV	7(9-3)
E	Cluster 4 note Segments T 3 7 (9)	7(9-3) (6-5)
		7(9-5)

A

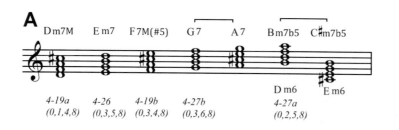

B

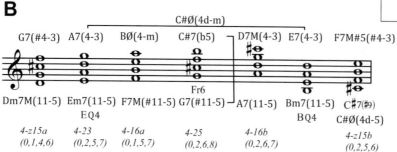

C

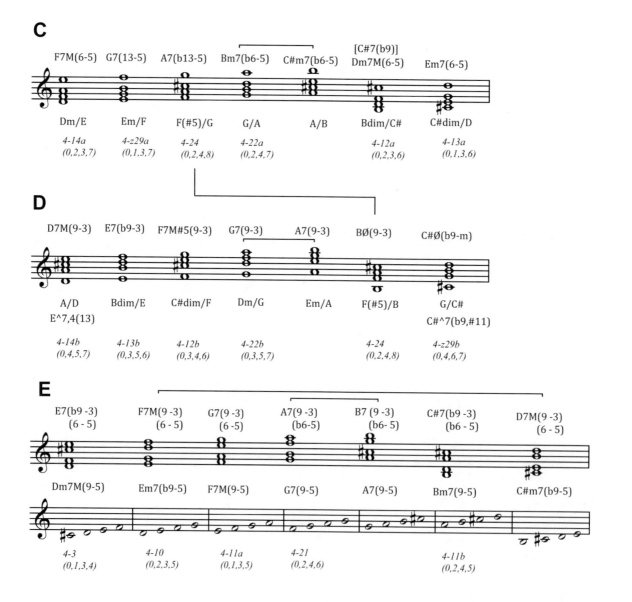

4.9.4   7-32b Harmonic Major Scale

Card 4		
A	Seventh Chords	7
B	Quartal Chords	7(4-3) 7(11-5)
C	Triad / II	7(6-5)
D	Triad / IV	7(9-3)
E	Cluster 4 note Segments T 3 7 (9)	7(9-3) (6-5) 7(9-5)

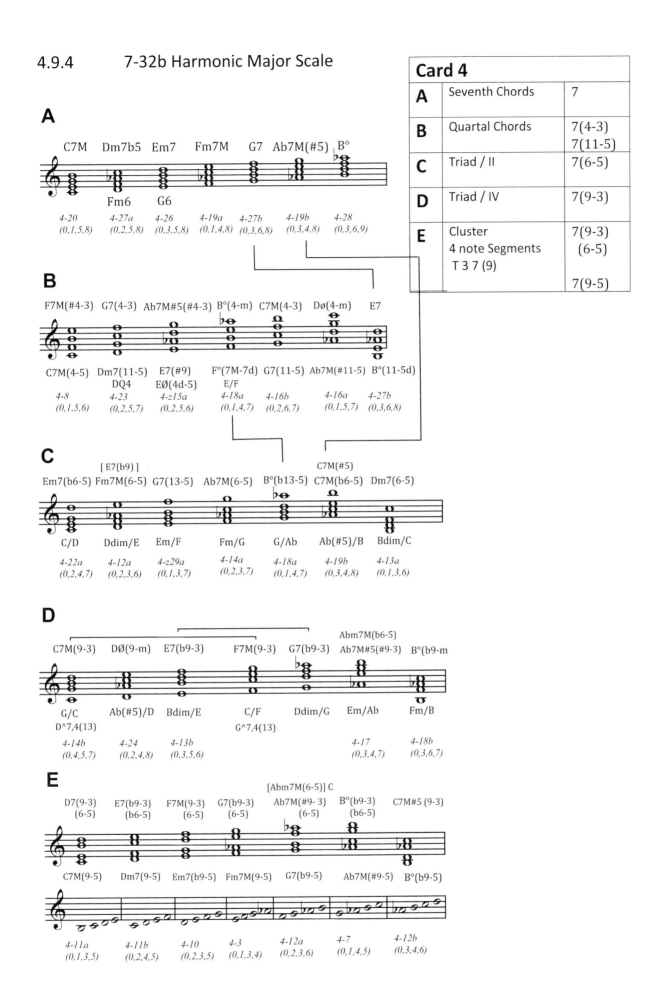

4.9.5

8-28 Octatonic Scale
Messiaen 2

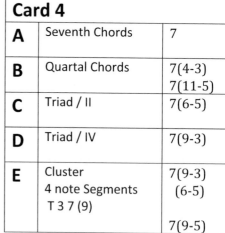

Card 4		
A	Seventh Chords	7
B	Quartal Chords	7(4-3) 7(11-5)
C	Triad / II	7(6-5)
D	Triad / IV	7(9-3)
E	Cluster 4 note Segments T 3 7 (9)	7(9-3) (6-5) 7(9-5)

A

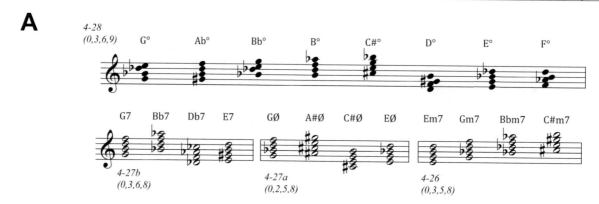

B

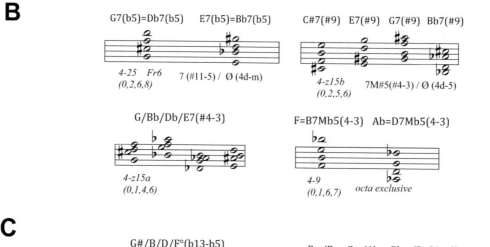

C

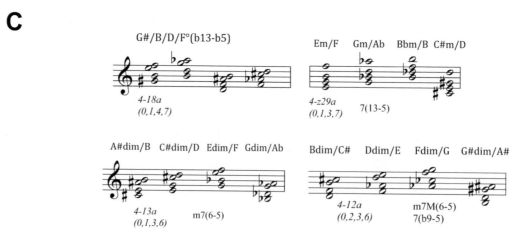

D

E/G G/Bb Bb/Db Db/E

4-17
(0,3,4,7) m7M(b6-5) (add#9)

Em/Bb Gm/Db Bbm/E C#m/G

4-18b
(0,3,6,7) °(b9-m)

G/C# Bb/E Db/G E/Bb

4-z29b Ø (b9-m)
(0,4,6,7)

Bdim/E Ddim/A Fdim/Bb G#dim/C#

4-13b
(0,3,5,6)

Gdim/B Bbdim/D C#dim/F Edim/G#

4-12b
(0,3,4,6) 7M#5(9-3)

E

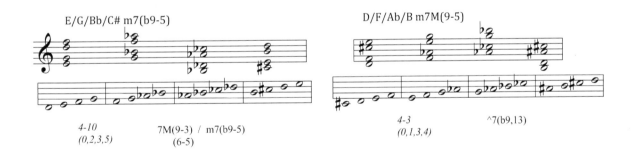

E/G/Bb/C# m7(b9-5)

4-10
(0,2,3,5) 7M(9-3) / m7(b9-5)
(6-5)

D/F/Ab/B m7M(9-5)

4-3
(0,1,3,4) ^7(b9,13)

9-12 Nonatonic Scale
Messiaen 3

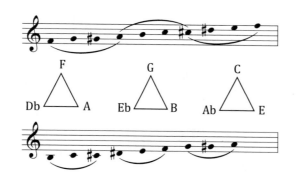

Card 4		
A	Seventh Chords	7
B	Quartal Chords	7(4-3)
		7(11-5)
C	Triad / II	7(6-5)
D	Triad / IV	7(9-3)
E	Cluster	7(9-3)
	4 note Segments	(6-5)
	T 3 7 (9)	
		7(9-5)

A

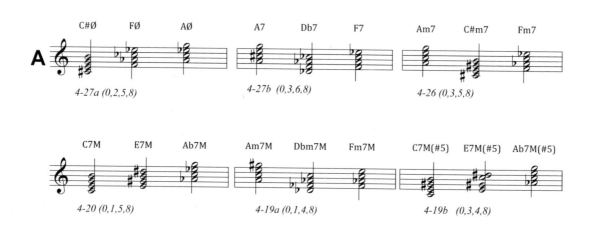

B

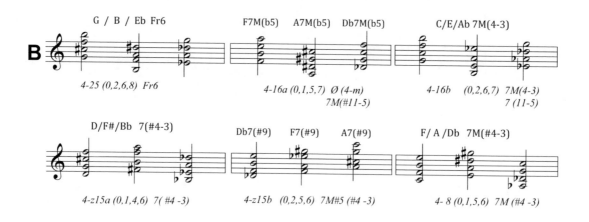

6-35 Whole-Tone Scale
Messiaen 1

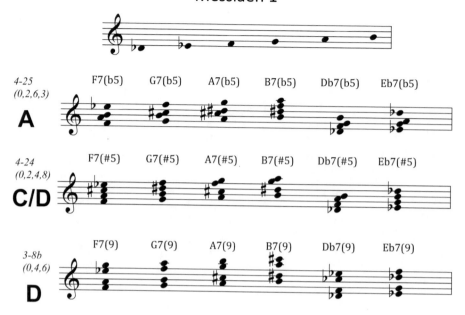

6-20 Augmented Scale
Subset of Messiaen 3

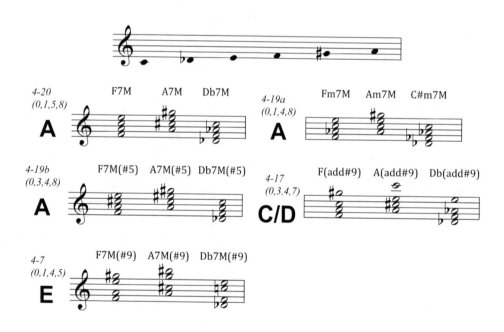

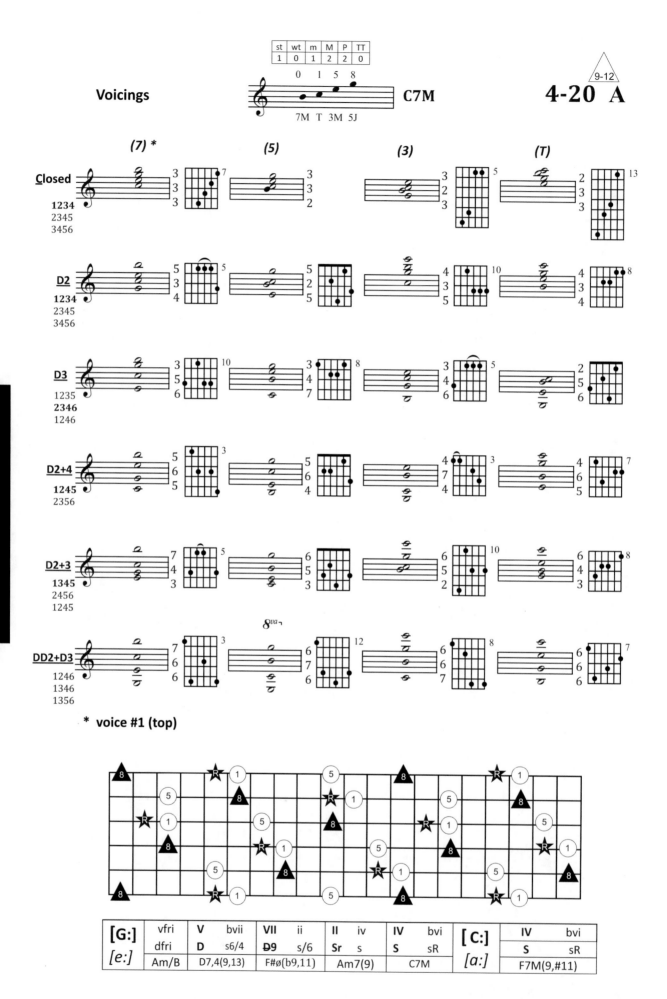

Voicings — C7M

st	wt	m	M	P	TT
1	0	1	2	2	0

0 1 5 8

7M T 3M 5J

4.10 FOUR-NOTE CHORDS

* voice #1 (top)

Voicings

Dm7M   **4-19a A**

9-12

7M T 3m 5J

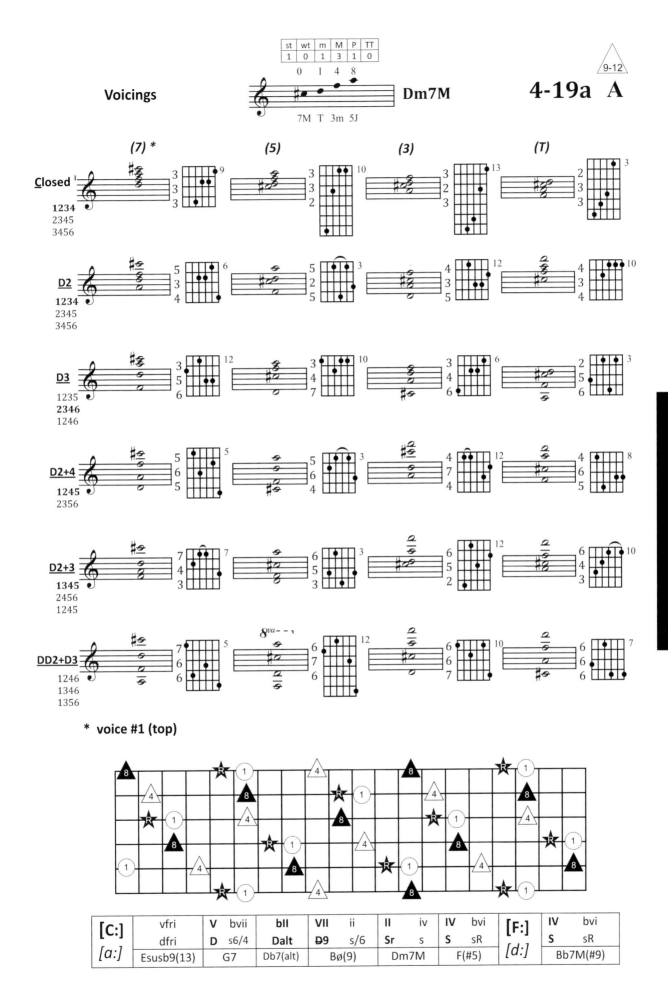

(7) *   (5)   (3)   (T)

Closed
1234
2345
3456

D2
1234
2345
3456

D3
1235
2346
1246

D2+4
1245
2356

D2+3
1345
2456
1245

DD2+D3
1246
1346
1356

* voice #1 (top)

4.10 FOUR-NOTE CHORDS

[C:]	vfri	V	bvii	bII	VII	ii	II	iv	IV	bvi	[F:]	IV	bvi
	dfri	D	s6/4	Dalt	D9	s/6	Sr	s	S	sR		S	sR
[a:]	Esusb9(13)		G7	Db7(alt)		Bø(9)		Dm7M		F(#5)	[d:]		Bb7M(#9)

st	wt	m	M	P	TT
1	0	1	3	1	0

0 3 4 8

Voicings

F7M(#5)   **4-19b**   **A**   9-12

5A 7M T 3M

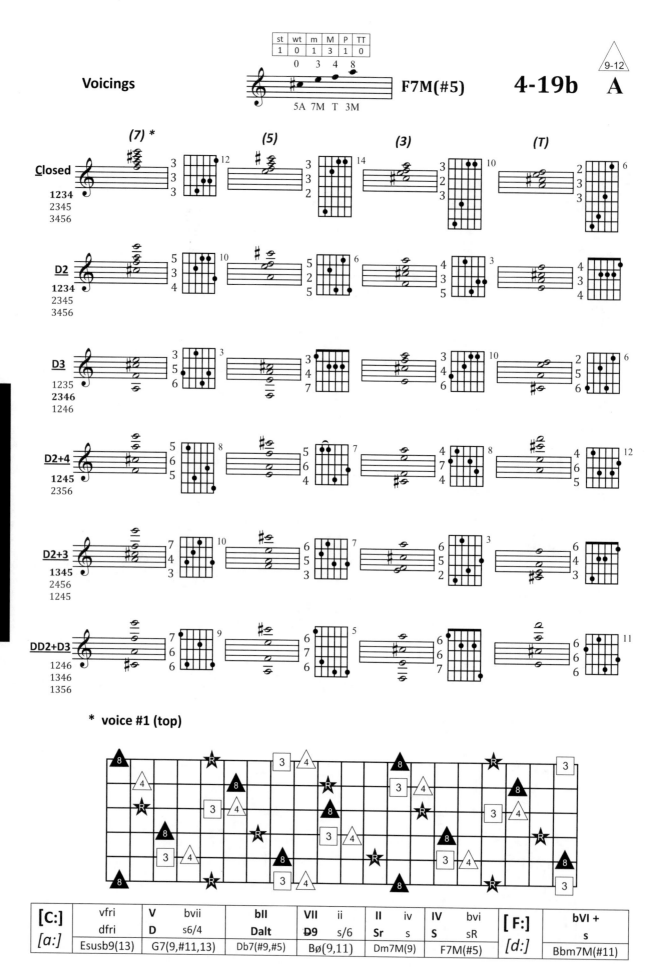

(7) *   *(5)*   *(3)*   *(T)*

Closed
1234
2345
3456

D2
1234
2345
3456

D3
1235
2346
1246

D2+4
1245
2356

D2+3
1345
2456
1245

DD2+D3
1246
1346
1356

* voice #1 (top)

[C:]	vfri	V	bvii	bII	VII	ii	II	iv	IV	bvi	[F:]	bVI +
[a:]	dfri	D	s6/4	Dalt	D9	s/6	Sr	s	S	sR	[d:]	s
	Esusb9(13)	G7(9,#11,13)		Db7(#9,#5)	Bø(9,11)		Dm7M(9)		F7M(#5)			Bbm7M(#11)

Voicings

st	wt	m	M	P	TT
1	0	1	2	2	0

F7M

7M T 3M 5J

4.10 FOUR-NOTE CHORDS

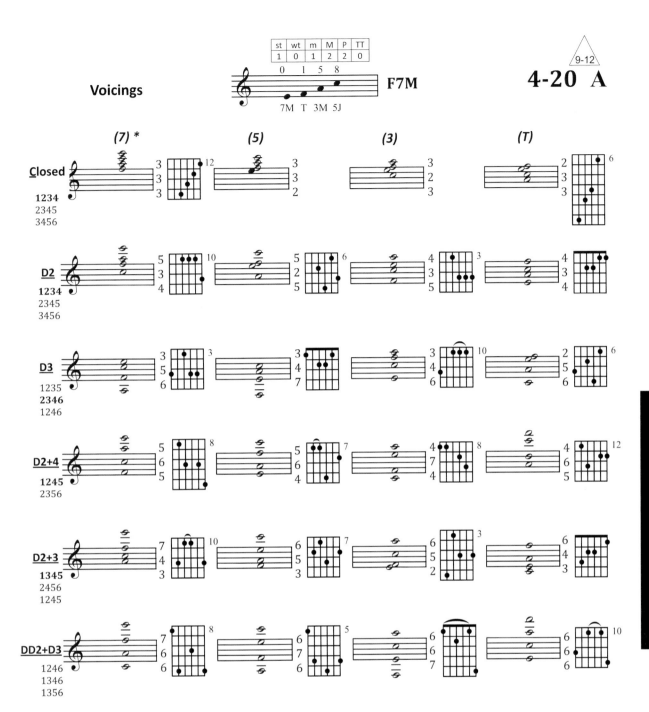

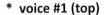

* **voice #1 (top)**

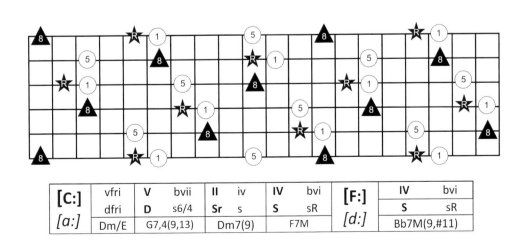

[C:]	vfri	**V**	bvii	**II**	iv	**IV**	bvi	**[F:]**	**IV**	bvi
	dfri	**D**	s6/4	**Sr**	s	**S**	sR		**S**	sR
[a:]	Dm/E	G7,4(9,13)		Dm7(9)		F7M		**[d:]**	Bb7M(9,#11)	

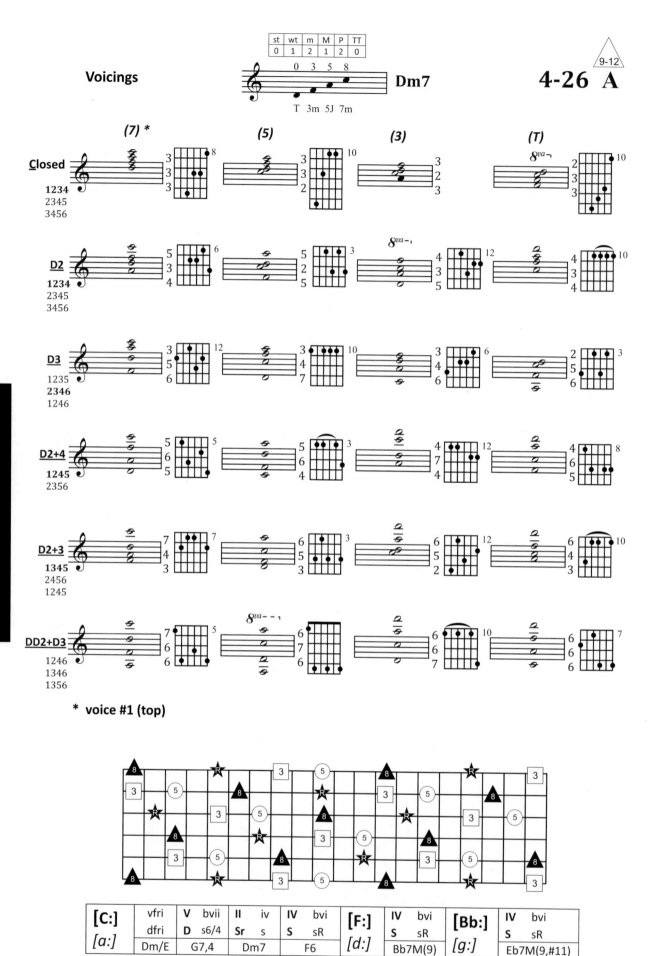

4.10 FOUR-NOTE CHORDS

Voicings

Dm7

4-26 A

st	wt	m	M	P	TT
0	1	2	1	2	0

0 3 5 8

T 3m 5J 7m

(7) * (5) (3) (T)

Closed
1234
2345
3456

D2
1234
2345
3456

D3
1235
2346
1246

D2+4
1245
2356

D2+3
1345
2456
1245

DD2+D3
1246
1346
1356

* voice #1 (top)

[C:]	vfri	V	bvii	II	iv	IV	bvi	[F:]	IV	bvi	[Bb:]	IV	bvi
[a:]	dfri	D	s6/4	Sr	s	S	sR	[d:]	S	sR	[g:]	S	sR
	Dm/E	G7,4		Dm7		F6			Bb7M(9)			Eb7M(9,#11)	

COMBINATORIAL HARMONY - BY JULIO HERRLEIN - MEL BAY

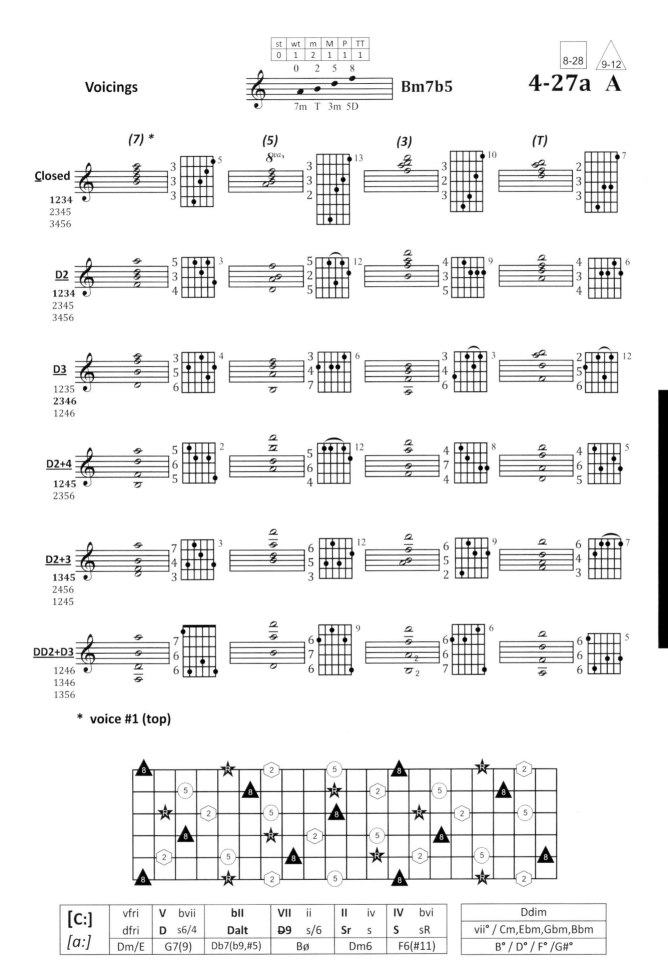

* voice #1 (top)

[C:]	vfri	V	bvii	bII		VII	ii	II	iv	IV	bvi	Ddim	
	dfri	D	s6/4	Dalt		D9	s/6	Sr	s	S	sR	vii° / Cm,Ebm,Gbm,Bbm	
[a:]	Dm/E	G7(9)		Db7(b9,#5)		Bø		Dm6		F6(#11)		B° / D° / F° /G#°	

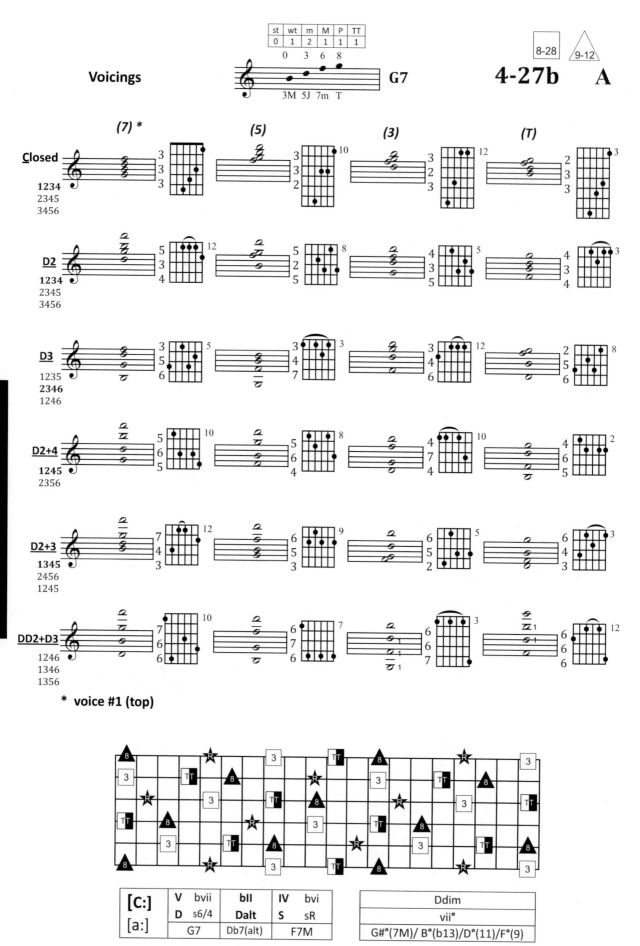

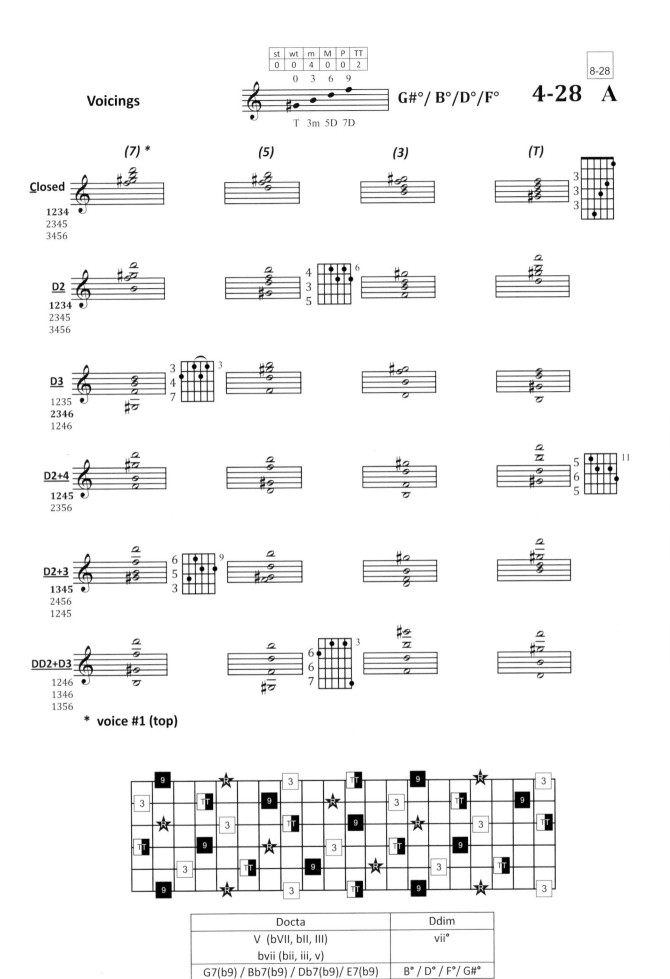

Docta	Ddim
V (bVII, bII, III)	vii°
bvii (bii, iii, v)	
G7(b9) / Bb7(b9) / Db7(b9)/ E7(b9)	B° / D° / F°/ G#°

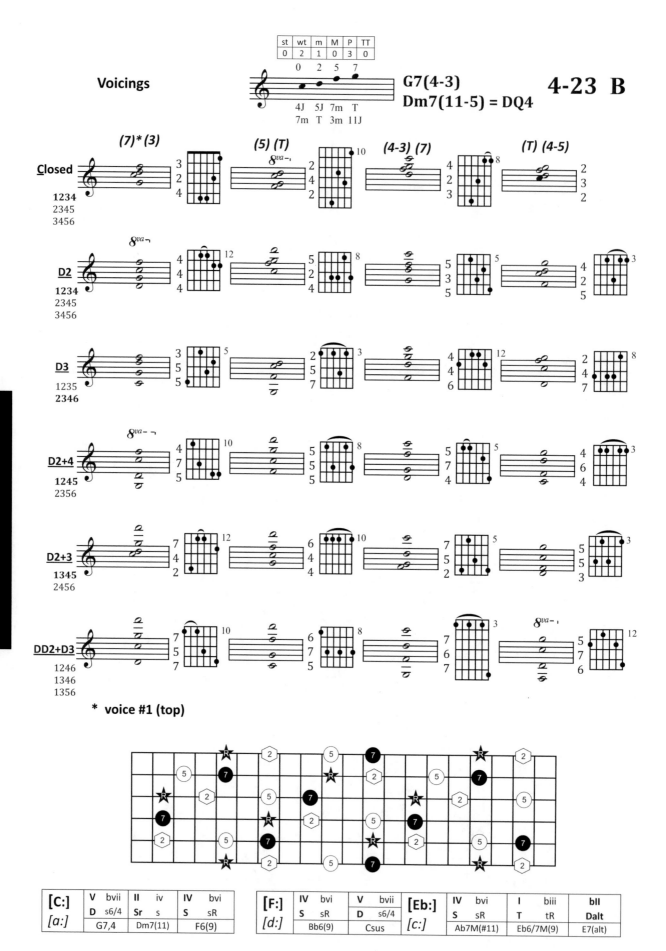

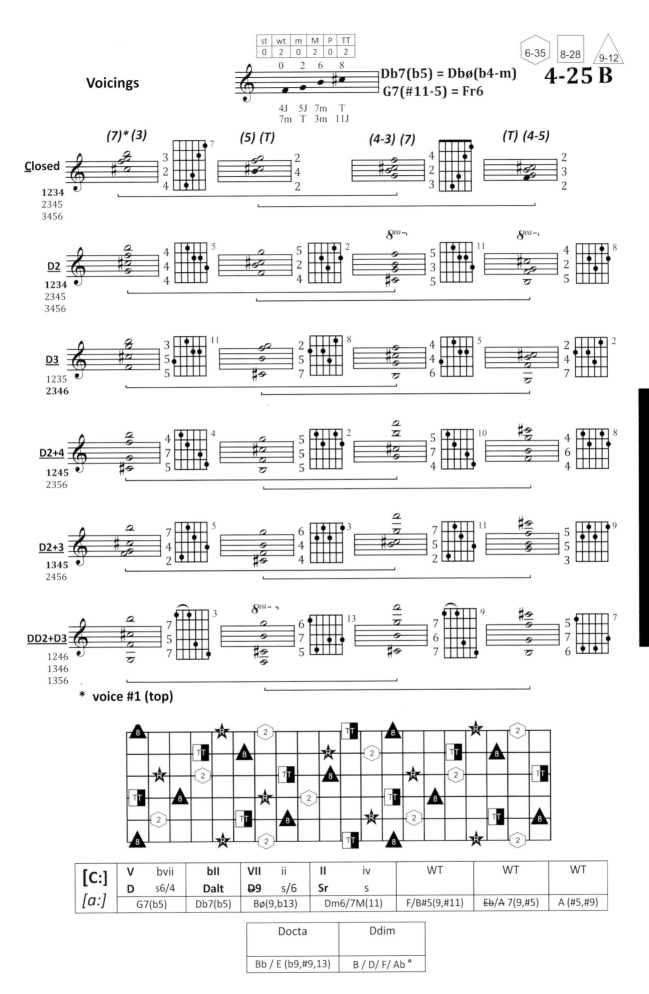

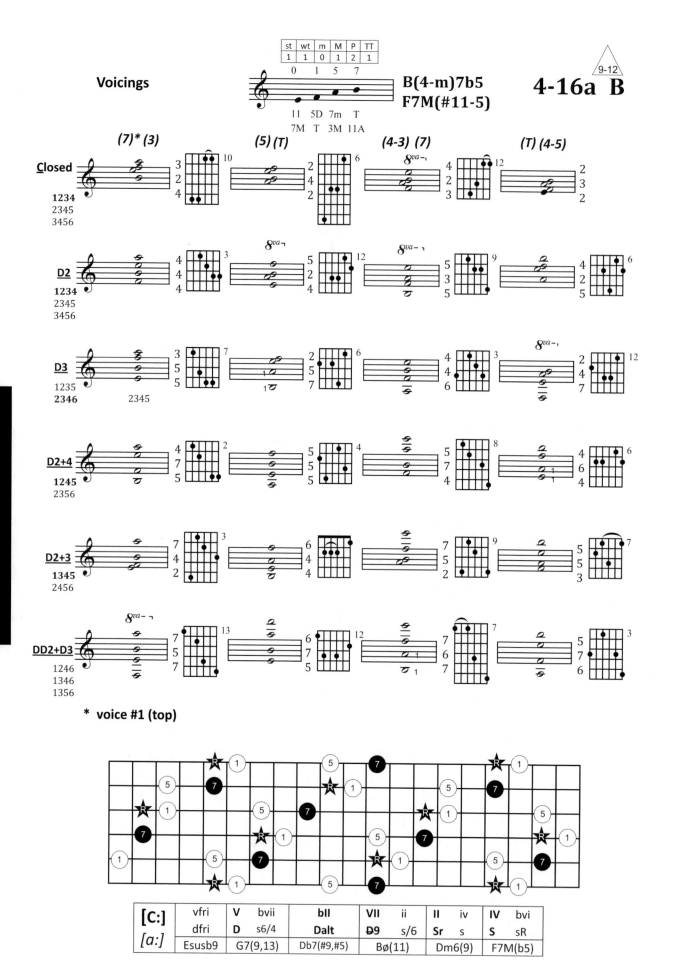

	wt	m	M	P	TT
st	wt	m	M	P	TT
1	1	0	1	2	1

Voicings

B(4-m)7b5
F7M(#11-5)

4-16a B

9-12

* voice #1 (top)

[C:]	vfri	**V**	bvii	**bII**	**VII**	ii	**II**	iv	**IV**	bvi
[a:]	dfri	**D**	s6/4	**Dalt**	**D9**	s/6	**Sr**	s	**S**	sR
	Esusb9	G7(9,13)		Db7(#9,#5)	Bø(11)		Dm6(9)		F7M(b5)	

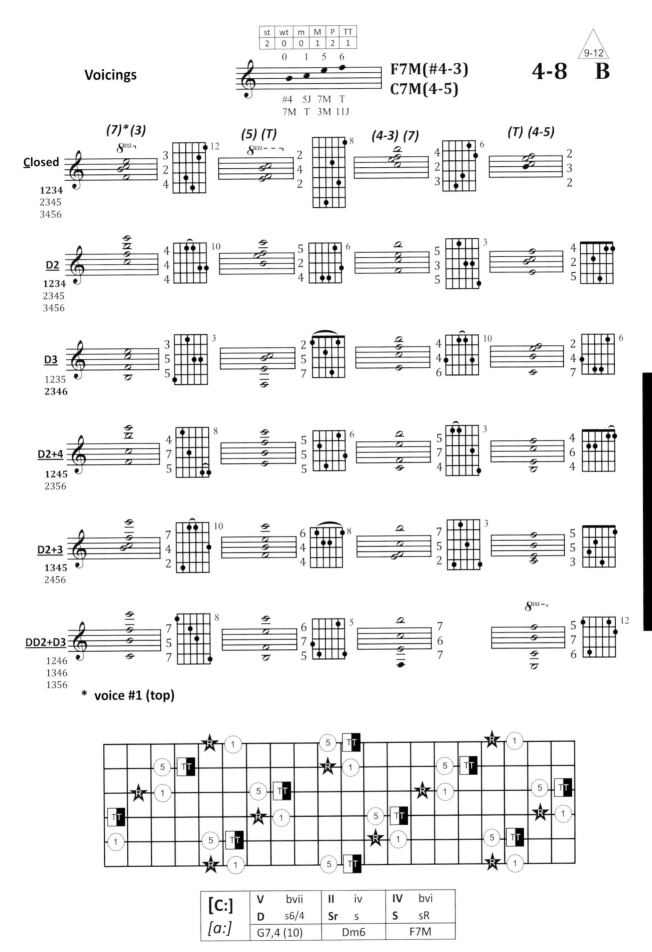

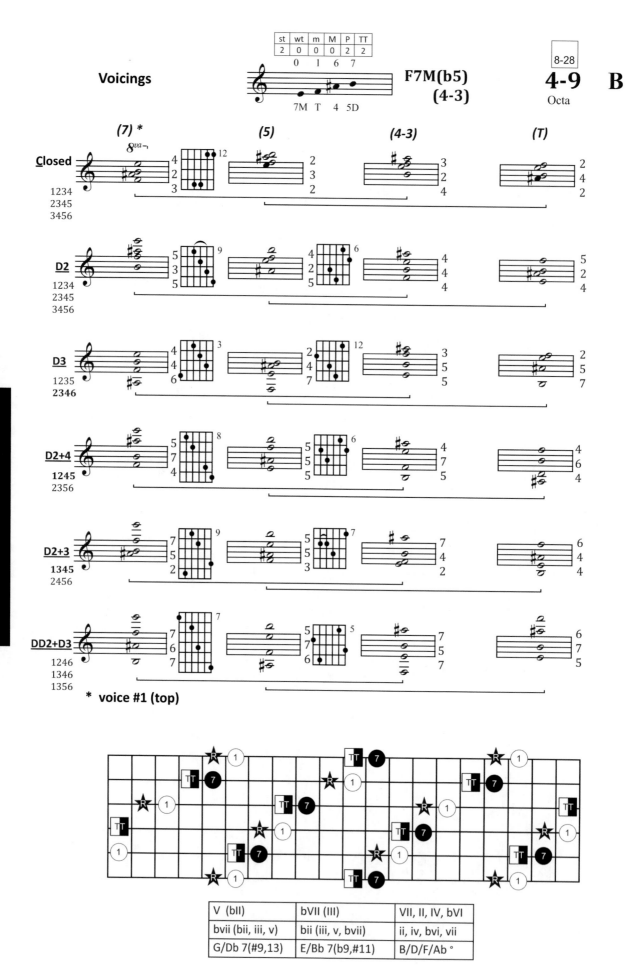

Voicings

st	wt	m	M	P	TT
2	0	0	0	2	2

0 1 6 7

F7M(b5)
(4-3)

8-28

4-9   B

Octa

7M T 4 5D

V (bII)	bVII (III)	VII, II, IV, bVI
bvii (bii, iii, v)	bii (iii, v, bvii)	ii, iv, bvi, vii
G/Db 7(#9,13)	E/Bb 7(b9,#11)	B/D/F/Ab °

* voice #1 (top)

Voicings

st	wt	m	M	P	TT
1	1	0	1	2	1
0	2	6	7		

C7M(4-3)
G7(11-5)

4J 5J 7M T
7m T 3M 11J

4-16b   B

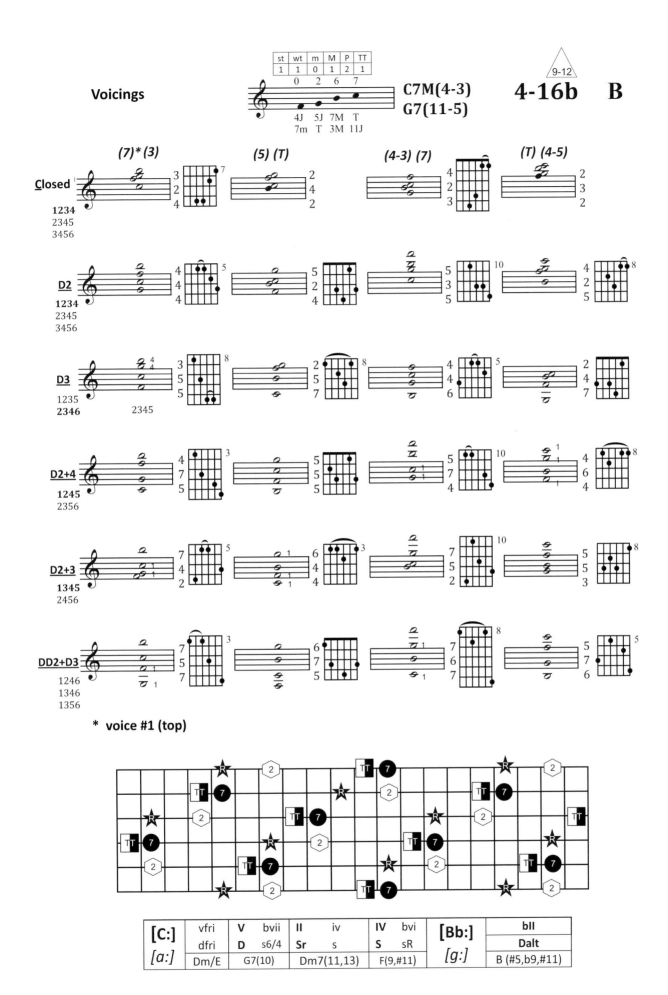

* voice #1 (top)

[C:]	vfri	V	bvii	II	iv	IV	bvi	[Bb:]	bII
	dfri	D	s6/4	Sr	s	S	sR		Dalt
[a:]	Dm/E	G7(10)		Dm7(11,13)		F(9,#11)		[g:]	B (#5,b9,#11)

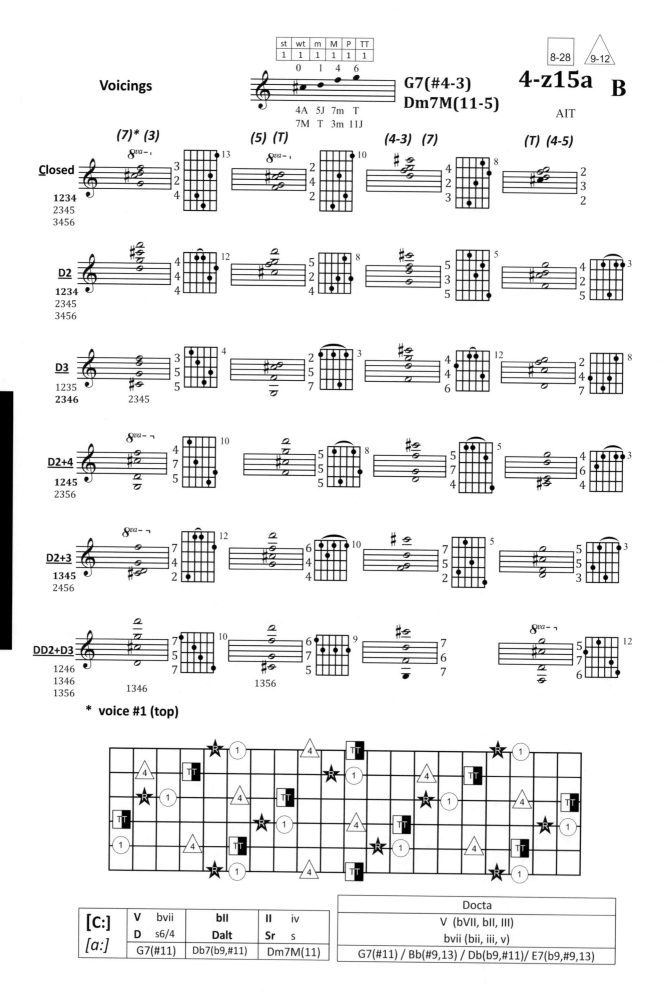

Voicings

G7(#4-3)
Dm7M(11-5)

4-z15a B

8-28 9-12

AIT

	st	wt	m	M	P	TT
	1	1	1	1	1	1
	0	1	4	6		

4A 5J 7m T
7M T 3m 11J

(7)* (3)   (5) (T)   (4-3) (7)   (T) (4-5)

Closed
1234
2345
3456

D2
1234
2345
3456

D3
1235
2346   2345

D2+4
1245
2356

D2+3
1345
2456

DD2+D3
1246
1346   1346   1356
1356

* voice #1 (top)

[C:]	V	bvii	bII	II	iv
[a:]	D	s6/4	Dalt	Sr	s
	G7(#11)		Db7(b9,#11)	Dm7M(11)	

Docta
V (bVII, bII, III)
bvii (bii, iii, v)
G7(#11) / Bb(#9,13) / Db(b9,#11)/ E7(b9,#9,13)

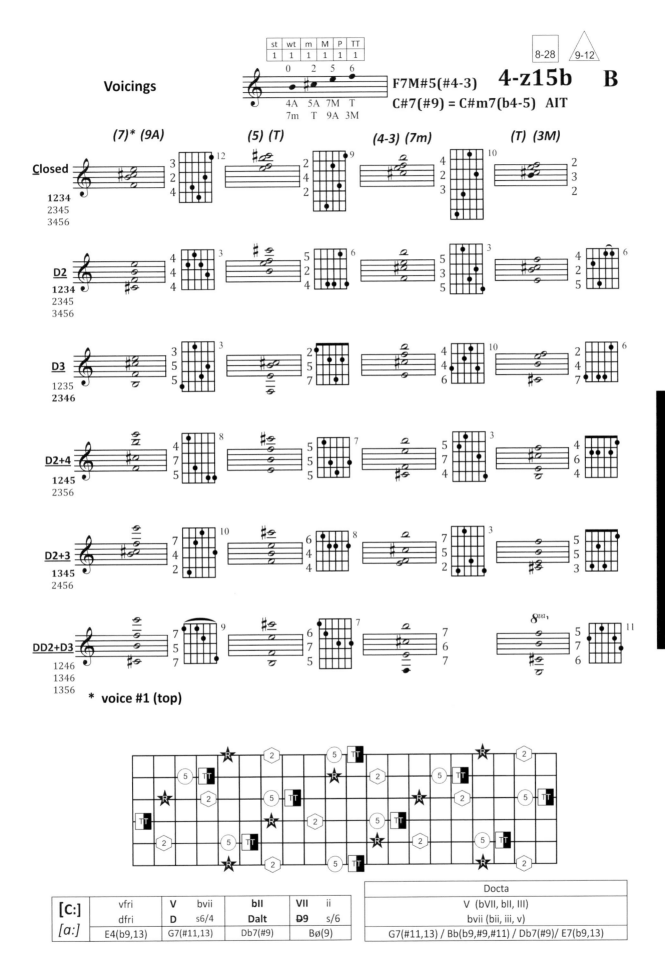

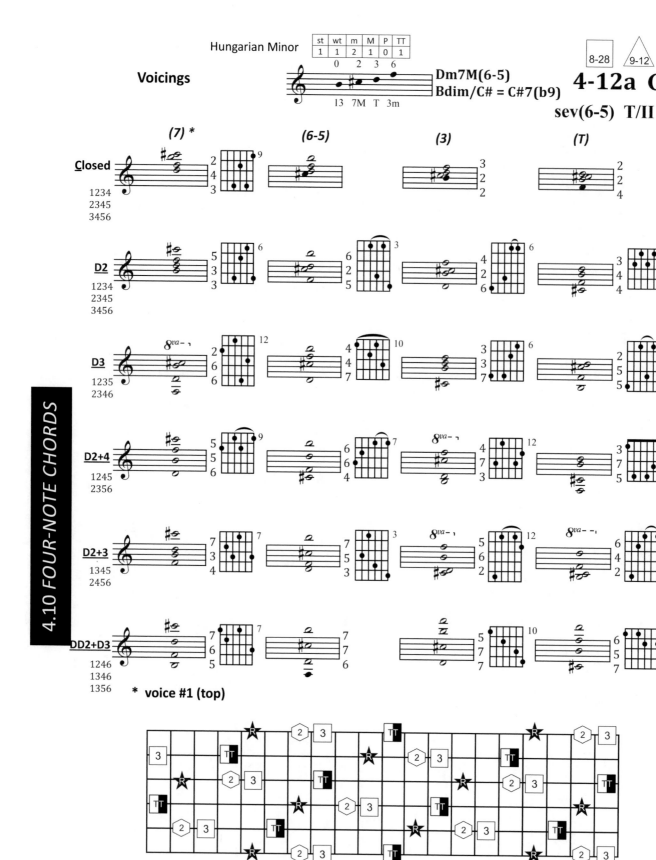

4.10 FOUR-NOTE CHORDS

Hungarian Minor

st	wt	m	M	P	TT
1	1	2	1	0	1

8-28 9-12

Voicings

Dm7M(6-5)
Bdim/C# = C#7(b9)

4-12a C

sev(6-5) T/II

13 7M T 3m

(7) *   (6-5)   (3)   (T)

Closed

D2

D3

D2+4

D2+3

DD2+D3

* voice #1 (top)

[C:] [a:]	vfri dfri	V D	bvii s6/4	bII Dalt	VII D9	ii s/6	II Sr	iv s
	E7,4(b9,13)	G7(#11)		Db7(b9)		Bø(9)		Dm6/7M

Docta
V (bVII, bII, III)
bvii (bii, iii, v)
G7(#11) / Bb(b9,#9) / Db7(b9) / E7(b9,13)

COMBINATORIAL HARMONY - BY JULIO HERRLEIN - MEL BAY

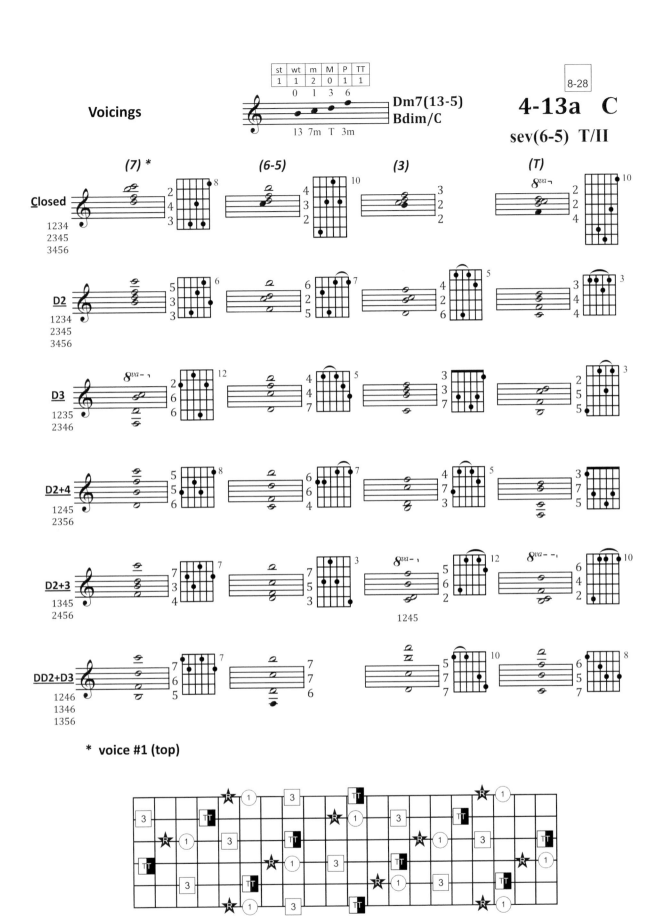

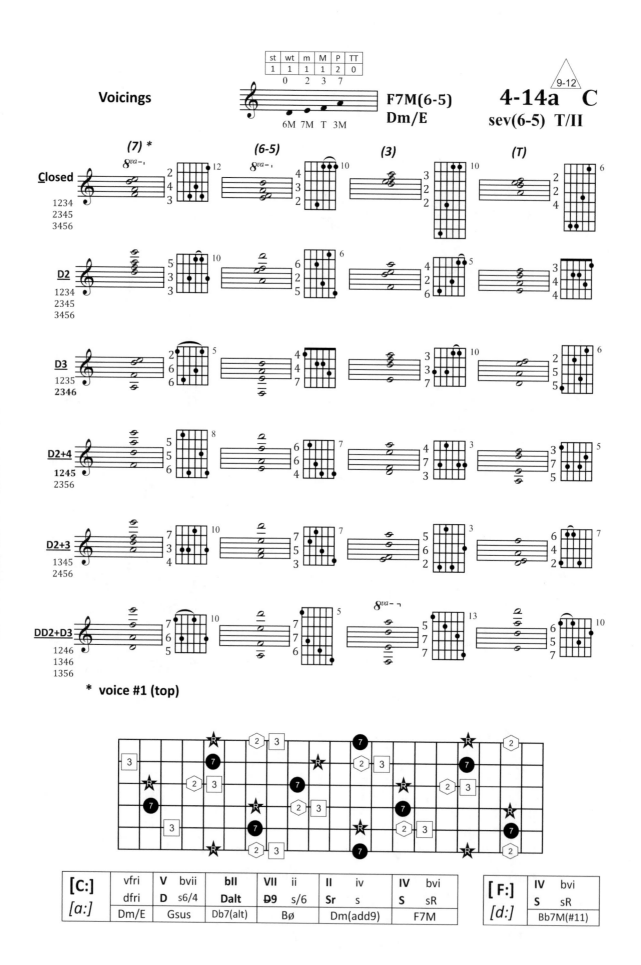

4.10 FOUR-NOTE CHORDS

Voicings

st	wt	m	M	P	TT
1	1	1	1	2	0
0		2	3	7	

F7M(6-5)
Dm/E

4-14a   C

sev(6-5) T/II

* voice #1 (top)

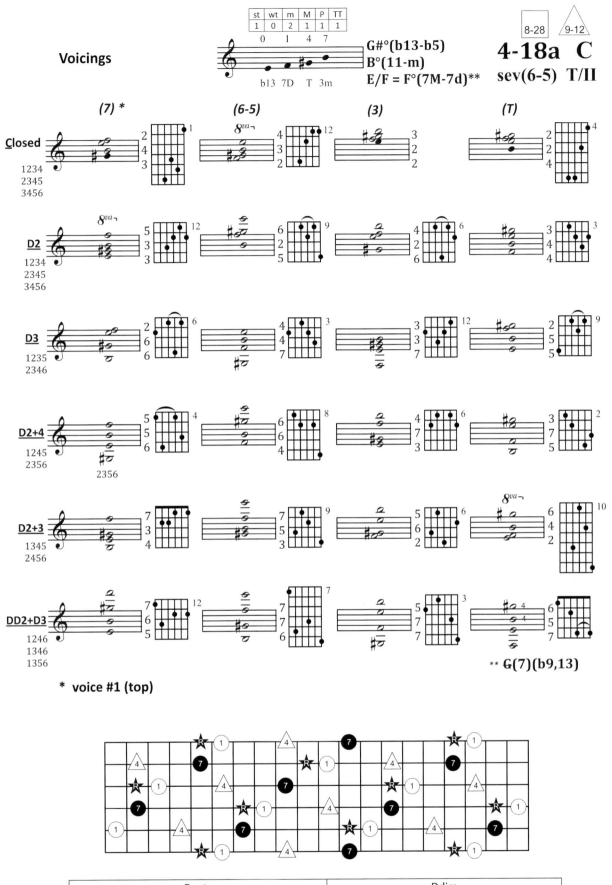

Voicings

st	wt	m	M	P	TT
1	0	2	1	1	1
0	1	4	7		

b13 7D   T   3m

G#°(b13-b5)
B°(11-m)
E/F = F°(7M-7d)**

8-28   9-12

4-18a   C
sev(6-5)   T/II

*(7) ** *   *(6-5)*   *(3)*   *(T)*

Closed
1234
2345
3456

D2
1234
2345
3456

D3
1235
2346

D2+4
1245
2356
2356

D2+3
1345
2456

DD2+D3
1246
1346
1356

** G(7)(b9,13)

* **voice #1 (top)**

4.10 FOUR-NOTE CHORDS

Docta	Ddim
V (bVII, bII, III)	vii°
bvii (bii, iii, v)	
G7(b9,13) / Bb(b9,#11,5J) / Db(#9,5J)/ E(addb9)	B°(11-m) / D°(9-R) / F°(7M-7d)/G#°(b13-5d)

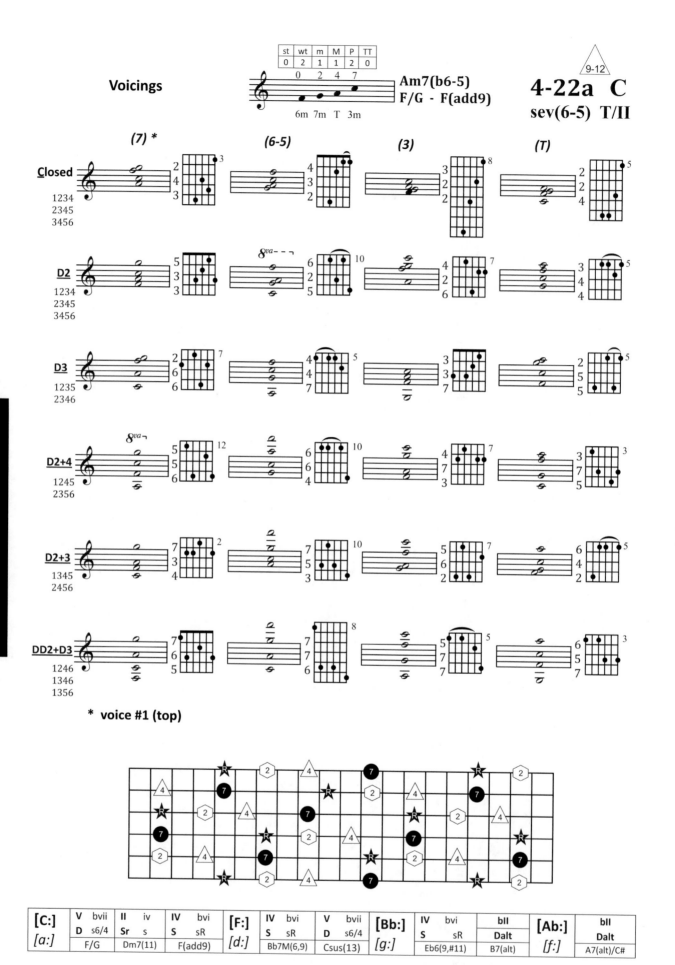

4.10 FOUR-NOTE CHORDS

Voicings

st	wt	m	M	P	TT
0	2	1	1	2	0

Am7(b6-5)
F/G - F(add9)

9-12

4-22a C
sev(6-5) T/II

6m 7m T 3m

* voice #1 (top)

[C:]	V	bvii	II	iv	IV	bvi	[F:]	IV	bvi	V	bvii	[Bb:]	IV	bvi	bII	[Ab:]	bII
[a:]	D	s6/4	Sr	s	S	sR	[d:]	S	sR	D	s6/4	[g:]	S	sR	Dalt	[f:]	Dalt
	F/G		Dm7(11)		F(add9)			Bb7M(6,9)		Csus(13)			Eb6(9,#11)		B7(alt)		A7(alt)/C#

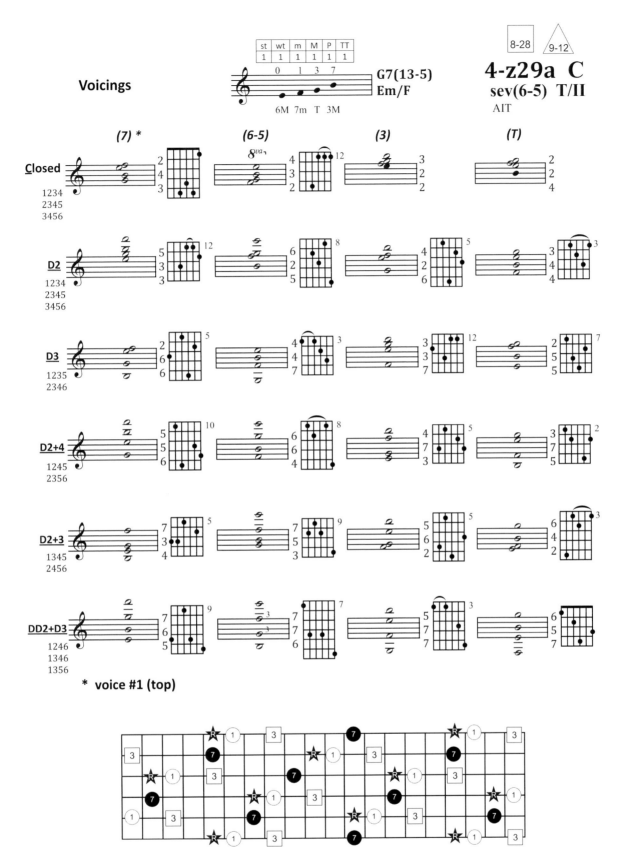

Voicings

st	wt	m	M	P	TT
1	1	1	1	1	1

G7(13-5)
Em/F

4-z29a C
sev(6-5) T/II
AIT

8-28   9-12

Closed
1234
2345
3456

D2
1234
2345
3456

D3
1235
2346

D2+4
1245
2356

D2+3
1345
2456

DD2+D3
1246
1346
1356

* voice #1 (top)

4.10 FOUR-NOTE CHORDS

[C:]	V	bvii	bII		VII	ii	II	iv	IV	bvi
	D	s6/4	Dalt		D9	s/6	Sr	s	S	sR
[a:]	G7(13)		Db7(#11,13)		Bø(11,b13)		Dm6(9,11)		F7M(9,#11)	

Docta	Ddim
V (bVII, bII, III)	vii°
bvii (bii, iii, v)	
G/Bb/Db/E 7	B / D/ F/ G#°

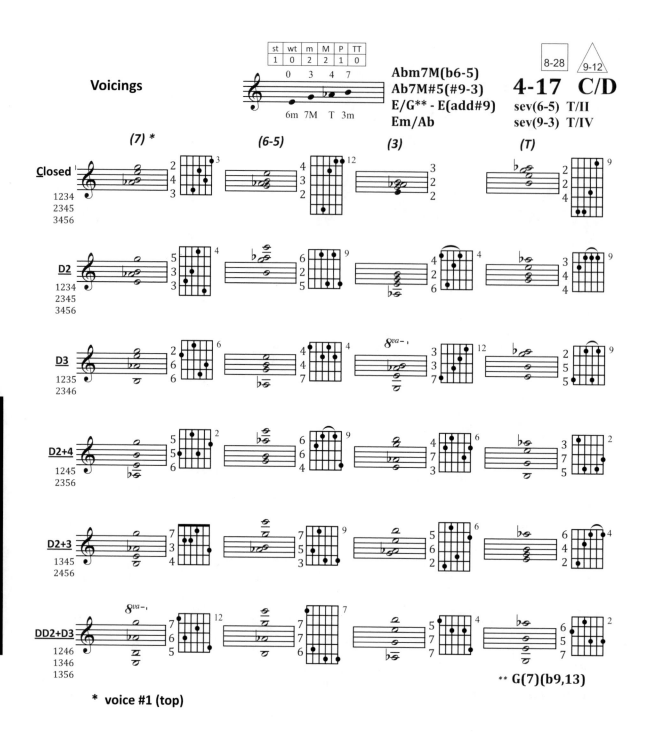

Voicings

st	wt	m	M	P	TT
1	0	2	2	1	0

Abm7M(b6-5)
Ab7M#5(#9-3)
E/G** - E(add#9)
Em/Ab

8-28   9-12

4-17 C/D

sev(6-5) T/II
sev(9-3) T/IV

(7) *   **(6-5)**   **(3)**   **(T)**

Closed
1234
2345
3456

D2
1234
2345
3456

D3
1235
2346

D2+4
1245
2356

D2+3
1345
2456

DD2+D3
1246
1346
1356

** G(7)(b9,13)

* voice #1 (top)

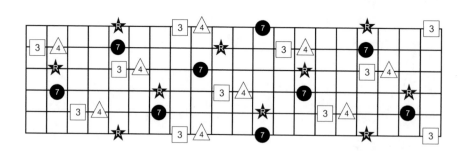

Docta	Ddim
V (bVII, bII, III)	vii°
bvii (bii, iii, v)	
G7(b9,13) / Bb(b9,#11,13) / Db(#9,#11)/ E(add#9)	B°(11,b13) / D°(11) / F°(7M,9)/G#°(7M,b13)

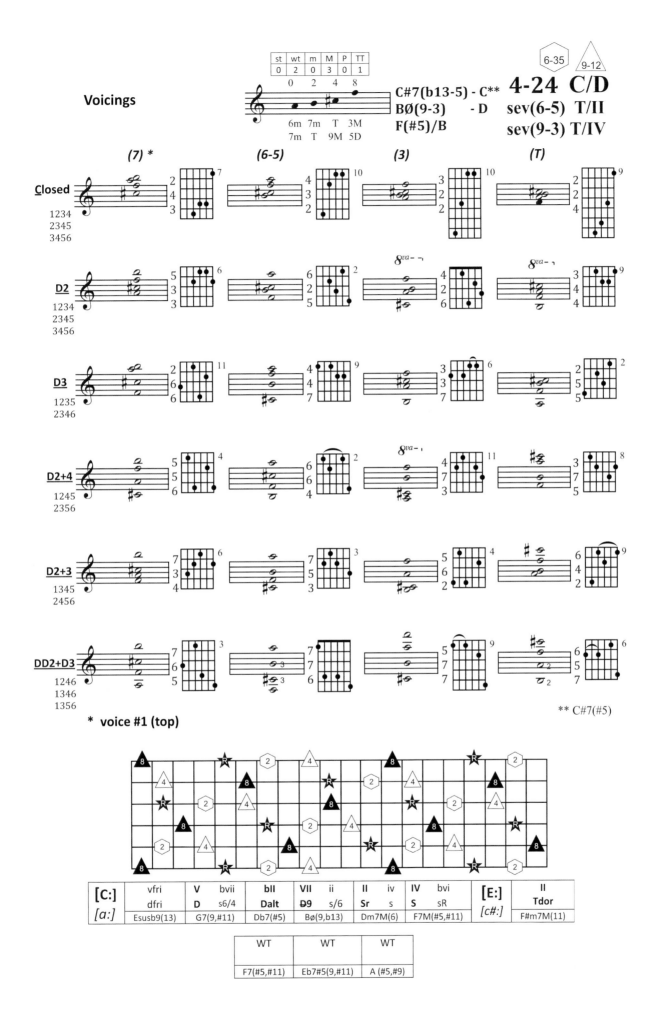

Hungarian Major

st	wt	m	M	P	TT
1	1	2	1	0	1

0 3 4 6

Voicings

F7M#5(9-3)   **4-12b**   **D**
C#dim/F   sev(9-3)   T/IV **

8-28   9-12

5A 7M T 9

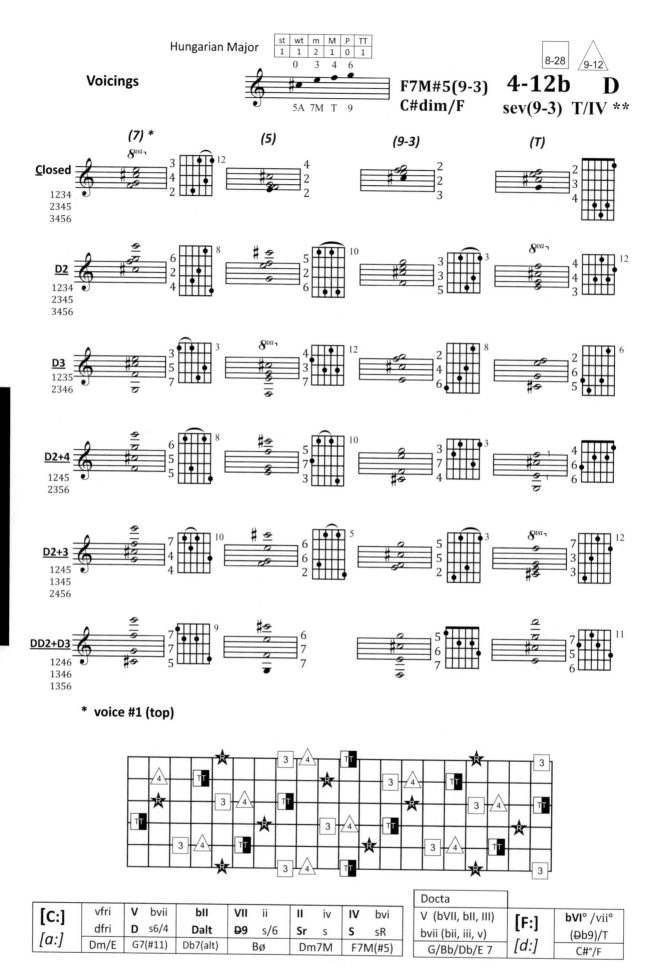

(7) *   (5)   (9-3)   (T)

Closed
1234
2345
3456

D2
1234
2345
3456

D3
1235
2346

D2+4
1245
2356

D2+3
1245
1345
2456

DD2+3
1246
1346
1356

* **voice #1 (top)**

[C:]	vfri	V	bvii	bII	VII	ii	II	iv	IV	bvi
[a:]	dfri	D	s6/4	Dalt	~~D9~~	s/6	Sr	s	S	sR
	Dm/E	G7(#11)		Db7(alt)	Bø		Dm7M		F7M(#5)	

Docta		
V (bVII, bII, III)	**[F:]**	bVI° /vii°
bvii (bii, iii, v)	[d:]	(~~Db9~~)/T
G/Bb/Db/E 7		C#°/F

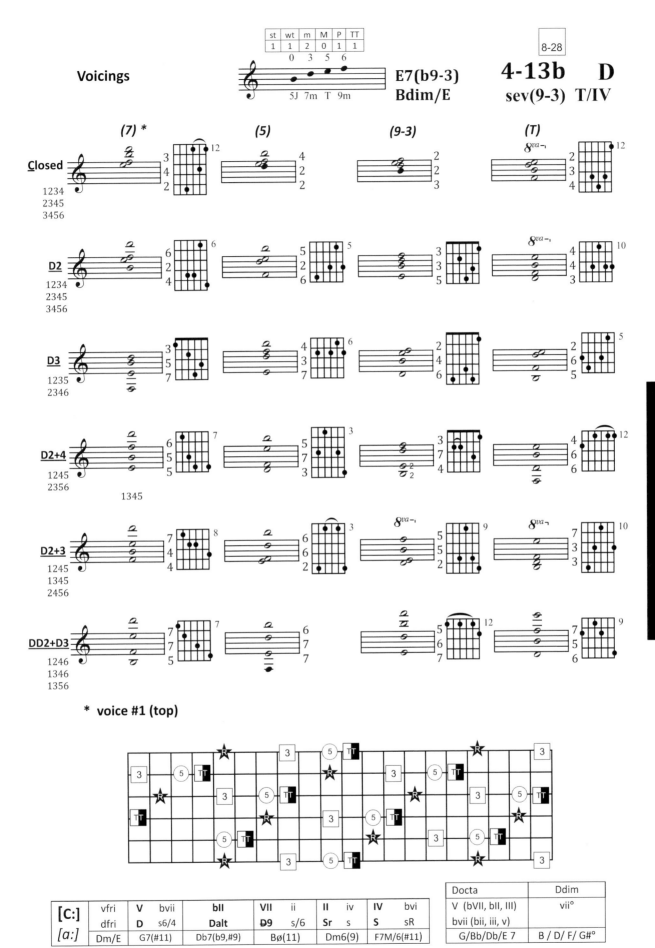

Voicings

E7(b9-3)
Bdim/E

4-13b   D
sev(9-3) T/IV

8-28

st	wt	m	M	P	TT
1	1	2	0	1	1
	0	3	5	6	

5J 7m T 9m

(7) *   **(5)**   **(9-3)**   **(T)**

Closed
1234
2345
3456

D2
1234
2345
3456

D3
1235
2346

D2+4
1245
2356
1345

D2+3
1245
1345
2456

DD2+D3
1246
1346
1356

* voice #1 (top)

[C:]	vfri	V	bvii	bII	VII	ii	II	iv	IV	bvi
[a:]	dfri	D	s6/4	**Dalt**	~~D9~~	s/6	Sr	s	S	sR
	Dm/E	G7(#11)		Db7(b9,#9)	Bø(11)		Dm6(9)		F7M/6(#11)	

Docta		Ddim
V (bVII, bII, III)		vii°
bvii (bii, iii, v)		
G/Bb/Db/E 7		B / D/ F/ G#°

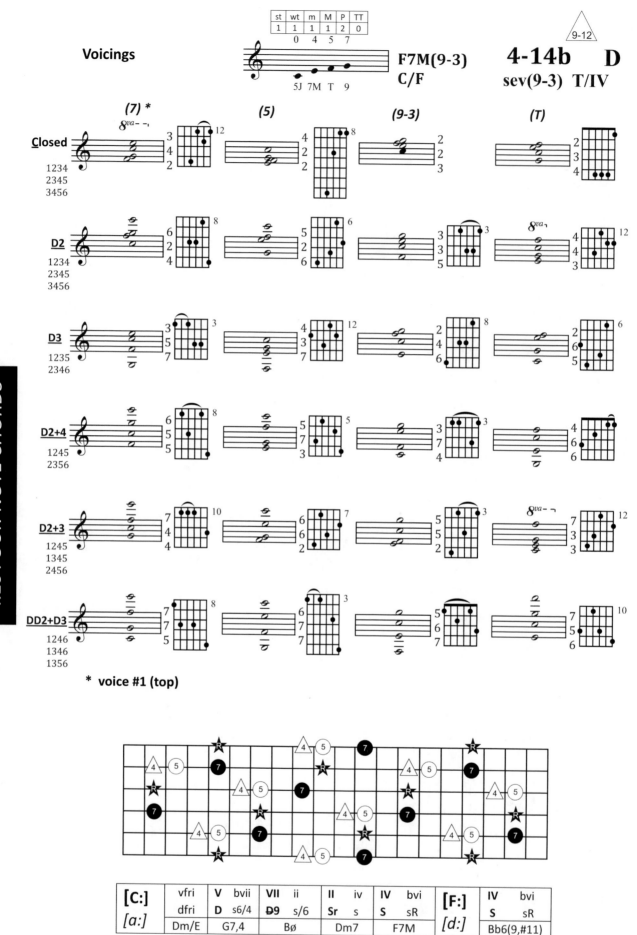

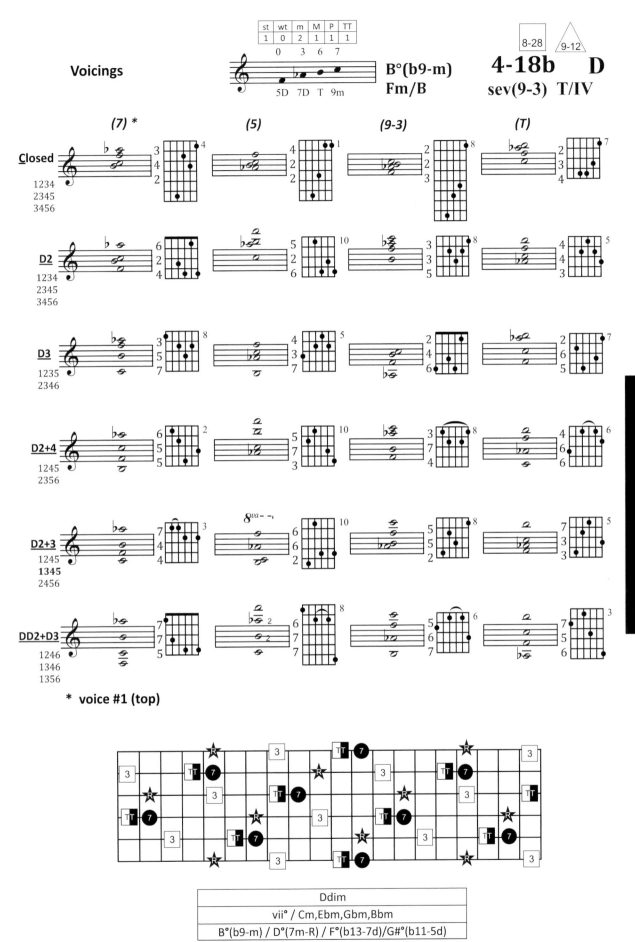

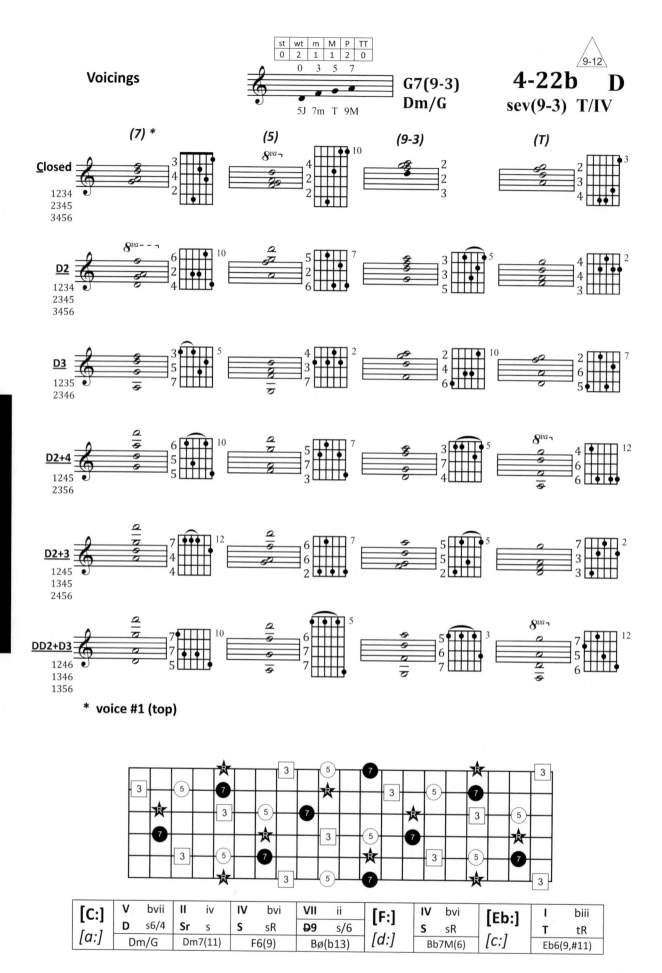

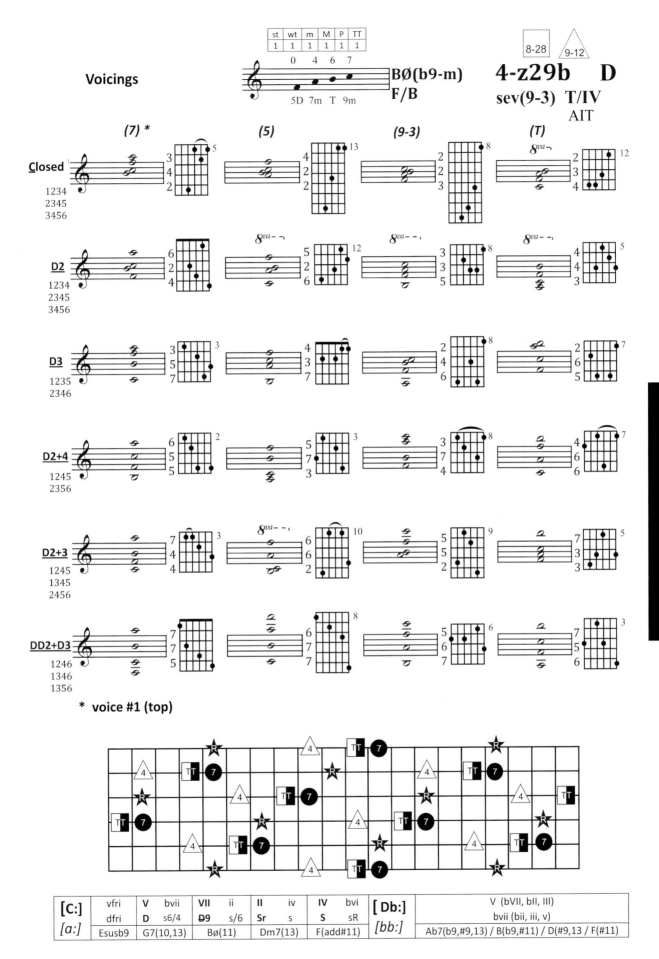

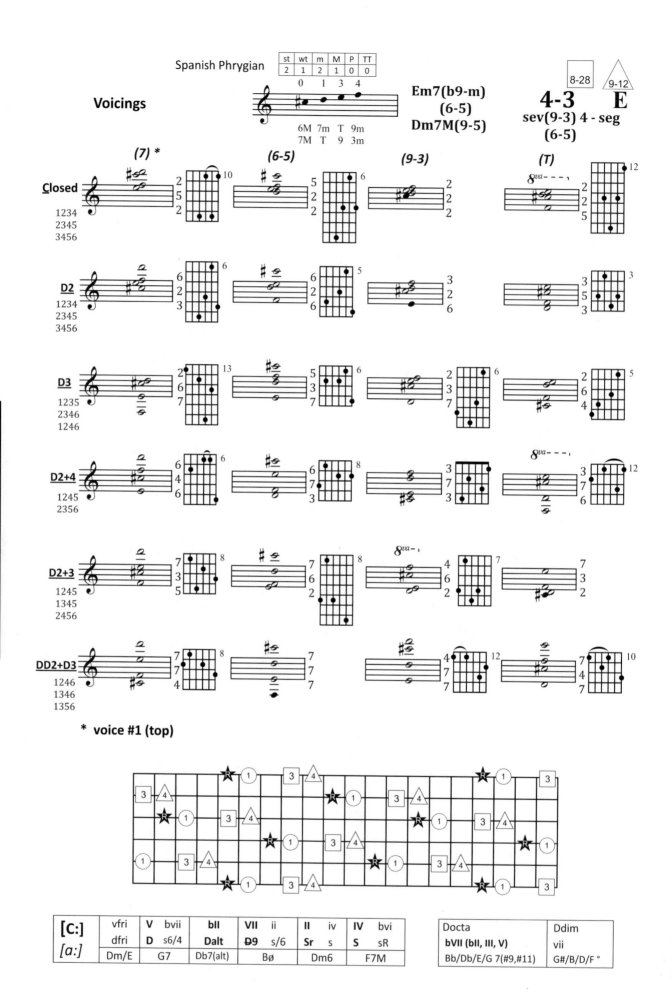

Spanish Phrygian

st	wt	m	M	P	TT
2	1	2	1	0	0
0	1	3	4		

Voicings

Em7(b9-m)
(6-5)
Dm7M(9-5)

6M 7m T 9m
7M T 9 3m

8-28   9-12

4-3   E
sev(9-3) 4 - seg
(6-5)

(7) *   (6-5)   (9-3)   (T)

Closed
1234
2345
3456

D2
1234
2345
3456

D3
1235
2346
1246

D2+4
1245
2356

D2+3
1245
1345
2456

DD2+D3
1246
1346
1356

* voice #1 (top)

[C:]	vfri	V	bvii	bII	VII	ii	II	iv	IV	bvi
	dfri	D	s6/4	Dalt	D9	s/6	Sr	s	S	sR
[a:]	Dm/E	G7		Db7(alt)	Bø		Dm6		F7M	

Docta	Ddim
bVII (bII, III, V)	vii
Bb/Db/E/G 7(#9,#11)	G#/B/D/F °

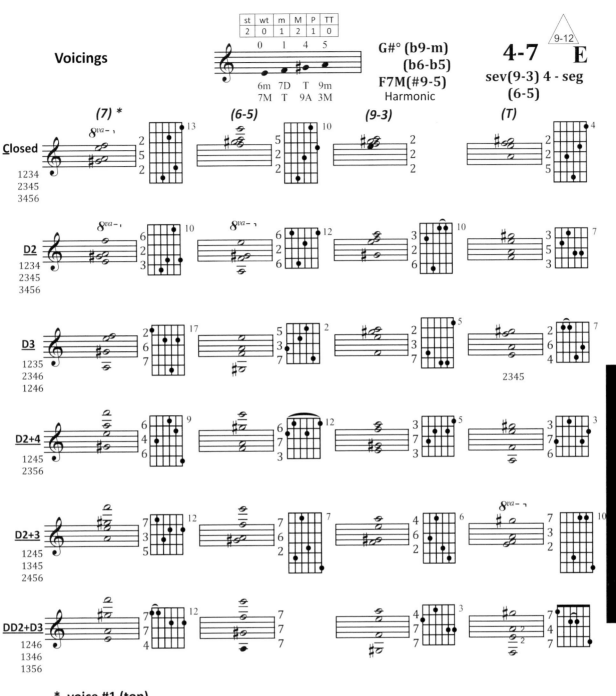

Voicings

st	wt	m	M	P	TT
2	0	1	2	1	0

G#° (b9-m)
(b6-b5)
F7M(#9-5)
Harmonic

4-7 △(9-12) **E**
sev(9-3) 4 - seg
(6-5)

* voice #1 (top)

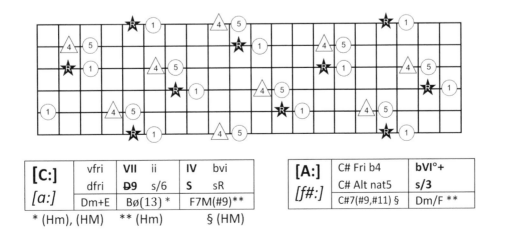

[C:]	vfri	**VII**	ii	**IV**	bvi
[a:]	dfri	~~D9~~	s/6	S	sR
	Dm+E	Bø(13) *		F7M(#9)**	

* (Hm), (HM)   ** (Hm)   § (HM)

[A:]	C# Fri b4	bVI°+
[f#:]	C# Alt nat5	s/3
	C#7(#9,#11) §	Dm/F **

4.10 FOUR-NOTE CHORDS

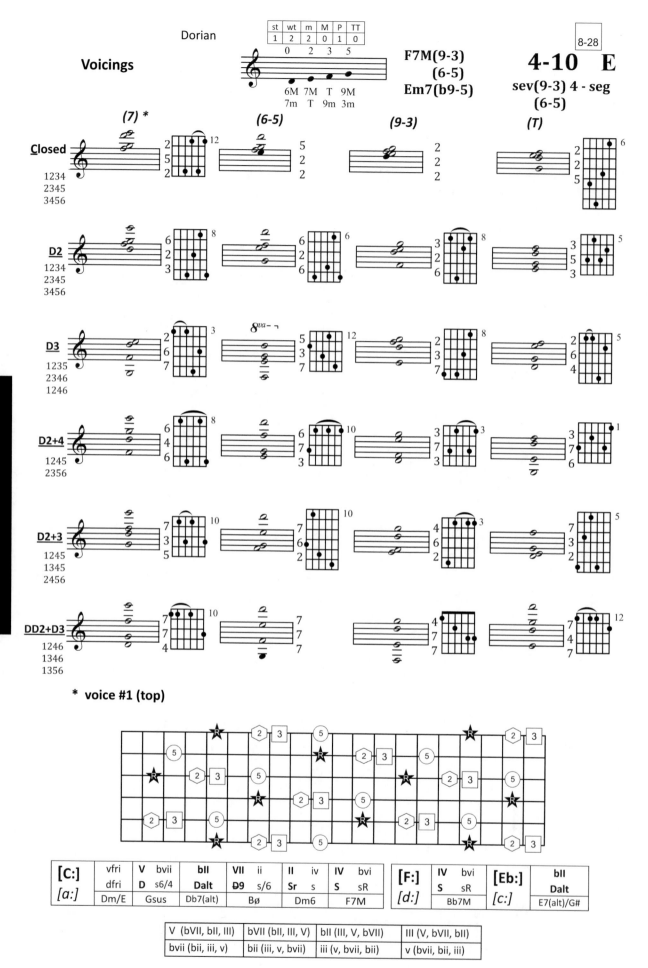

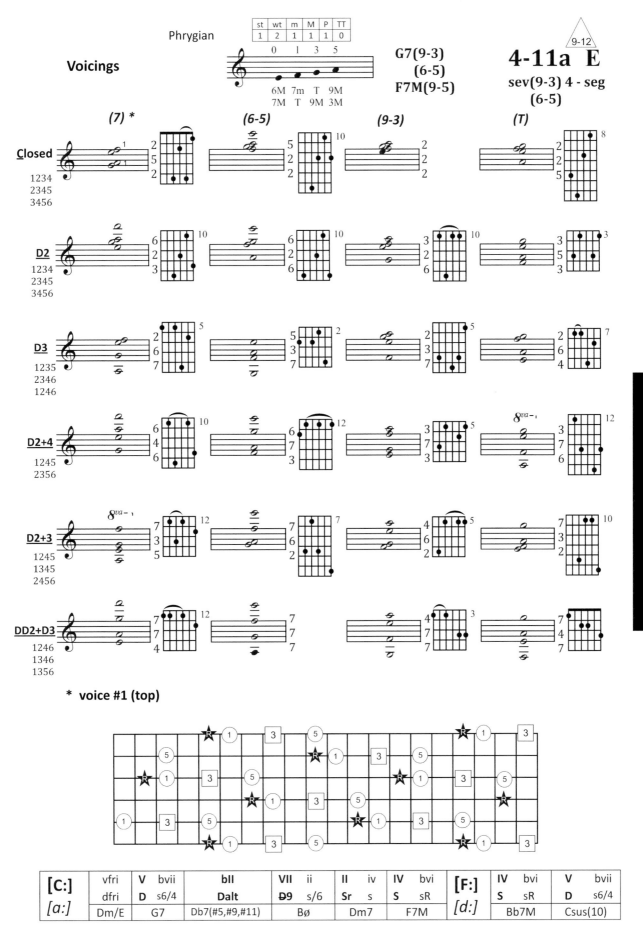

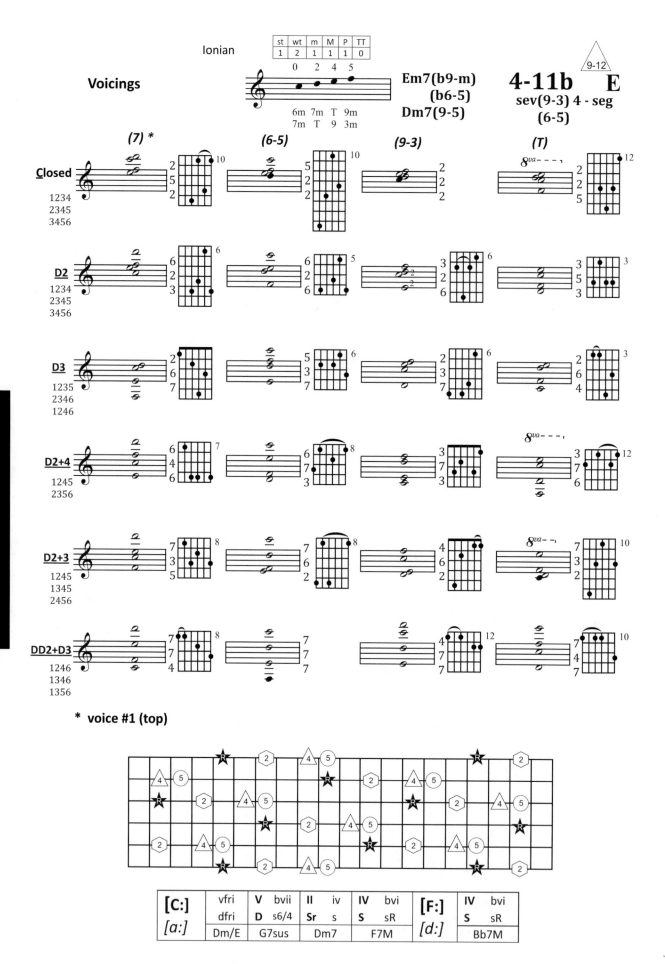

4.10 FOUR-NOTE CHORDS

* voice #1 (top)

[C:]	vfri	V	bvii	II	iv	IV	bvi	[F:]	IV	bvi
[a:]	dfri	D	s6/4	Sr	s	S	sR	[d:]	S	sR
	Dm/E	G7sus		Dm7		F7M			Bb7M	

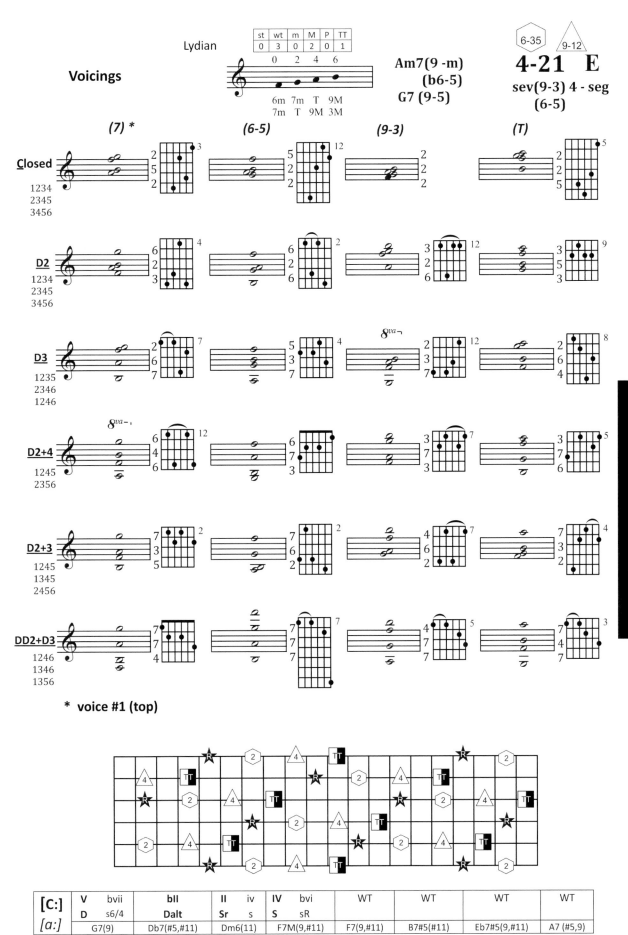

* voice #1 (top)

[C:]	V	bvii	bII	II	iv	IV	bvi	WT	WT	WT	WT
	D	s6/4	Dalt	Sr	s	S	sR				
[a:]	G7(9)		Db7(#5,#11)	Dm6(11)		F7M(9,#11)		F7(9,#11)	B7#5(#11)	Eb7#5(9,#11)	A7 (#5,9)

4.11. CARD 4 - MELODIC EXERCISES

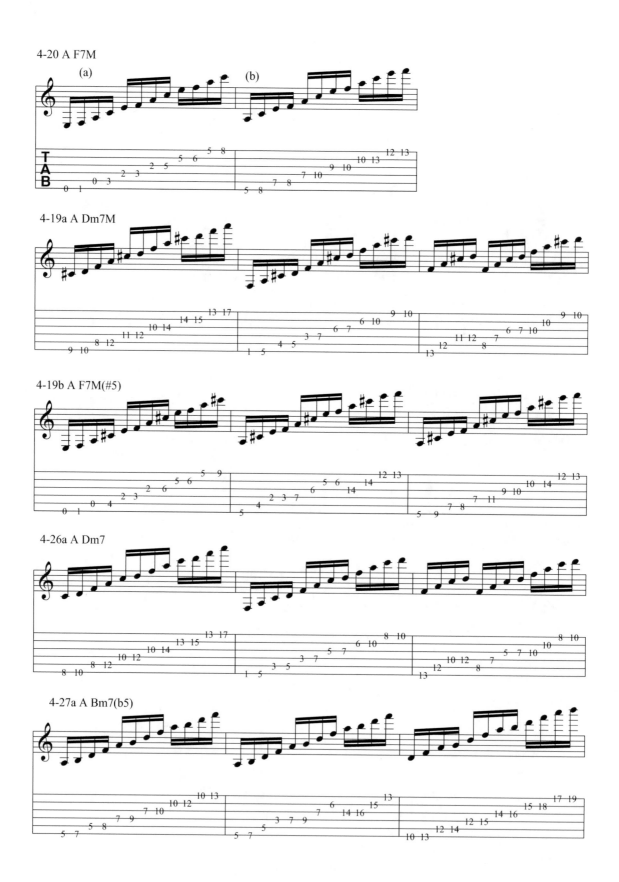

4-20 A F7M

4-19a A Dm7M

4-19b A F7M(#5)

4-26a A Dm7

4-27a A Bm7(b5)

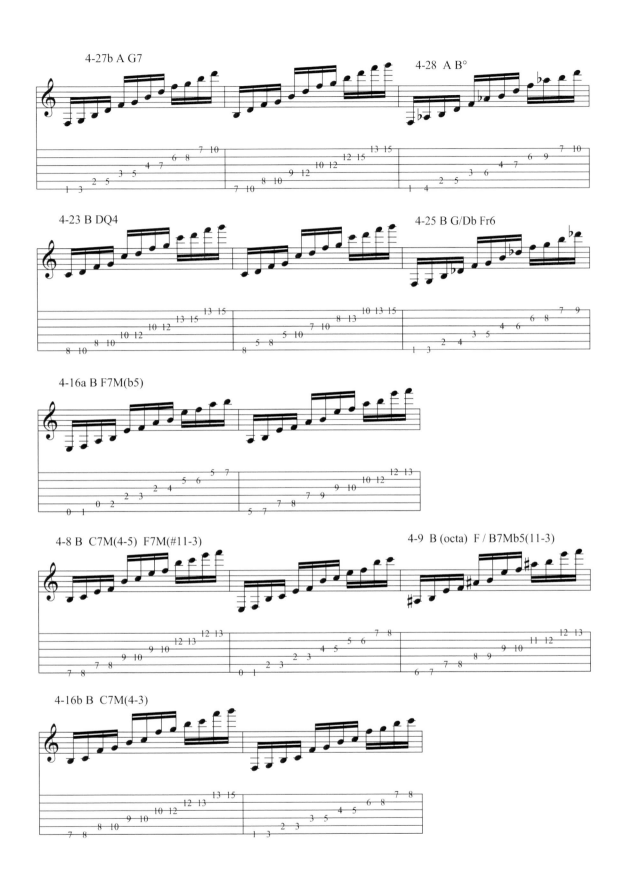

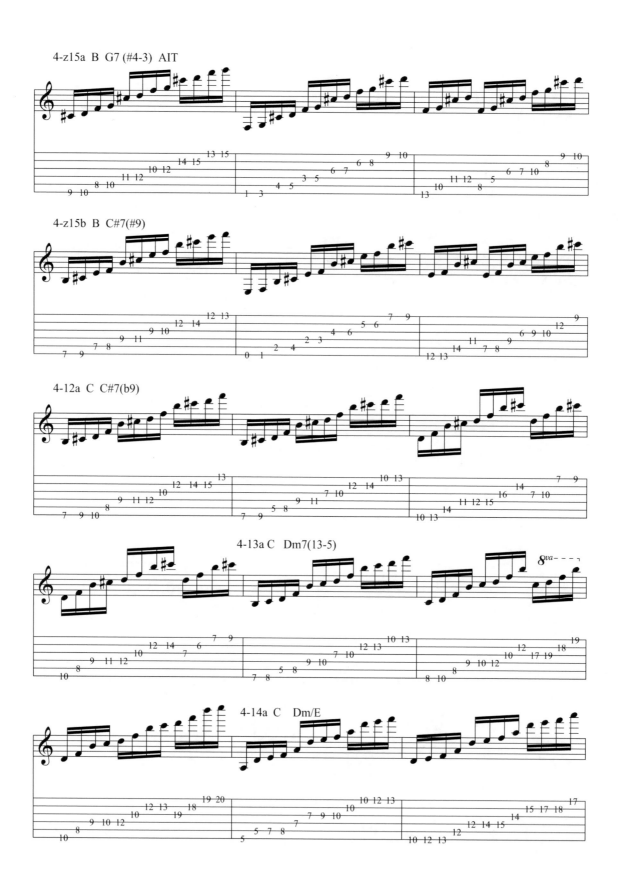

4-z15a B G7 (#4-3) AIT

4-z15b B C#7(#9)

4-12a C C#7(b9)

4-13a C   Dm7(13-5)

4-14a C   Dm/E

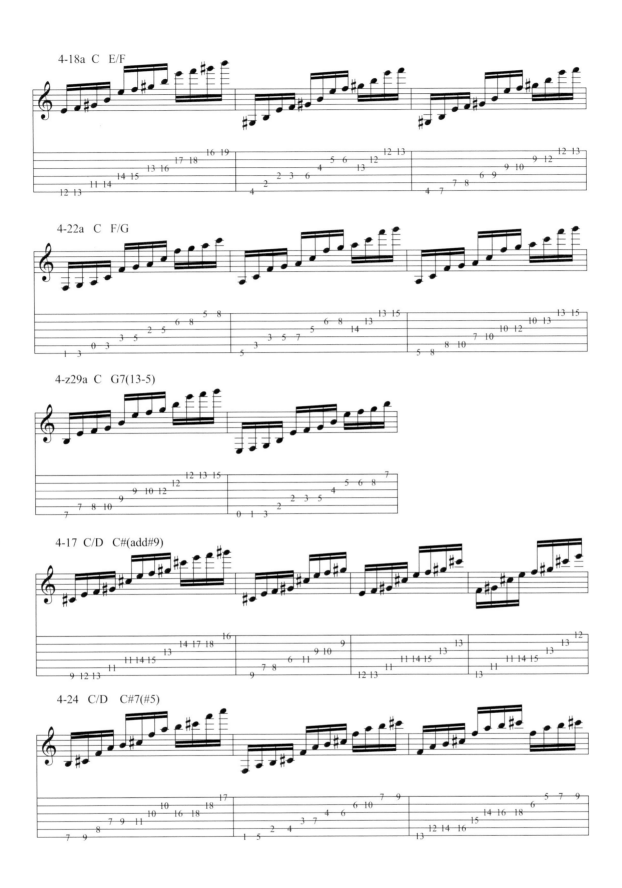

5. CARD 5 - TYPOLOGY

5.1 7-35 Diatonic Scale

Card 5		
A	Ninth Chords Third Stack	7(9)
B	Quartal-5 Chords	7(4)
E	Cluster 5-Note Segments T 3 5 (9, 11)	Triad (^9-11)

A

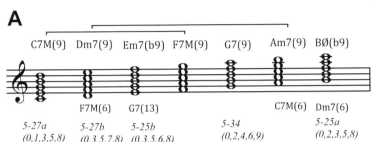

C7M(9) Dm7(9) Em7(b9) F7M(9) G7(9) Am7(9) BØ(b9)

F7M(6) G7(13)   C7M(6) Dm7(6)

5-27a   5-27b   5-25b   5-34   5-25a
(0,1,3,5,8) (0,3,5,7,8) (0,3,5,6,8)   (0,2,4,6,9) (0,2,3,5,8)

B

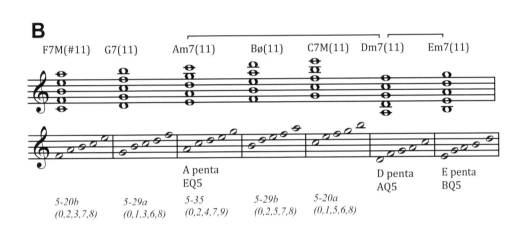

F7M(#11) G7(11) Am7(11) BØ(11) C7M(11) Dm7(11) Em7(11)

A penta   D penta E penta
EQ5   AQ5   BQ5

5-20b   5-29a   5-35   5-29b   5-20a
(0,2,3,7,8) (0,1,3,6,8) (0,2,4,7,9) (0,2,5,7,8) (0,1,5,6,8)

E

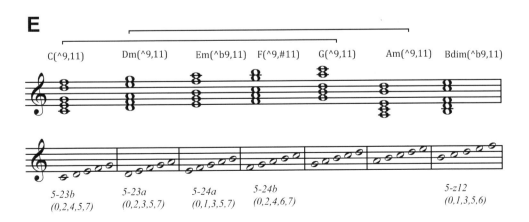

C(^9,11) Dm(^9,11) Em(^b9,11) F(^9,#11) G(^9,11) Am(^9,11) Bdim(^b9,11)

5-23b   5-23a   5-24a   5-24b   5-z12
(0,2,4,5,7) (0,2,3,5,7) (0,1,3,5,7) (0,2,4,6,7) (0,1,3,5,6)

5.2 7-34 Acoustic Scale (Melodic Minor)

Card 5		
A	Ninth Chords Third Stack	7(9)
B	Quartal-5 Chords	7(4)
E	Cluster 5-Note Segments T 3 5 (9, 11)	Triad (^9-11)

A

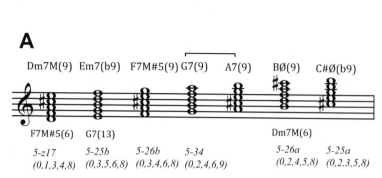

Dm7M(9) Em7(b9) F7M#5(9) G7(9) A7(9) BØ(9) C#Ø(b9)

F7M#5(6) G7(13) Dm7M(6)

5-z17 *5-25b* *5-26b* *5-34* *5-26a* *5-25a*
(0,1,3,4,8) *(0,3,5,6,8)* *(0,3,4,6,8)* *(0,2,4,6,9)* *(0,2,4,5,8)* *(0,2,3,5,8)*

B

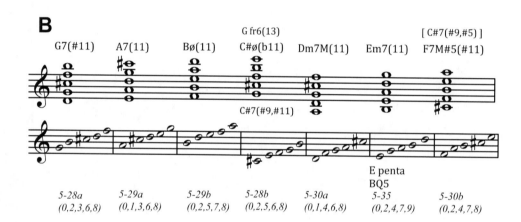

G7(#11) A7(11) BØ(11) G fr6(13) Dm7M(11) Em7(11) [C#7(#9,#5)]
                        C#Ø(b11)   F7M#5(#11)

C#7(#9,#11)

E penta
BQ5

5-28a *5-29a* *5-29b* *5-28b* *5-30a* *5-35* *5-30b*
(0,2,3,6,8) *(0,1,3,6,8)* *(0,2,5,7,8)* *(0,2,5,6,8)* *(0,1,4,6,8)* *(0,2,4,7,9)* *(0,2,4,7,8)*

E

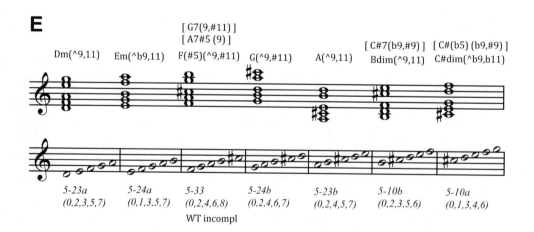

                [G7(9,#11)]
                [A7#5 (9)]
Dm(^9,11) Em(^b9,11) F(#5)(^9,#11) G(^9,#11) A(^9,11) [C#7(b9,#9)] [C#(b5) (b9,#9)]
                                                           Bdim(^9,11) C#dim(^b9,b11)

5-23a *5-24a* *5-33* *5-24b* *5-23b* *5-10b* *5-10a*
(0,2,3,5,7) *(0,1,3,5,7)* *(0,2,4,6,8)* *(0,2,4,6,7)* *(0,2,4,5,7)* *(0,2,3,5,6)* *(0,1,3,4,6)*
                        WT incompl

5.3 7-32 Harmonic Minor Scale

Card 5		
A	Ninth Chords Third Stack	7(9)
B	Quartal-5 Chords	7(4)
E	Cluster 5-Note Segments T 3 5 (9, 11)	Triad (^9-11)

A

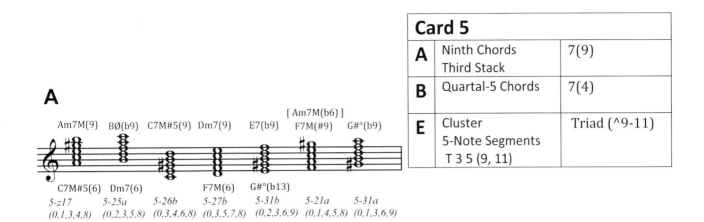

B

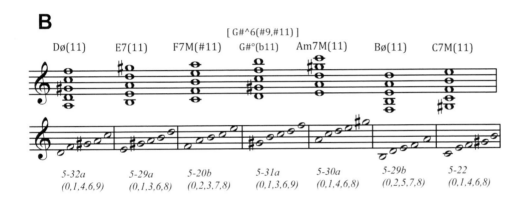

E

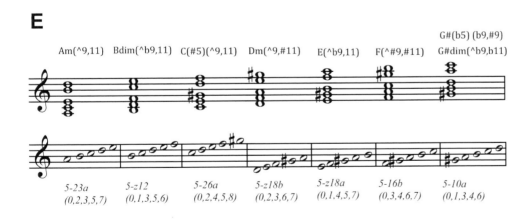

5.4　7-32b Harmonic Major Scale

Card 5		
A	Ninth Chords Third Stack	7(9)
B	Quartal-5 Chords	7(4)
E	Cluster 5-Note Segments T 3 5 (9, 11)	Triad (^9-11)

A

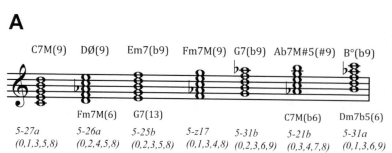

C7M(9)　DØ(9)　Em7(b9)　Fm7M(9)　G7(b9)　Ab7M#5(#9)　B°(b9)

Fm7M(6)　G7(13)　　　　　　　C7M(b6)　Dm7b5(6)

5-27a　*5-26a*　*5-25b*　*5-z17*　*5-31b*　*5-21b*　*5-31a*
(0,1,3,5,8)　*(0,2,4,5,8)*　*(0,2,3,5,8)*　*(0,1,3,4,8)*　*(0,2,3,6,9)*　*(0,3,4,7,8)*　*(0,1,3,6,9)*

B

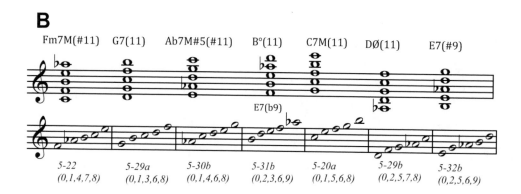

Fm7M(#11)　G7(11)　Ab7M#5(#11)　B°(11)　C7M(11)　DØ(11)　E7(#9)

E7(b9)

5-22　*5-29a*　*5-30b*　*5-31b*　*5-20a*　*5-29b*　*5-32b*
(0,1,4,7,8)　*(0,1,3,6,8)*　*(0,1,4,6,8)*　*(0,2,3,6,9)*　*(0,1,5,6,8)*　*(0,2,5,7,8)*　*(0,2,5,6,9)*

E

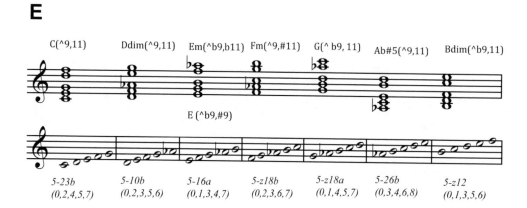

C(^9,11)　Ddim(^9,11)　Em(^b9,b11)　Fm(^9,#11)　G(^ b9, 11)　Ab#5(^9,11)　Bdim(^b9,11)

E (^b9,#9)

5-23b　*5-10b*　*5-16a*　*5-z18b*　*5-z18a*　*5-26b*　*5-z12*
(0,2,4,5,7)　*(0,2,3,5,6)*　*(0,1,3,4,7)*　*(0,2,3,6,7)*　*(0,1,4,5,7)*　*(0,3,4,6,8)*　*(0,1,3,5,6)*

Pentatonic Sets   7-35

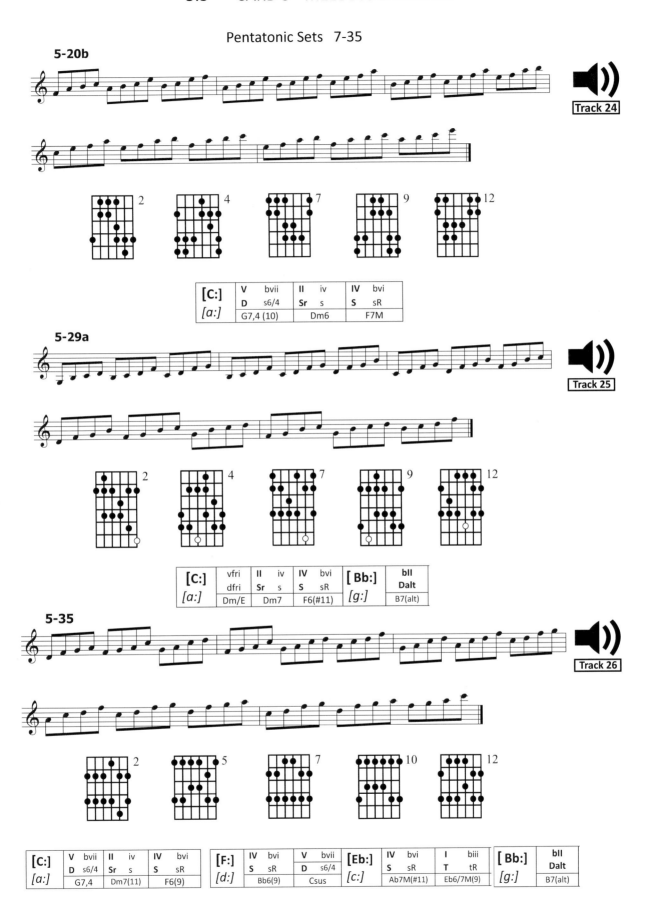

5-20b — Track 24

[C:]	V	bvii	II	iv	IV	bvi
[a:]	D	s6/4	Sr	s	S	sR
	G7,4 (10)		Dm6		F7M	

5-29a — Track 25

[C:]	vfri		II	iv	IV	bvi	[Bb:]	bII
[a:]	dfri		Sr	s	S	sR	[g:]	Dalt
	Dm/E		Dm7		F6(#11)			B7(alt)

5-35 — Track 26

[C:]	V	bvii	II	iv	IV	bvi	[F:]	IV	bvi	V	bvii	[Eb:]	IV	bvi	I	biii	[Bb:]	bII
[a:]	D	s6/4	Sr	s	S	sR	[d:]	S	sR	D	s6/4	[c:]	S	sR	T	tR	[g:]	Dalt
	G7,4		Dm7(11)		F6(9)			Bb6(9)		Csus			Ab7M(#11)		Eb6/7M(9)			B7(alt)

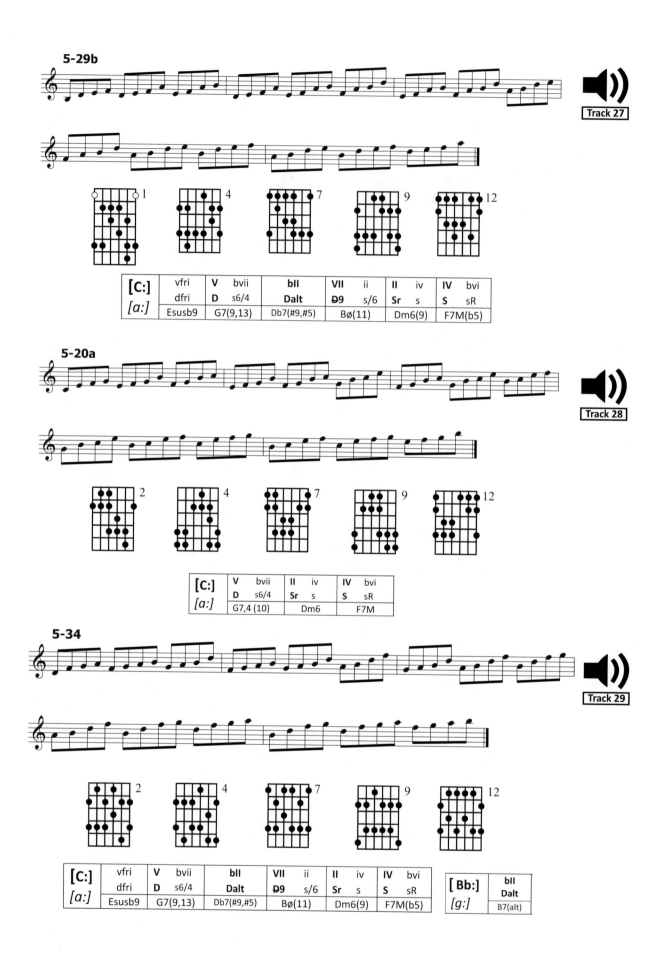

5-29b

Track 27

[C:]	vfri	V	bvii	bII	VII	ii	II	iv	IV	bvi
[a:]	dfri	D	s6/4	Dalt	D9	s/6	Sr	s	S	sR
	Esusb9	G7(9,13)		Db7(#9,#5)	Bø(11)		Dm6(9)		F7M(b5)	

5-20a

Track 28

[C:]	V	bvii	II	iv	IV	bvi
[a:]	D	s6/4	Sr	s	S	sR
	G7,4 (10)		Dm6		F7M	

5-34

Track 29

[C:]	vfri	V	bvii	bII	VII	ii	II	iv	IV	bvi		[Bb:]	bII
[a:]	dfri	D	s6/4	Dalt	D9	s/6	Sr	s	S	sR		[g:]	Dalt
	Esusb9	G7(9,13)		Db7(#9,#5)	Bø(11)		Dm6(9)		F7M(b5)				B7(alt)

5-30a

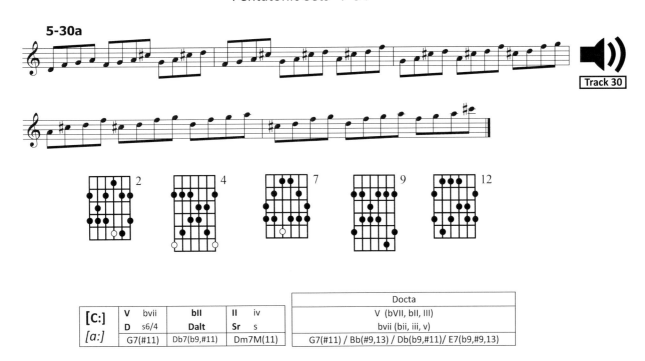

Track 30

[C:]	V	bvii	bII		II	iv
	D	s6/4	**Dalt**		**Sr**	s
[a:]	G7(#11)		Db7(b9,#11)		Dm7M(11)	

Docta
V (bVII, bII, III)
bvii (bii, iii, v)
G7(#11) / Bb(#9,13) / Db(b9,#11)/ E7(b9,#9,13)

5-30b

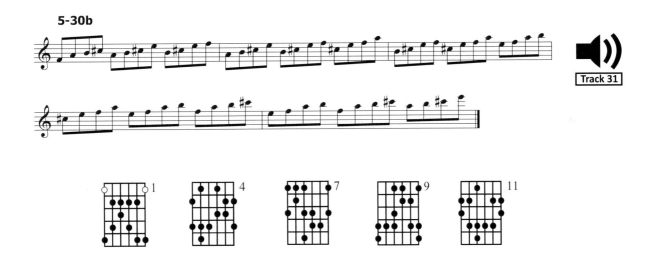

Track 31

[C:]	vfri	V	bvii	bII	VII	ii	II	iv	IV	bvi
	dfri	D	s6/4	**Dalt**	~~D9~~	s/6	**Sr**	s	**S**	sR
[a:]	Esusb9	G7(9,13)		Db7(#9,#5)	Bø(11)		Dm6(9)		F7M(b5)	

5.5.1 PENTATONIC SUBSETS OF 8-28 SCALE

Pentatonic Sets 8-28

The following sets are subsets of the octatonic scale (8-28)
and can be played over the chords indicated below:

Docta	Ddim
V (bVII, bII, III)	vii°
bvii (bii, iii, v)	
G7(b9) / Bb7(b9) / Db7(b9)/ E7(b9)	B° / D° / F°/ G#°

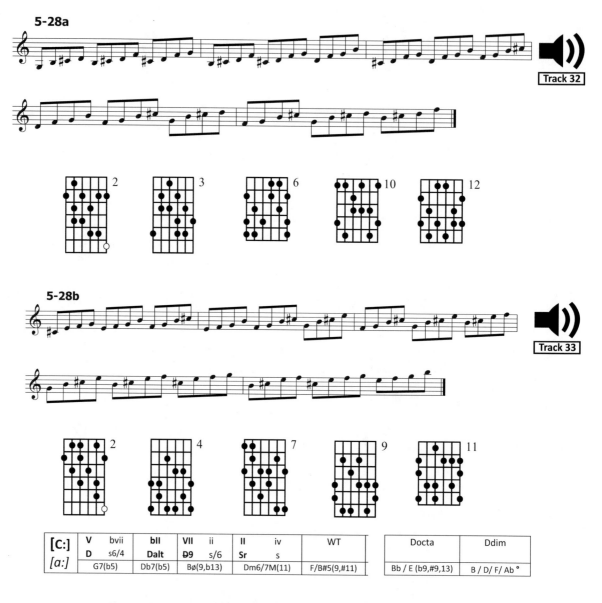

5-28a

Track 32

5-28b

Track 33

[C:]	V	bvii	**bII**	**VII**	ii	**II**	iv	WT		Docta	Ddim
	D	s6/4	**Dalt**	**D9**	s/6	**Sr**	s				
[a:]	G7(b5)		Db7(b5)	Bø(9,b13)		Dm6/7M(11)		F/B#5(9,#11)		Bb / E (b9,#9,13)	B / D/ F/ Ab °

The sets 5-28a and 5-28b also pertain to the scale 7-34. As the rest of the
8-28 (acatatonic) subsets, they can be freely tranposed by minor thirds
(Sesquitone Cycle)

COMBINATORIAL HARMONY - BY JULIO HERRLEIN - MEL BAY

Pentatonic Sets   8-28 (cont.)

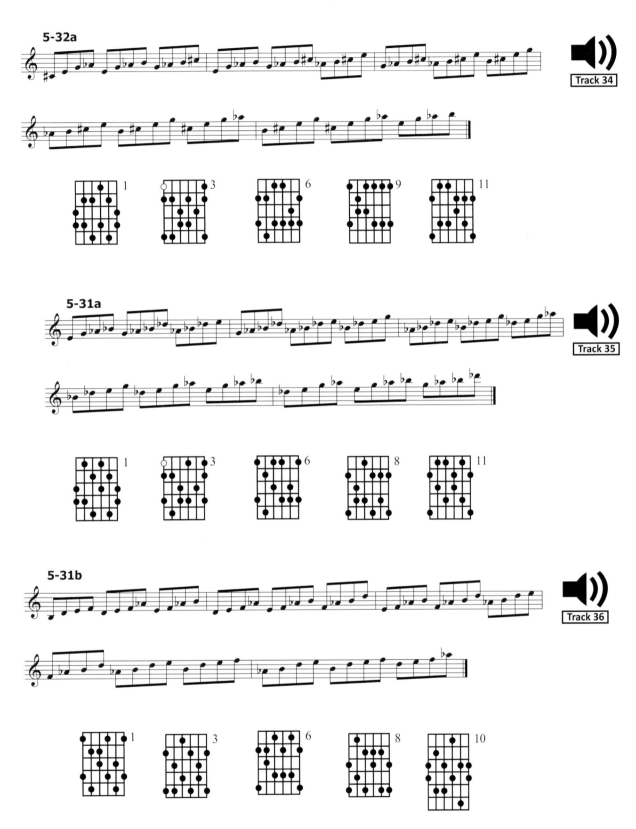

Pentatonic Sets   8-28 (cont.)

5-32b

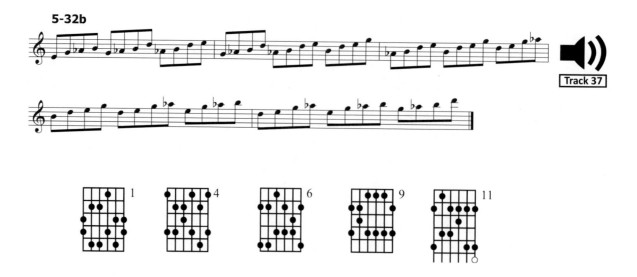

Track 37

Pentatonic Sets   7-32a/b

5-22

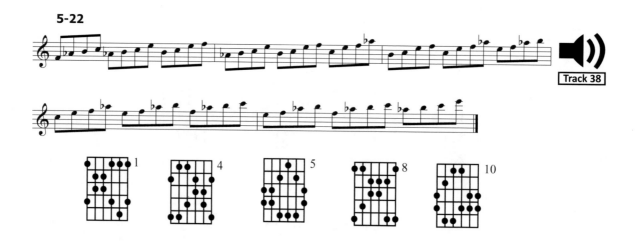

Track 38

Lydian Diminished

Fm7M(9,#11)

[C:]	bVI°+
	s/3
	Fm/Ab

6. COMBINATORIAL VOICE LEADING OF HEXATONICS

Voice leading is one of the most complex issues in music.

For each six-note set, there are ten different combinations (3+3) (Elliott Carter, Harmony Book, page 217). Each six-note set, i.e. two sets of three notes forming a set of six different notes, can be arranged in 10 mutually exclusive trichord pairs, called hexatonics.

I have found an interesting solution for implementing these combinations, which I have called combinatorial voice leading, in which each trichord that is part of the hexatonic is mapped as an ordered pair, related to its complementary trichord.

These pairs of trichords are arranged to produce typical paths of voice leading. On the first page of the exercises with hexatonics, we will show the kinds of mutually exclusive trichords obtained from hexachords, and the closest voice leading in each case.

Next, the typology of hexatonics contained in each scale will be presented, followed by harmonic and melodic exercises developed from an algorithm I created using the program "Pure Data" (freeware software similar to Max MSP, created by Miller Puckette). After inputting the hexachords into this program via MIDI, the voice leadings and the combinatorial exercises of hexatonics are listed.

These exercises are presented in the harmonic form (voice leading through the shortest path in open and closed position) and in the melodic form (melodic pattern using the same notes of the voice leading pattern) and can be used as fragments in improvisations and compositions.

6. COMBINATORIAL VOICE LEADING OF HEXACHORDS

VOICE LEADING TYPES

Hexachord´s FORTE number.

6-32 ↗

→ Hexachord arranged sequentially, in thirds and in fourths.

1

A A

C   Dm

→ Similar motion - all voices in the same direction by diatonic seconds.

2

A C

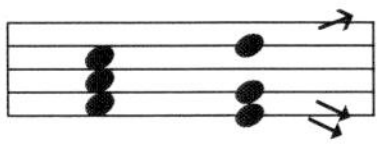

F   E^m7

→ Two voices in one direction stepwise and a third voice in contrary motion stepwise.

3

A D

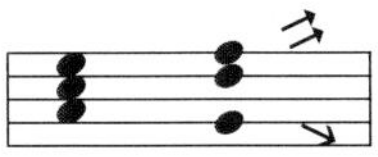

Am   G^7(5)

→ Two voices in one direction stepwise and a third voice in contrary motion stepwise.

4

B B

EQ3   GQ3

→ Two voices in one direction stepwise and a third voice in contrary motion stepwise.

5

B D

AQ3   F^7M(5)

→ Two voices in one direction stepwise and a third voice in contrary motion by a third.

6

B C

DQ3   F7M(¬5)

→ Two voices in one direction stepwise and a third voice in contrary motion by a third.

7

D C

A^7(5) D^m7

→ Two voices in one direction stepwise and a third voice in contrary motion by a third.

STEPWISE MOVEMENT (all voices)

TWO VOICES STEPWISE, ONE BY THIRD.

8

C E

A^m7   E^7(b9)

→

9

D E

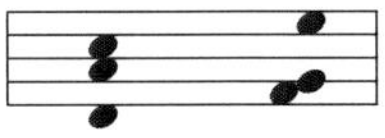

D^7(5)   F^7M(9)

→

10

E E

D^7(9)   G^7(9)

→

MORE MELODIC USE.

7-35 DIAT HEXATONICS - Trichord pairs - Combinatorial Voice Leading

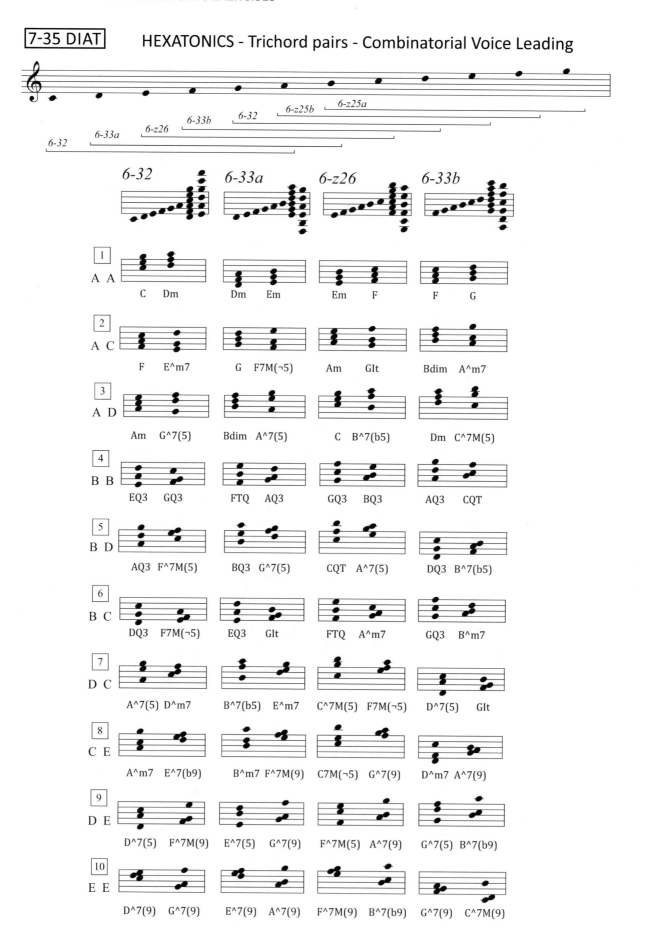

6-32 No tritone

2 Suggested chord: Dm7

3 F7M

4 Dm7

5 Dm7

Suggested chord: Dm7

6-33a

6-z26

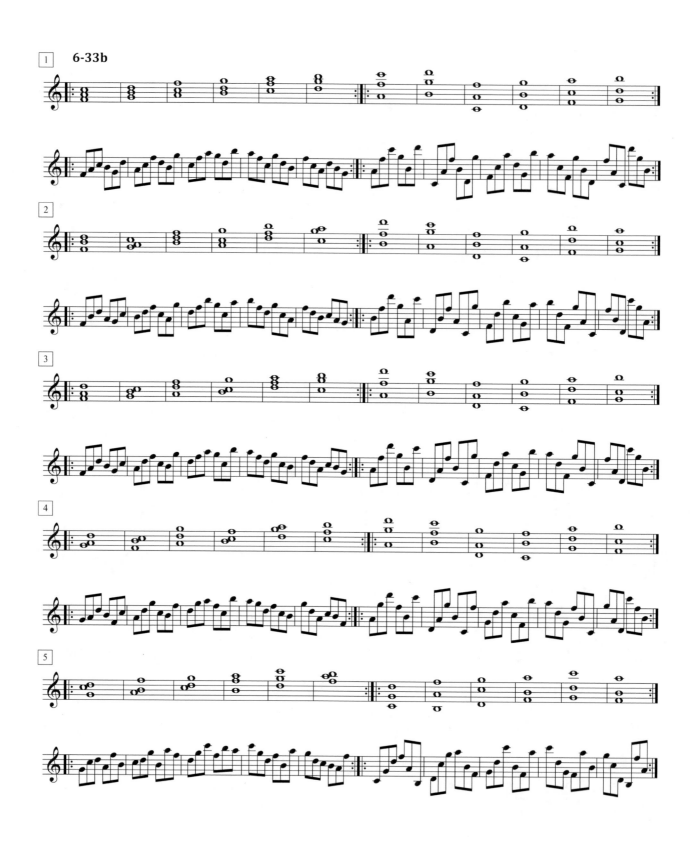

6-33b

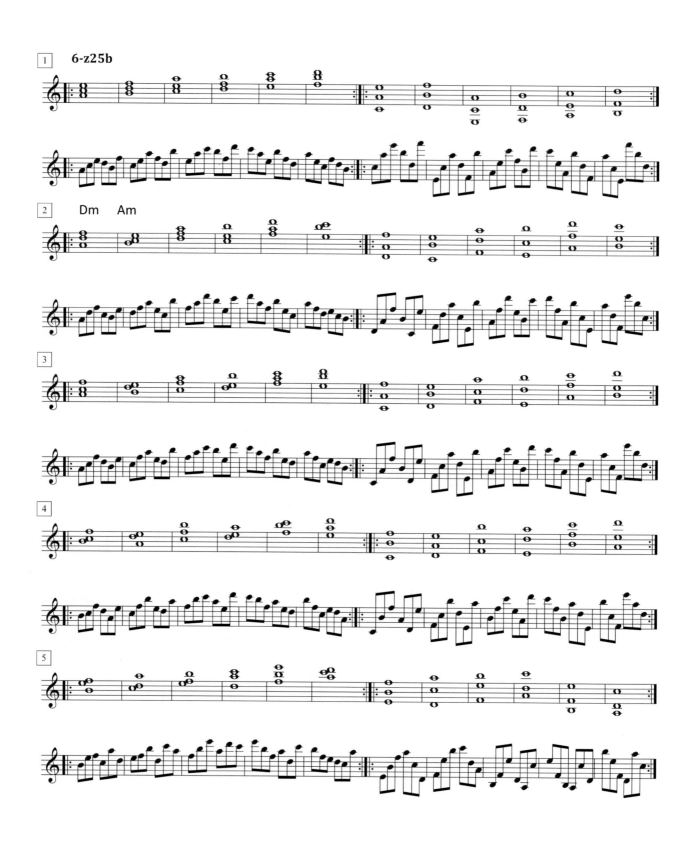

HEXATONICS - Trichord pairs - Combinatorial Voice Leading

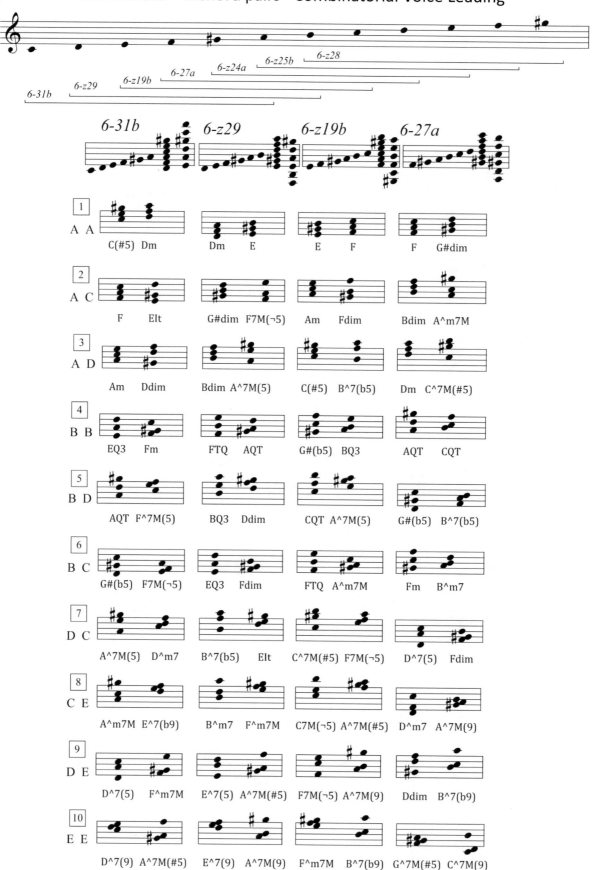

6-31b Hm 9-12

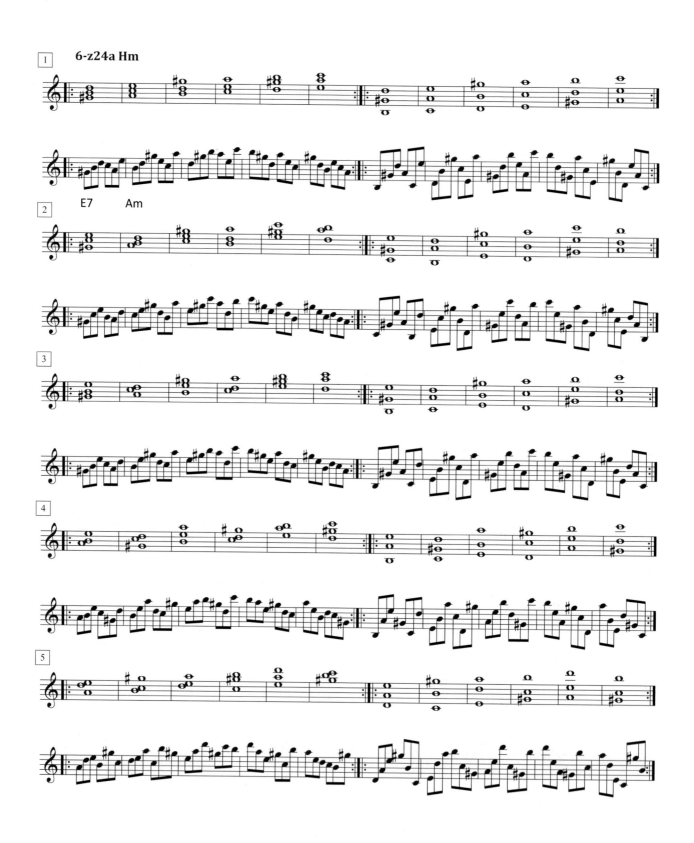

HEXATONICS - Trichord pairs - Combinatorial Voice Leading

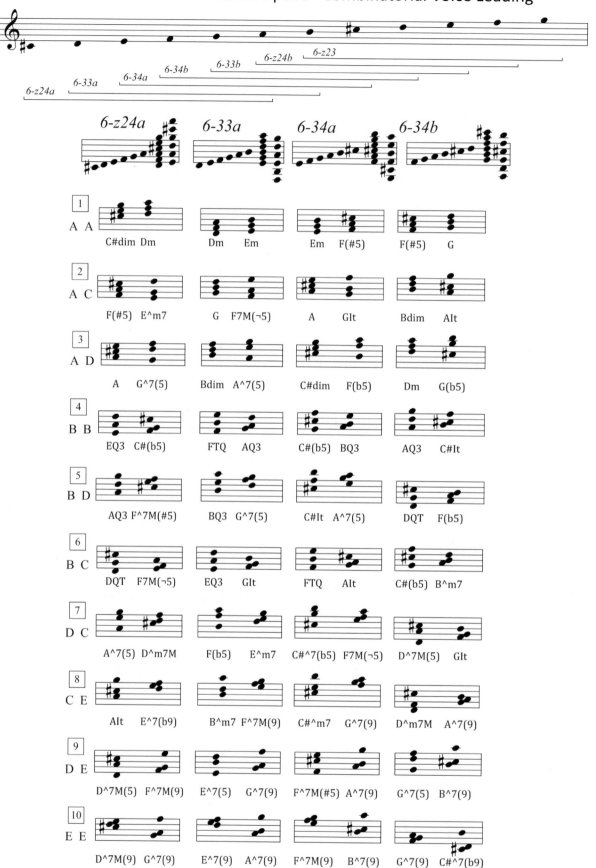

6-34a AC △9-12 Suggested chords: Bø(9) , G7(9,#11), C#7(alt), Dm7M,F7M(#5),E7susb9,A7(#5).

Suggested chords: Bø(9) , G7(9,#11), C#7(alt), Dm7M,F7M(#5),E7susb9,A7(#5).

7-32b Harmonic Major (HM)

HEXATONICS - Trichord pairs - Combinatorial Voice Leading

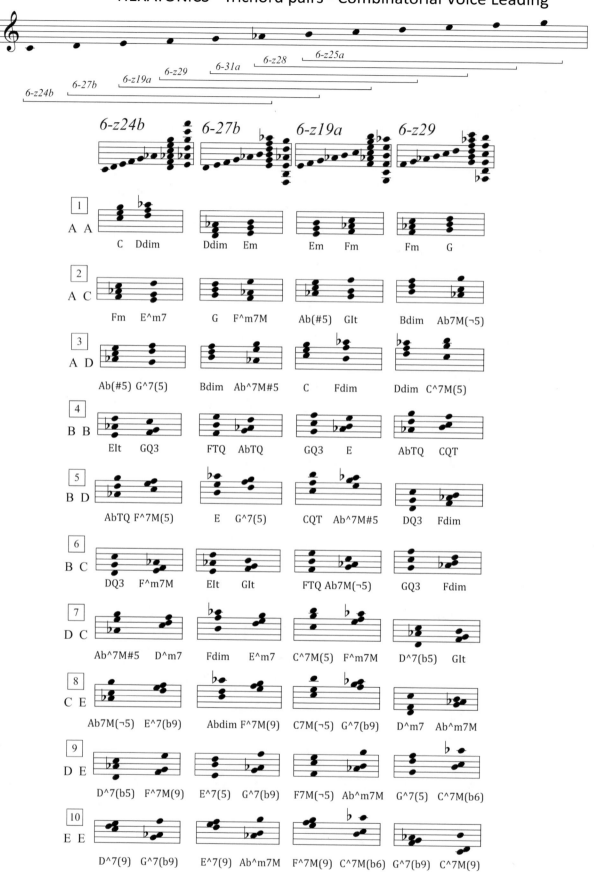

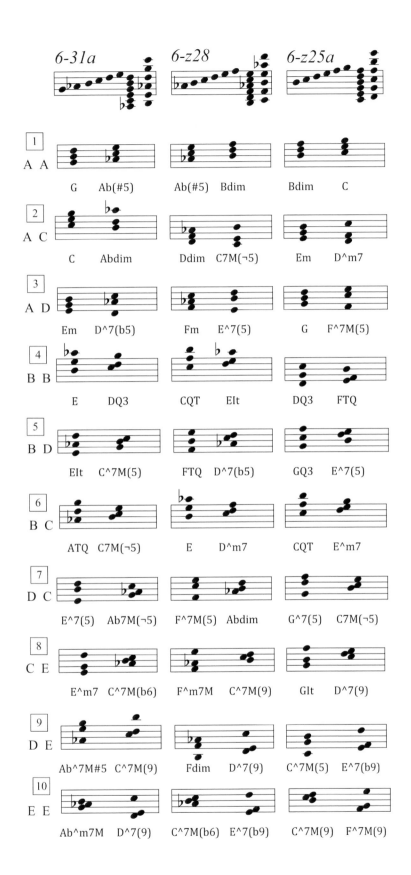

7-31a Octatonic Subset 1

HEXATONICS - Trichord pairs - Combinatorial Voice Leading

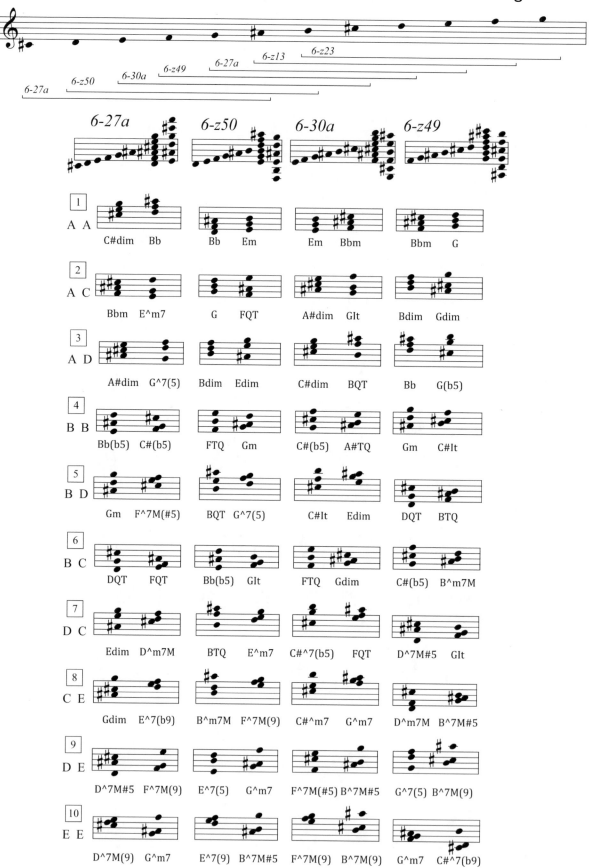

7-31b Octatonic Subset 2

HEXATONICS - Trichord pairs - Combinatorial Voice Leading

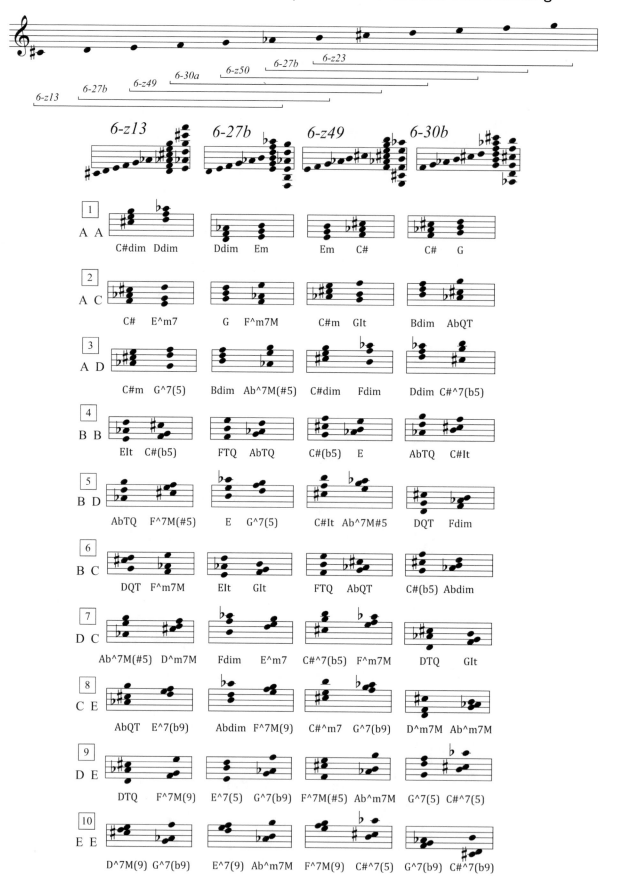

	6-z13	6-27b	6-z49	6-30b
1 A A	C#dim Ddim	Ddim Em	Em C#	C# G
2 A C	C# E^m7	G F^m7M	C#m GIt	Bdim AbQT
3 A D	C#m G^7(5)	Bdim Ab^7M(#5)	C#dim Fdim	Ddim C#^7(b5)
4 B B	EIt C#(b5)	FTQ AbTQ	C#(b5) E	AbTQ C#It
5 B D	AbTQ F^7M(#5)	E G^7(5)	C#It Ab^7M#5	DQT Fdim
6 B C	DQT F^m7M	EIt GIt	FTQ AbQT	C#(b5) Abdim
7 D C	Ab^7M(#5) D^m7M	Fdim E^m7	C#^7(b5) F^m7M	DTQ GIt
8 C E	AbQT E^7(b9)	Abdim F^7M(9)	C#^m7 G^7(b9)	D^m7M Ab^m7M
9 D E	DTQ F^7M(9)	E^7(5) G^7(b9)	F^7M(#5) Ab^m7M	G^7(5) C#^7(5)
10 E E	D^7M(9) G^7(b9)	E^7(9) Ab^m7M	F^7M(9) C#^7(5)	G^7(b9) C#^7(b9)

COMBINATORIAL HARMONY - BY JULIO HERRLEIN - MEL BAY

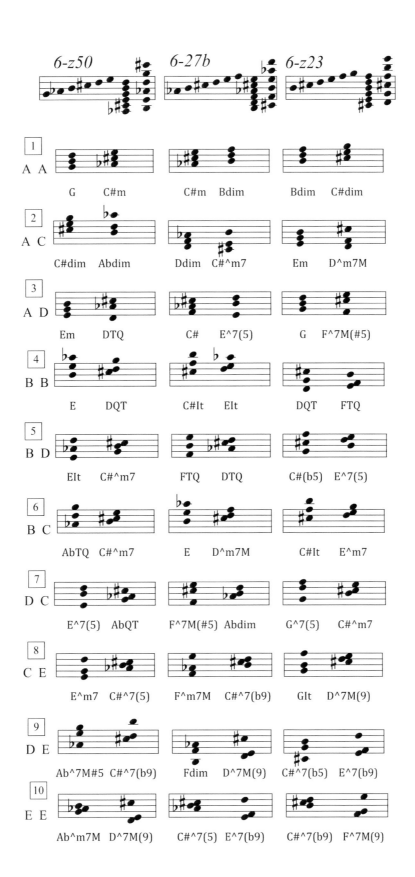

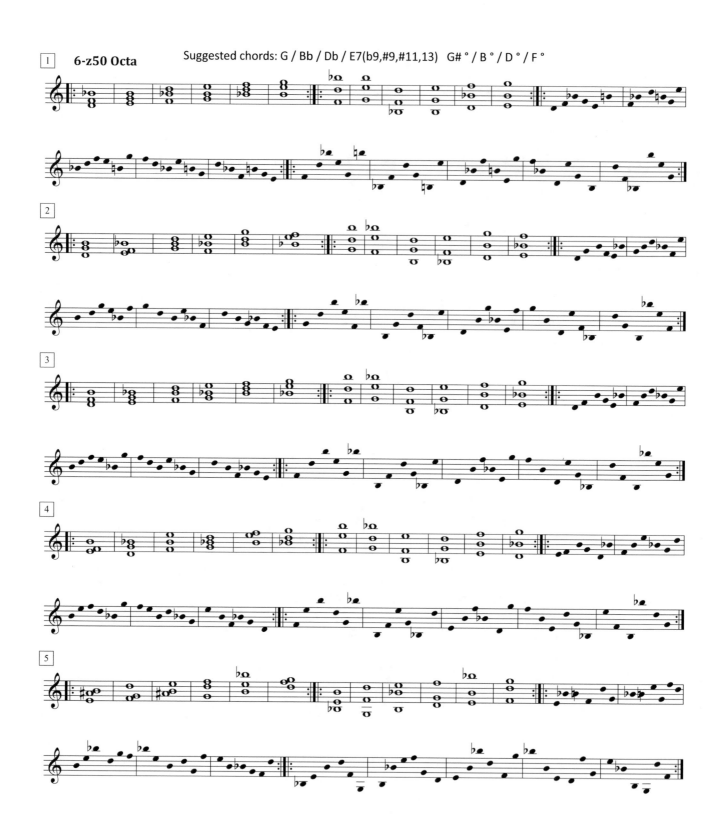

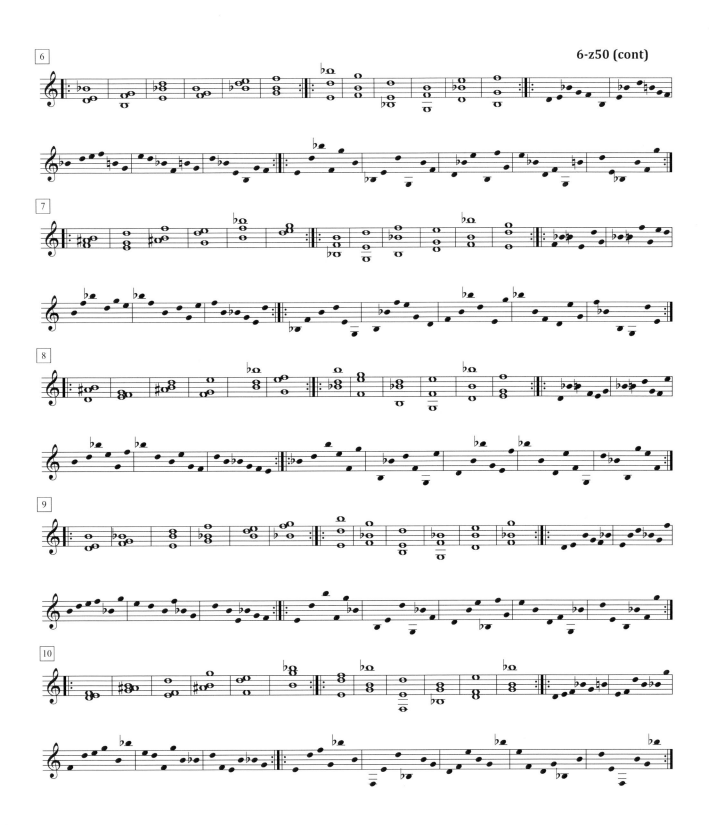

6-30a Octa subset of 8-25 (messiaen 6)   Suggested chords: G / Bb / Db / E7(b9,#9,#11,13)   G# ° / B ° / D ° / F °

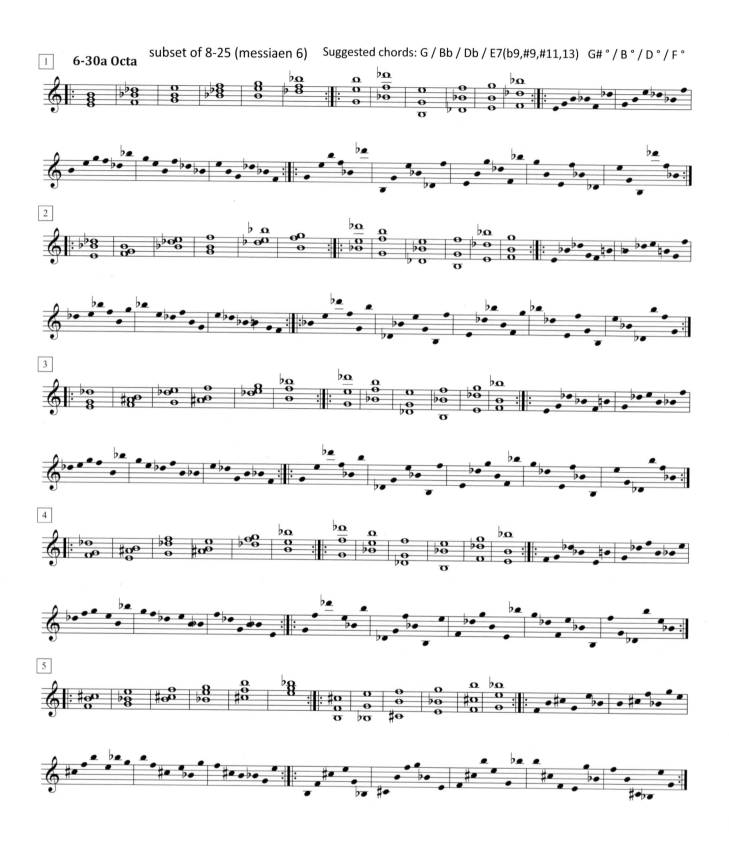

COMBINATORIAL HARMONY - BY JULIO HERRLEIN - MEL BAY

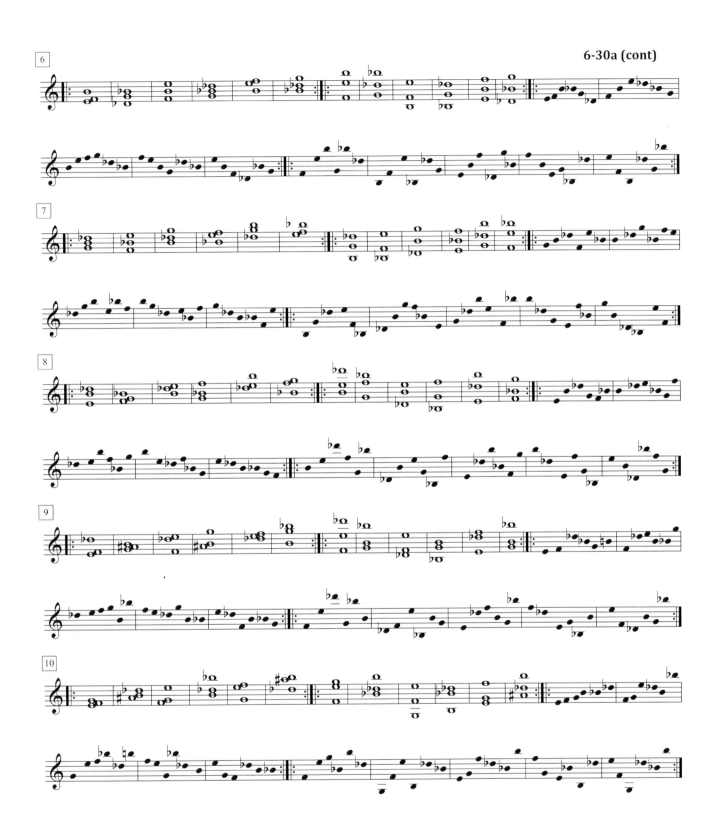

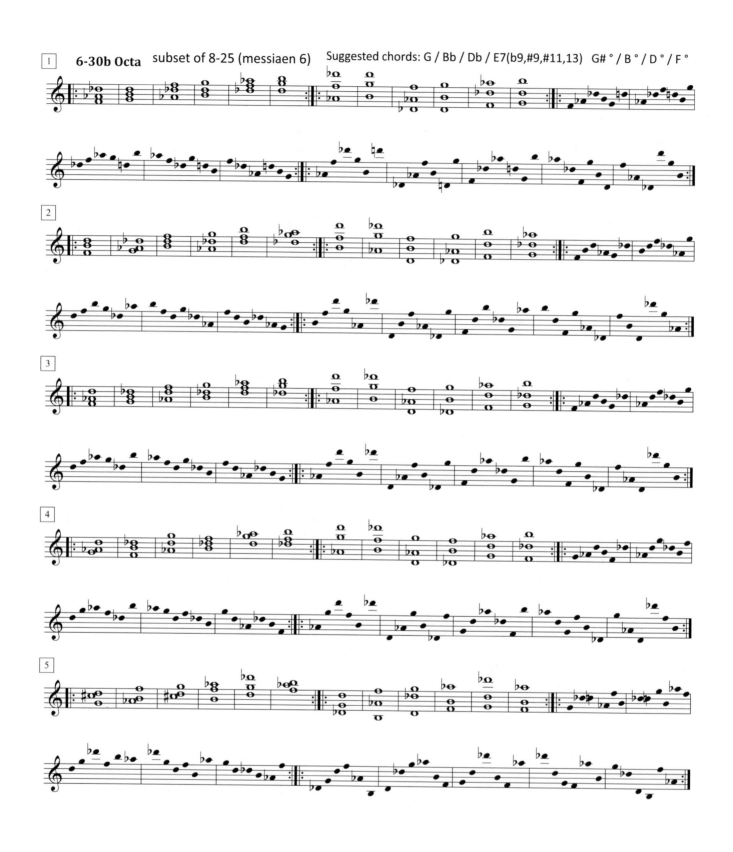

1   **6-30b Octa**   subset of 8-25 (messiaen 6)   Suggested chords: G / Bb / Db / E7(b9,#9,#11,13)   G#° / B° / D° / F°

         COMBINATORIAL HARMONY - BY JULIO HERRLEIN - MEL BAY

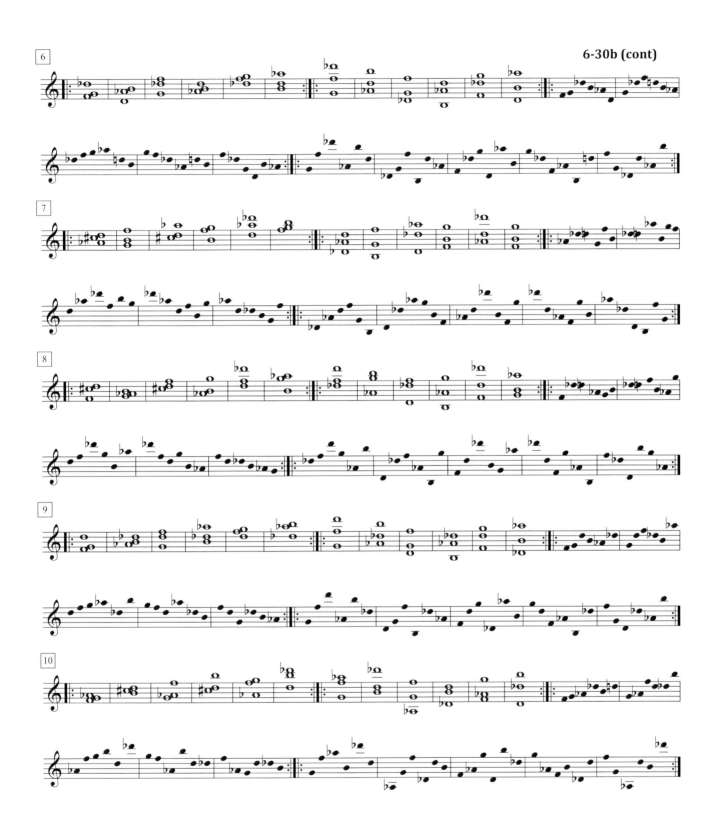

6-z49 Octa 9-12

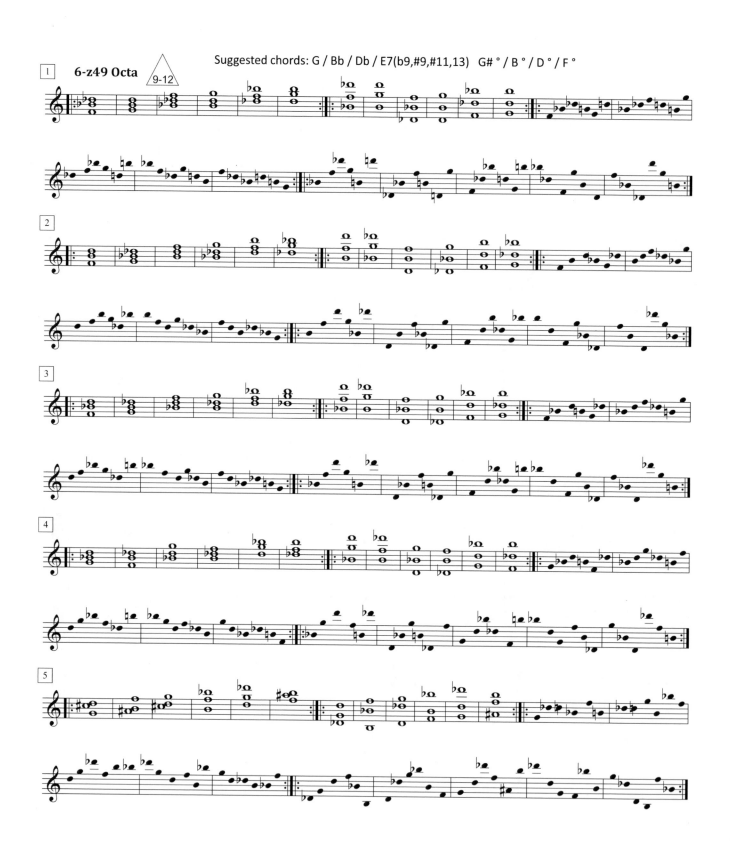

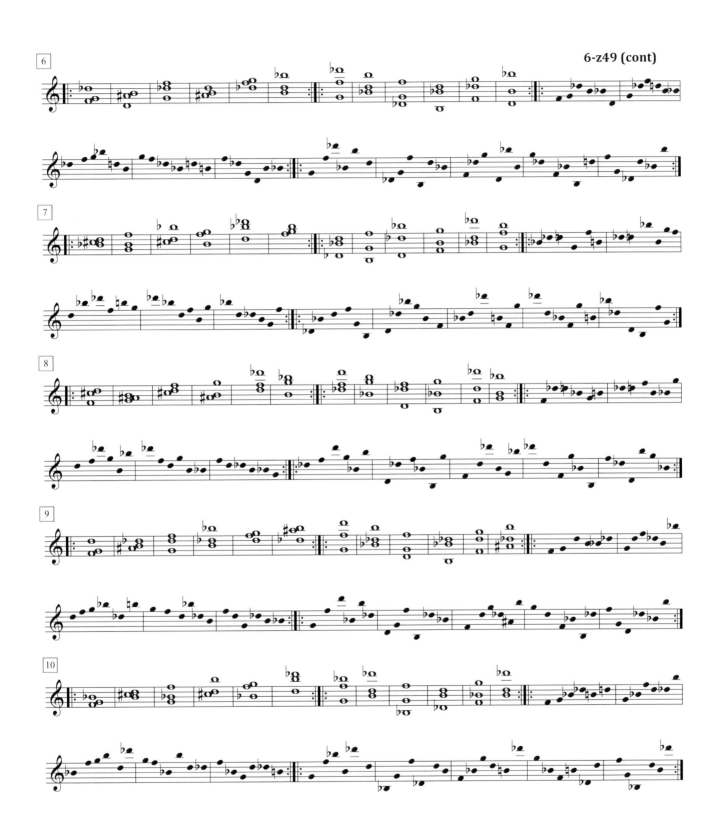

6-27a Octa, Hm

Suggested chords: G / Bb / Db / E7(b9,#9,#11,13)   G#° / B° / D° / F°

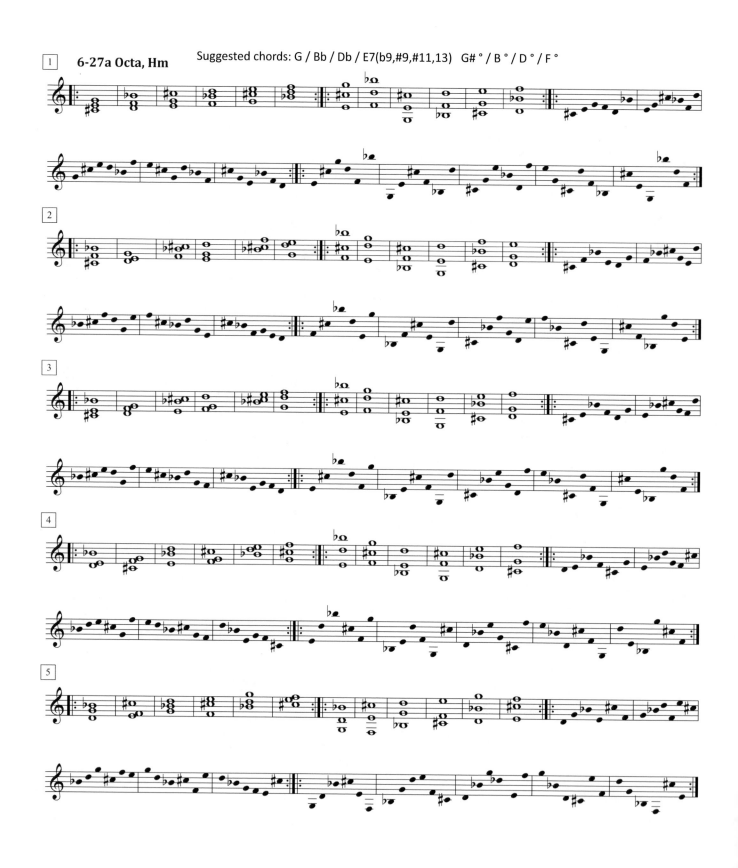

COMBINATORIAL HARMONY - BY JULIO HERRLEIN - MEL BAY

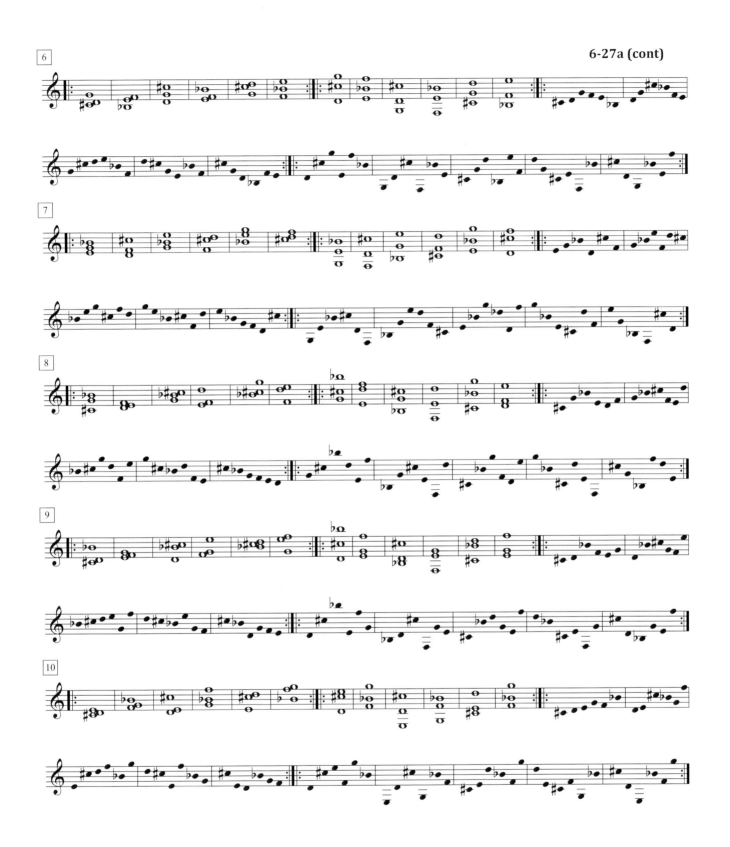

1 **6-z23 Octa, AC**   Suggested chords: G / Bb / Db / E7(b9,#9,#11,13)   G# ° / B ° / D ° / F °

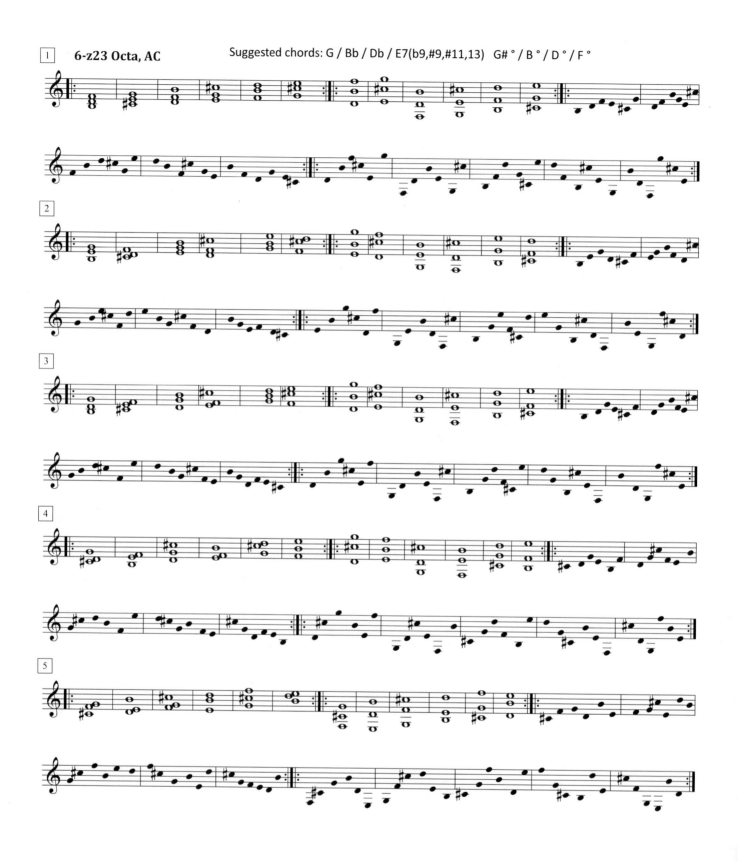

         COMBINATORIAL HARMONY - BY JULIO HERRLEIN - MEL BAY

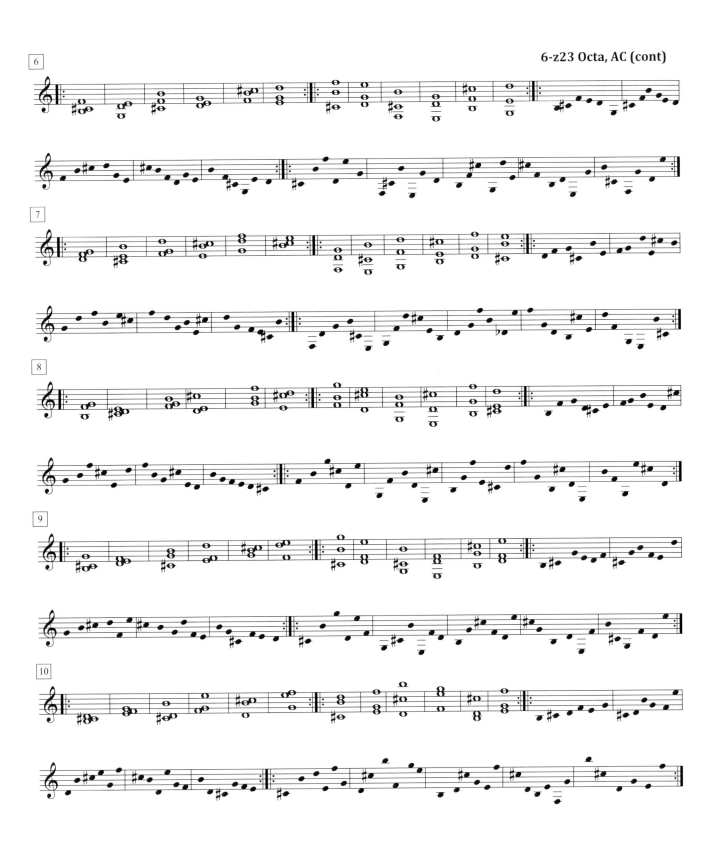

6-z13 Octa

Suggested chords: G / Bb / Db / E7(b9,#9,#11,13)   G# ° / B ° / D ° / F °

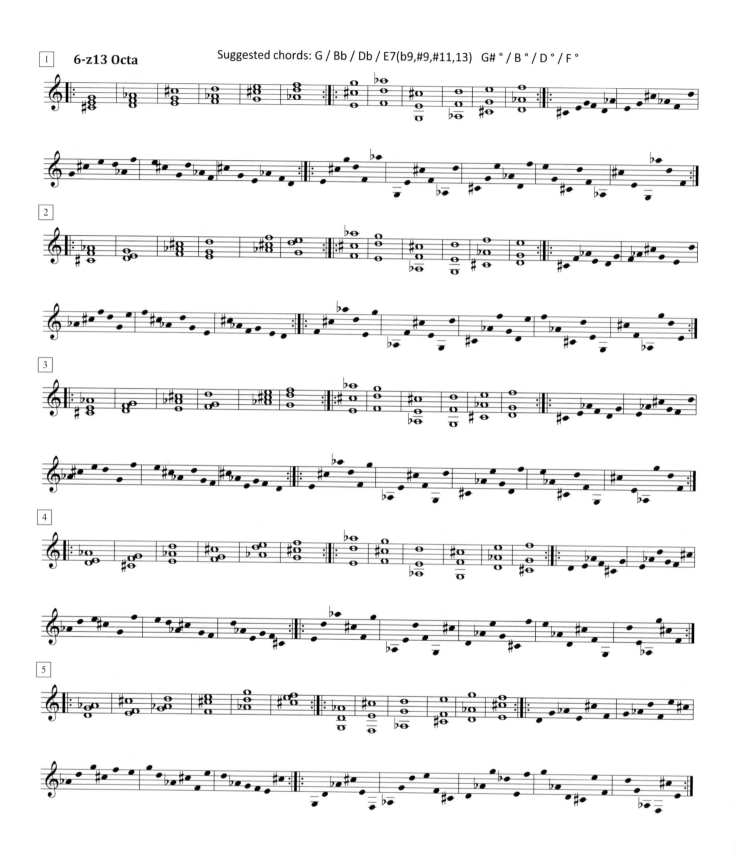

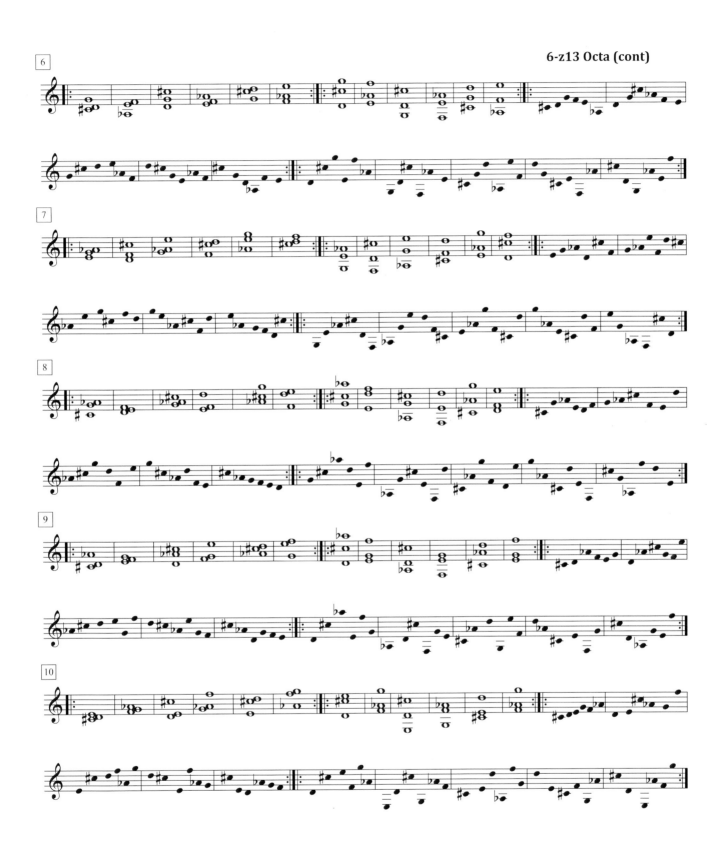

6-27b Octa ,HM Suggested chords: G / Bb / Db / E7(b9,#9,#11,13) G# ° / B ° / D ° / F °

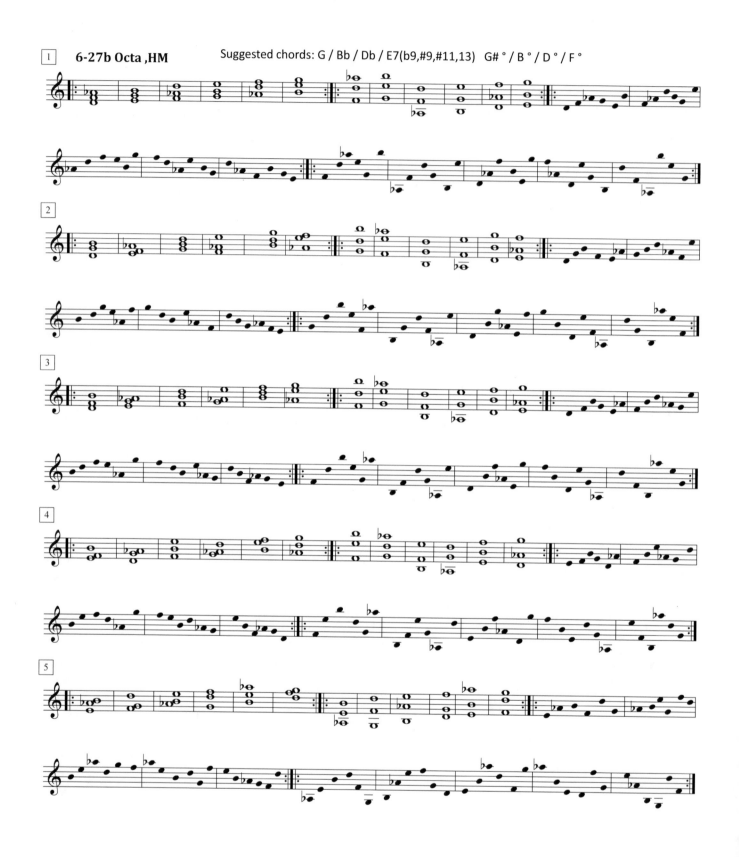

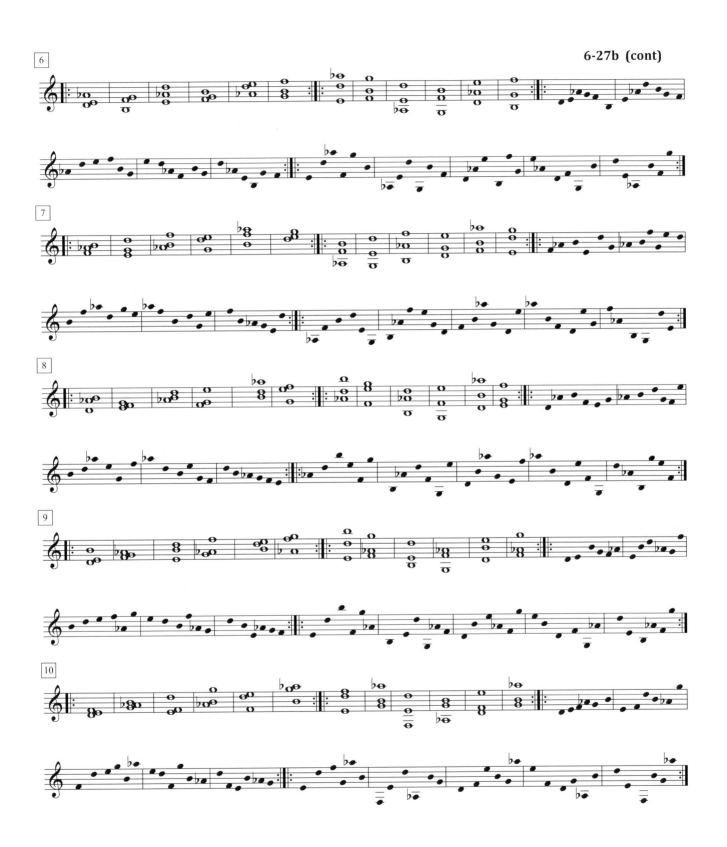

6-35 Whole-Tone

HEXATONICS - Trichord pairs - Combinatorial Voice Leading

6-35

1 A A	F(#5) G(#5)	G(#5) A(#5)	A(#5) B(#5)	B(#5) C#(#5)
2 A C	B(b5) AIt	C#(b5) BIt	D#(b5) C#It	F(b5) D#It
3 A D	FIt G(b5)	GIt A(b5)	AIt B(b5)	BIt C#(b5)
4 B B	Eb(b5) C#It	F(b5) D#It	G(b5) FIt	A(b5) GIt
5 B D	EbIt F(b5)	FIt G(b5)	GIt A(b5)	AIt B(b5)
6 B C	C#(b5) BIt	D#(b5) C#It	F(b5) D#It	G(b5) FIt
7 D C	A(b5) GIt	B(b5) AIt	C#(b5) BIt	D#(b5) C#It
8 C E	D#^7(9) A^7(9)	F^7(9) B^7(9)	G^7(9) C#^7(9)	A^7(9) D#^7(9)
9 D E	F^7(9) B^7(9)	G^7(9) C#^7(9)	A^7(9) D#^7(9)	B^7(9) F^7(9)
10 E E	G^7(9) C#^7(9)	A^7(9) D#^7(9)	B^7(9) F^7(9)	C#^7(9) G^7(9)

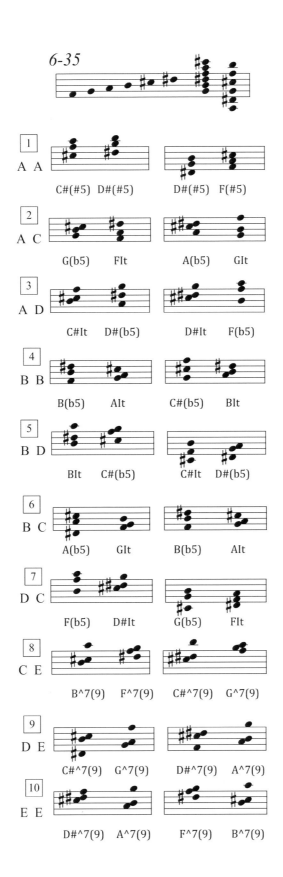

6-35 WT

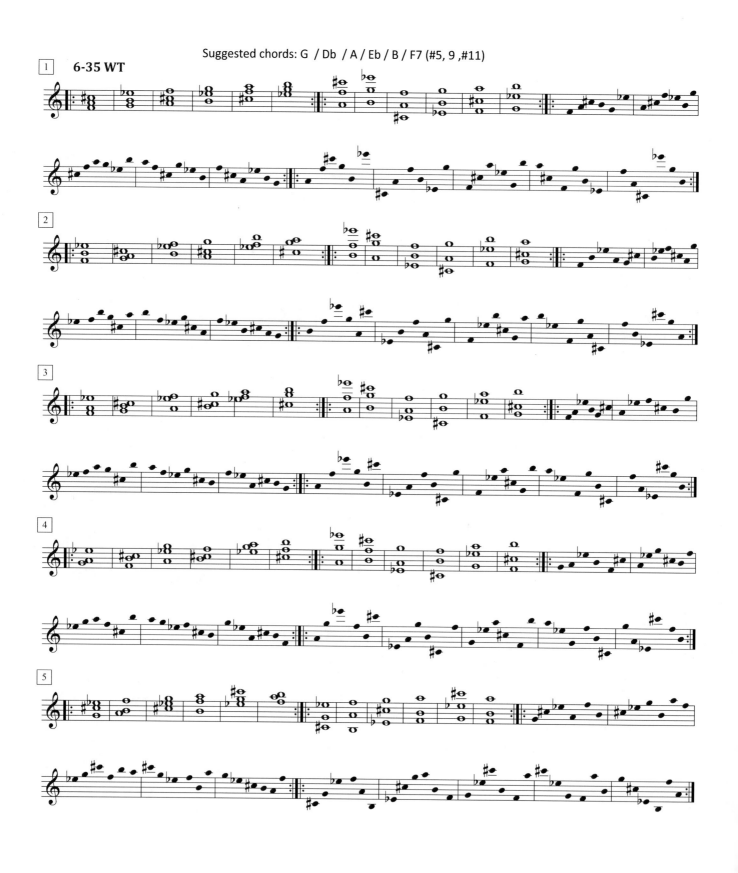

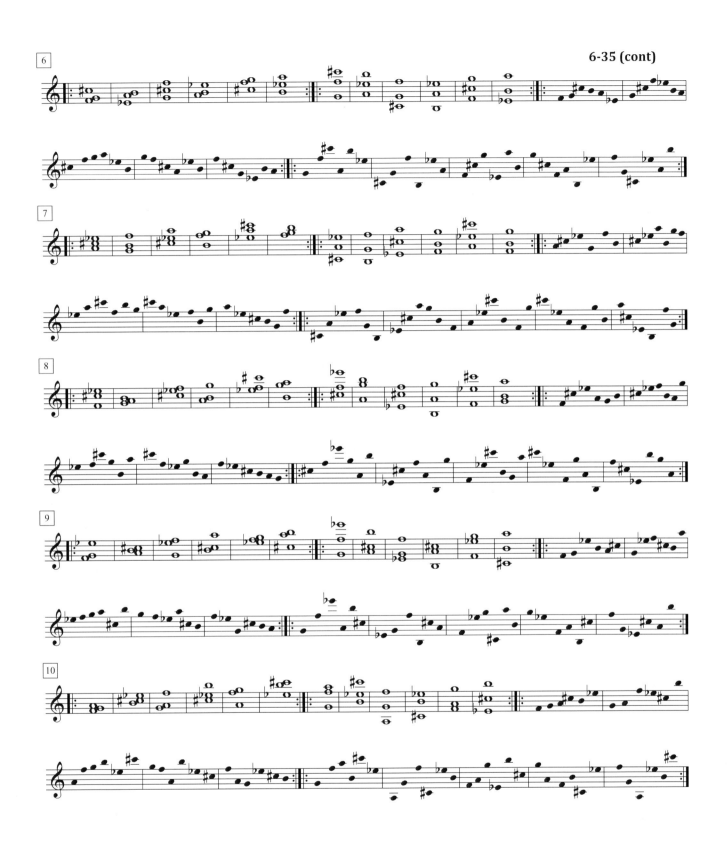

6-20 Augmented (9-12 messiaen 3 subset)

HEXATONICS - Trichord pairs - Combinatorial Voice Leading

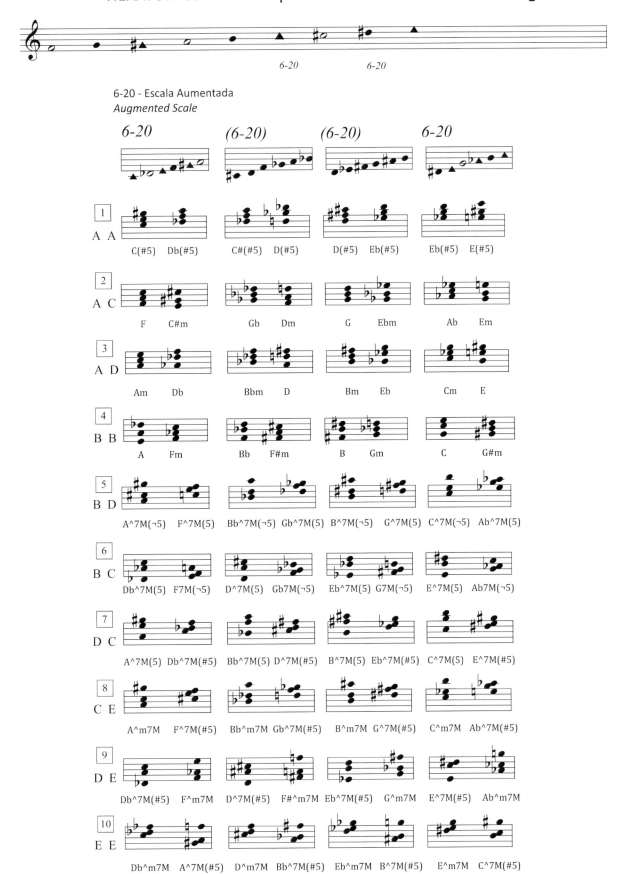

6-20 - Escala Aumentada
Augmented Scale

6-20 Aug - Nonatonic (9-12)

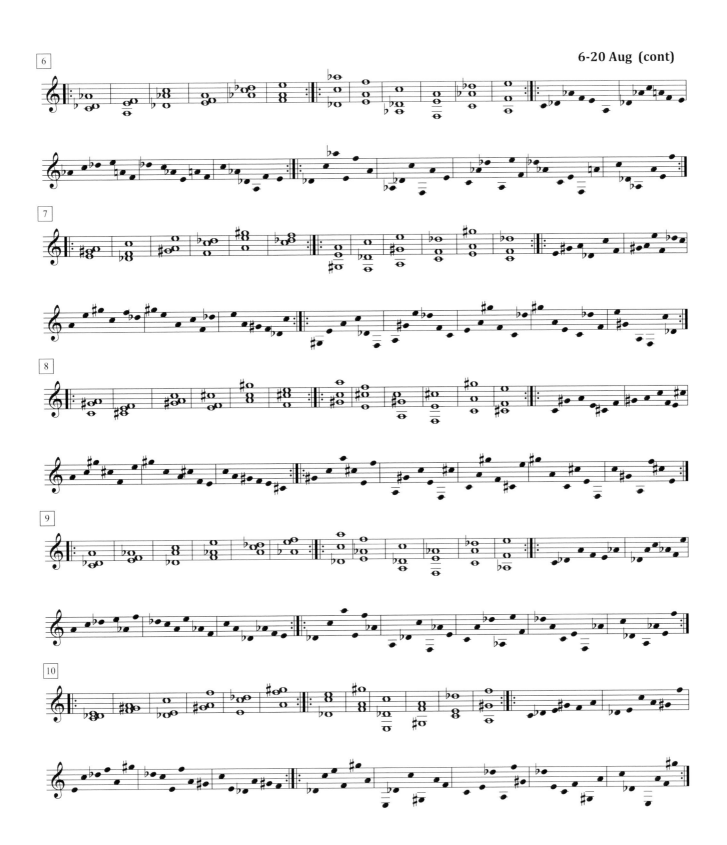

6-z17a All Trichord Hexachord

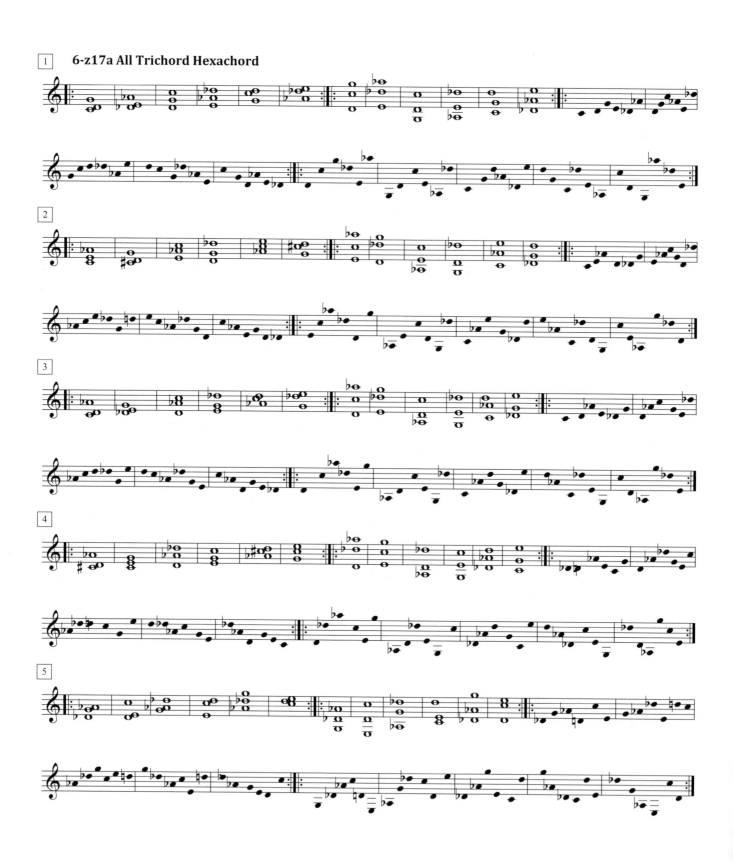

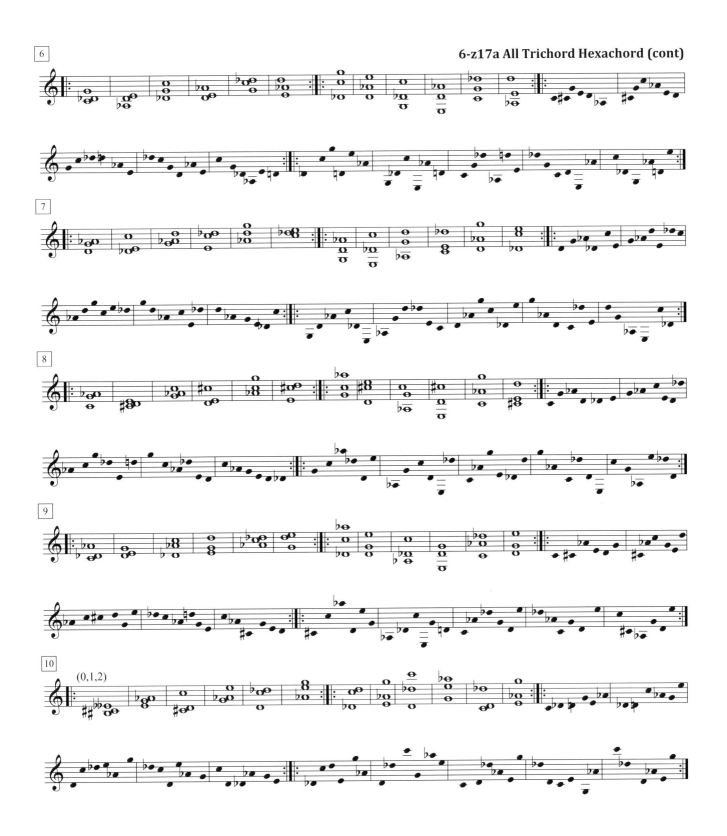

7. CADENCES AND CHORD PROGRESSIONS

7.1 TONAL AXES

We can link different tonalities from tonal axes generated by harmonic structures of limited transpositions (diminished chords and augmented chords, for example) that are shared by several tonal centers. One of the examples is obtained from the superimposition of two circles (the chromatic circle and the circle of fourths) that produces, in the vertices indicated in the center, a 4-25 chord (called Fr6 or French sixth chord), i.e. a chord of 7(b5) type. This chord will serve as a pivot for the modulations among the four tonal centers that form the tetratonic axis of the ex 7.1. The 4-25 chord is of limited transposition (6), so G7(b5) is identical in content to Db7(b5). The diagram 7.1 shows how a single chord can link four different tonal centers.

7.1   *Fr6 Chord Axis*

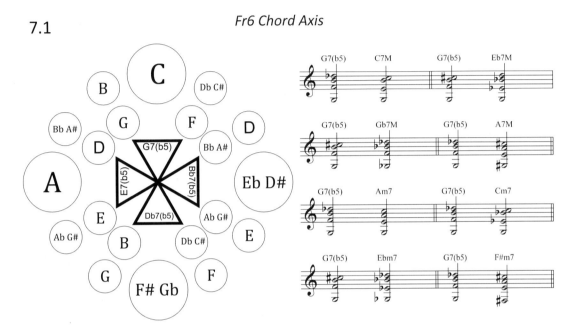

7.2 CADENTIAL GRAVITY

Chord progressions are characterized by a feeling of a cadential gravity or movement toward a goal. Successions of chords, in contrast, are characterized by harmonic movements that suggest vagueness, with no sense of direction toward a tonic center. The functions, in order of gravity (tonal cycle) are shown in 7.2.

7.2

[M:]

S	s	D	T		
S	s	DFri	D	T	

[m:]

s	d	d+	t	
s	d	dfri	d+	t

[M:] – Maior / *Major*

[m:] – Menor / *Minor*

As we are dealing with several connected tonal centers, it is convenient to introduce the harmonic functions mentioned in Chapter 2 in all tonal centers. From them, we may discuss the cadences and chord progressions. This summary will enable an overview of all the tonal centers and their harmonic functions.

COMBINATORIAL HARMONY - BY JULIO HERRLEIN - MEL BAY   243

[C:] / [a:]

	VI	i	I	biii	III	v	vfri	v+	vii°+	Vfri	V	bvii	bII	VI+	VII	ii	II	iv	IV	bvi	bVI°+
	Tr	t	T	tR	Ta	d	dfri	d+	Đb9	Dfri	D	s6/4	Dalt	Đ/Sr	Đ9	s/6	Sr	s	S	sR	s/3
	Am7		C		Em7		Dm/E	E7	G#°+	Fm/G	G7		Db7(alt)	C#fr6/A	Bø		Dm7		F7M		Fm/Ab

[F:] / [d:]

	VI	i	I	biii	III	v	vfri	v+	vii°+	Vfri	V	bvii	bII	VI+	VII	ii	II	iv	IV	bvi	bVI°+
	Tr	t	T	tR	Ta	d	dfri	d+	Đb9	Dfri	D	s6/4	Dalt	Đ/Sr	Đ9	s/6	Sr	s	S	sR	s/3
	Dm7		F		Am7		Gm/A	A7	C#°+	Bbm/C	C7		Gb7(alt)	F#fr6/D	Eø		Gm7		Bb7M		Bbm/Db

[Bb:] / [g:]

	VI	i	I	biii	III	v	vfri	v+	vii°+	Vfri	V	bvii	bII	VI+	VII	ii	II	iv	IV	bvi	bVI°+
	Tr	t	T	tR	Ta	d	dfri	d+	Đb9	Dfri	D	s6/4	Dalt	Đ/Sr	Đ9	s/6	Sr	s	S	sR	s/3
	Gm7		Bb		Dm7		Cm/D	D7	F#°+	Ebm/F	F7		B7(alt)	Bfr6/G	Aø		Cm7		Eb7M		Ebm/Gb

[Eb:] / [c:]

	VI	i	I	biii	III	v	vfri	v+	vii°+	Vfri	V	bvii	bII	VI+	VII	ii	II	iv	IV	bvi	bVI°+
	Tr	t	T	tR	Ta	d	dfri	d+	Đb9	Dfri	D	s6/4	Dalt	Đ/Sr	Đ9	s/6	Sr	s	S	sR	s/3
	Cm7		Eb		Gm7		Fm/G	G7	B°+	Abm/Bb	Bb7		E7(alt)	Efr6/C	Dø		Fm7		Ab7M		Abm/B

[Ab:] / [f:]

	VI	i	I	biii	III	v	vfri	v+	vii°+	Vfri	V	bvii	bII	VI+	VII	ii	II	iv	IV	bvi	bVI°+
	Tr	t	T	tR	Ta	d	dfri	d+	Đb9	Dfri	D	s6/4	Dalt	Đ/Sr	Đ9	s/6	Sr	s	S	sR	s/3
	Fm7		Ab		Cm7		Bbm/C	C7	E°+	Dbm/Eb	Eb7		A7(alt)	Afr6/F	Gø		Bbm7		Db7M		Dbm/E

[Db:] / [bb:]

	VI	i	I	biii	III	v	vfri	v+	vii°+	Vfri	V	bvii	bII	VI+	VII	ii	II	iv	IV	bvi	bVI°+
	Tr	t	T	tR	Ta	d	dfri	d+	Đb9	Dfri	D	s6/4	Dalt	Đ/Sr	Đ9	s/6	Sr	s	S	sR	s/3
	Bbm7		Db		Fm7		Ebm/F	F7	A°+	Gbm/Ab	Ab7		D7(alt)	Dfr6/Bb	Cø		Ebm7		Gb7M		Gbm/A

[Gb:]	**VI** i	**I** biii	**III** v	vfri	v+	vii°+	**Vfri**	**V** bvii	**bII**	**VI+**	**VII** ii	**II** iv	**IV** bvi	**bVI** °+
[eb:]	**Tr** t	**T** tR	**Ta** d	dfri	d+	Đb9	**Dfri**	**D** s6/4	**Dalt**	**Đ/Sr**	**Đ9** s/6	**Sr** s	**S** sR	**s/3**
	Ebm7	Gb	Bbm7	Abm/Bb	Bb7	D°+	Bm/Db	Db7	G7(alt)	Gfr6/Eb	Fø	Abm7	Cb7M	Bm/D

[B:]	**VI** i	**I** biii	**III** v	vfri	v+	vii°+	**Vfri**	**V** bvii	**bII**	**VI+**	**VII** ii	**II** iv	**IV** bvi	**bVI** °+
[g#:]	**Tr** t	**T** tR	**Ta** d	dfri	d+	Đb9	**Dfri**	**D** s6/4	**Dalt**	**Đ/Sr**	**Đ9** s/6	**Sr** s	**S** sR	**s/3**
	G#m7	B	D#m7	C#m/D#	D#7	G°+	Em/F#	F#7	C7(alt)	Cfr6/G#	A#ø	C#m7	E7M	Em/G

[E:]	**VI** i	**I** biii	**III** v	vfri	v+	vii°+	**Vfri**	**V** bvii	**bII**	**VI+**	**VII** ii	**II** iv	**IV** bvi	**bVI** °+
[c#:]	**Tr** t	**T** tR	**Ta** d	dfri	d+	Đb9	**Dfri**	**D** s6/4	**Dalt**	**Đ/Sr**	**Đ9** s/6	**Sr** s	**S** sR	**s/3**
	C#m7	E	G#m7	F#m/G#	G#7	C°+	Am/B	B7	F7(alt)	Ffr6/Db	D#ø	F#m7	A7M	Am/C

[A:]	**VI** i	**I** biii	**III** v	vfri	v+	vii°+	**Vfri**	**V** bvii	**bII**	**VI+**	**VII** ii	**II** iv	**IV** bvi	**bVI** °+
[f#:]	**Tr** t	**T** tR	**Ta** d	dfri	d+	Đb9	**Dfri**	**D** s6/4	**Dalt**	**Đ/Sr**	**Đ9** s/6	**Sr** s	**S** sR	**s/3**
	F#m7	A	C#m7	Bm/C#	C#7	F°+	Dm/E	E7	A#7(alt)	A#fr6/F#	G#ø	Bm7	D7M	Dm/F

[D:]	**VI** i	**I** biii	**III** v	vfri	v+	vii°+	**Vfri**	**V** bvii	**bII**	**VI+**	**VII** ii	**II** iv	**IV** bvi	**bVI** °+
[b:]	**Tr** t	**T** tR	**Ta** d	dfri	d+	Đb9	**Dfri**	**D** s6/4	**Dalt**	**Đ/Sr**	**Đ9** s/6	**Sr** s	**S** sR	**s/3**
	Bm7	D	F#m7	Em/F#	F#7	A#°+	Gm/A	A7	Eb7(alt)	Ebfr6/B	C#ø	Em7	G7M	Gm/Bb

[G:]	**VI** i	**I** biii	**III** v	vfri	v+	vii°+	**Vfri**	**V** bvii	**bII**	**VI+**	**VII** ii	**II** iv	**IV** bvi	**bVI** °+
[e:]	**Tr** t	**T** tR	**Ta** d	dfri	d+	Đb9	**Dfri**	**D** s6/4	**Dalt**	**Đ/Sr**	**Đ9** s/6	**Sr** s	**S** sR	**s/3**
	Em7	G	Bm7	Am/B	B7	D#°+	Cm/D	D7	G#7(alt)	G#fr6/E	F#ø	Am7	C7M	Cm/Eb

7.4 CADENTIAL MODELS

Cadences can be defined as the tendency of movement (or attraction) among the chords of a progression. We will use three basic kinds of cadences:

a) D - T, the first chord of the dominant axis and the second of the tonic axis
b) S - D, the first chord of the subdominant axis and the second of the dominant axis
c) S - s, the first chord of the subdominant axis and the second of the subdominant minor axis

From these kinds of cadences, we present 97 cadential models. Note that such models are always built by a two-chord progression. Longer progressions link the cadential models, enabling the existance of interpolated chords among them (chromatic passage chords, for example).

In example 7.4a, we have the functions of tonality [C:] and [a].

From the D-T cadential model, we can build in [C:] the four cadences of the example 7.4.b.

From the D-T cadential model, we can build in [a:] the four cadences of the example 7.4.c.

Note that the eight cadences in 7.4 were created within the same tonality: the first four in [C:] and the last four in [a:].

7.4.a

[C:] [a:]	VI Tr	i t	I T	biii tR	III Ta	v d	vfri dfri	v+ d+	vii°+ Db9	Vfri Dfri	V D	bvii s6/4	bII Dalt	VI+ D/Sr	VII D9	ii s/6	II Sr	iv s	IV S	bvi sR	bVI°+ s/3
	Am7		C		Em7		Dm/E	E7	G#°+		Fm/G	G7		Db7(alt) C#fr6/A		Bø		Dm7		F7M		Fm/Ab

7.4.b

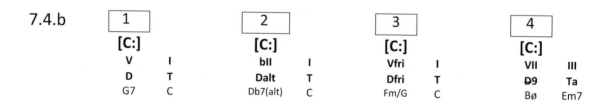

1		2		3		4	
[C:]		[C:]		[C:]		[C:]	
V	I	bII	I	Vfri	I	VII	III
D	T	Dalt	T	Dfri	T	D9	Ta
G7	C	Db7(alt)	C	Fm/G	C	Bø	Em7

7.4.c

5		6		7		8	
[a:]		[a:]		[a:]		[a:]	
v	i	v+	i	vfri	i	vii°+	i
d	t	d+	t	dfri	t	Db9	t
Em7	Am7	E7	Am7	Dm/E	Am7	G#°	Am7

In the following pages we present 97 cadential models. They are:

D - T Cadential Model:

1-8:   chaining chords in the same tonality

9-20:   chaining tonal centers linked by the tetratonic axis, i.e. that are related by minor thirds (sesquitone cycle)

21-42:   cadences based on tritonic axis (ditone cycle) allowing modulations to different tonal   centers

74-85:   D - T cadential model from close to distant tonal centers, progressively

S - D Cadential Model:

43-52:   chaining chords in the same tonality

53-61:   S – D cadential model chaining tonal centers linked by the tetratonic axis, i.e. related by minor thirds (sesquitone cycle)

86-97:   S - D cadential model from close to distant tonal centers, progressively

Cadences S - s Model:

62-73:   in the same tonality and by tonal centers apart

7.5   LIST OF CADENTIAL MODELS

D - T Cadential Model

1		2		3		4	
[C:]		**[C:]**		**[C:]**		**[C:]**	
V	I	bII	I	Vfri	I	VII	III
D	T	Dalt	T	Dfri	T	~~D9~~	Ta
G7	C	Db7(alt)	C	Fm/G	C	Bø	Em7

5		6		7		8	
[a:]		**[a:]**		**[a:]**		**[a:]**	
v	i	v+	i	vfri	i	vii°+	i
d	t	d+	t	dfri	t	~~Db9~~	t
Em7	Am7	E7	Am7	Dm/E	Am7	G#°	Am7

Tetratonic Axis

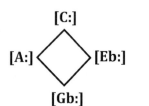

9	
[c:]	**[C:]**
v+	I
d+	T
G7	C

10	
[c:]	**[C:]**
vii°+	I
D̶b9	T
B°	C

11	
[c:]	**[C:]**
vfri	I
dfri	T
Fm/G	C

12	
[Eb:]	**[C:]**
V	I
D	T
Bb7	C

13	
[Eb:]	*[a:]*
bII	i
Dalt	t
E7(alt)	Am7

14	
[Eb:]	**[C:]**
VII	III
D̶9	Ta
Dø	Em7

15	
[Eb:]	*[a:]*
VII	i
D̶9	t
Dø	Am7

16	
[eb:]	**[C:]**
vfri	I
dfri	T
Abm/Bb	C

17	
[Gb:]	**[C:]**
V	I
D	T
Db7	C

18	
[Gb:]	**[C:]**
bII	I
Dalt	T
G7(alt)	C

19	
[A:]	*[a:]*
Vfri	i
Dfri	t
Dm/E	Am7

20	
[f#:]	**[C:]**
v+	I
d+	T
C#7	C

D - T Cadential Model

Tritonic Axis

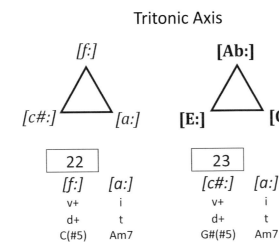

21	
[a:]	**[C:]**
v+	I
d+	**T**
E(#5)	C

22	
[f:]	*[a:]*
v+	i
d+	t
C(#5)	Am7

23	
[c#:]	*[a:]*
v+	i
d+	t
G#(#5)	Am7

24	
[C:]	
bII	I
Dalt	**T**
Db7(alt)	C

25	
[C:]	**[E:]**
bII	II
Dalt	**Tdor**
C#7(alt)	F#m7

26	
[C:]	**[Ab:]**
bII	II
Dalt	**Tdor**
Db7(alt)	Bbm7

27	
[Eb:]	**[B:]**
VI+	I
~~D~~/Sr	**T**
Efr6/C	B

28	
[Eb:]	**[Gb:]**
VI+	IV
~~D~~/Sr	**Tlyd**
Efr6/C	B

29	
[Eb:]	**[C:]**
VI+	IV
~~D~~/Sr	**Tlyd**
Efr6/C	F

30	
[Eb:]	**[F:]**
VI+	I
~~D~~/Sr	**T**
Efr6/C	F

31	
[C:]	
V	I
D	**T**
Gfr6	C

32	
[C:]	**[Gb:]**
V	I
D	**T**
Gfr6	Gb

33	
[C:]	**[A:]**
V	I
D	**T**
Gfr6	A

34	
[C:]	**[Eb:]**
V	I
D	**T**
Gfr6	Eb

35	
[C:]	**[G:]**
V	IV
D	**Tlyd**
Gfr6	C

36	
[C:]	**[Db:]**
V	IV
D	**Tlyd**
Gfr6	Gb

37	
[C:]	**[E:]**
V	IV
D	**Tlyd**
Gfr6	A

38	
[C:]	**[Bb:]**
V	IV
D	**Tlyd**
Gfr6	Eb

39	
[C:]	**[G:]**
V	II
D	**Tdor**
Gfr6	Am6

40	
[C:]	**[Db:]**
V	II
D	**Tdor**
Gfr6	Ebm6

41	
[C:]	**[E:]**
V	II
D	**Tdor**
Gfr6	F#m6

42	
[C:]	**[Bb:]**
V	II
D	**Tdor**
Gfr6	Cm6

S - D Cadential Model

[C:] and [a:] only

43			44			45			46	
[C:]			**[C:]**			**[C:]**			*[a:]*	
IV	V		II	V		II	bII		iv	v+
S	D		Sr	D		Sr	Dalt		s	d+
F7M	G7		Dm7	G7		Dm7	Db7(alt)		Dm7	E7

47			48			49			50	
[a:]			*[a:]*			**[C:]**			**[C:]**	
ii	v+		bvii	v+		bVI°+	V		bVI°+	bII
s/6	d+		s6/4	d+		s/3	D		s/3	Dalt
Bø	E7		G7	E7		Fm/Ab	G7		Fm/Ab	Db7(alt)

51			52		
[a:]			*[a:]*		
bvii	v+		bvii	vii°+	
sR	d+		sR	~~D~~b9	
F7M	E7		F7M	G#°+	

Tetratonic Axis

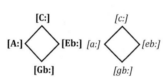

53			54			55			56	
[C:]	*[c:]*		**[C:]**	**[Eb:]**		**[C:]**	*[c:]*		**[C:]**	**[Eb:]**
II	v+		IV	bII		IV	vfri		IV	V
Sr	d+		S	Dalt		S	dfri		S	D
Dm7	G7(b13)		F7M	E7(alt)		F7M	Fm/G		F7M	Bb7

57			58			59			60	
[C:]	**[Gb:]**		**[C:]**	**[Gb:]**		*[a:]*	*[eb:]*		*[a:]*	*[eb:]*
II	V		II	bII		ii	v+		ii	vfri
Sr	D		Sr	Dalt		s/6	d+		s/6	dfri
Dm7	Db7		Dm7	G7(alt)		Bø	Bb7		Bø	Abm/Bb

61	
[C:]	**[A:]**
IV	Vfri
S	Dfri
F7M	Dm/E

S - s   Cadential Model

62	
[C:]	*[c:]*
IV	iv
S	s
F7M	Fm6

63	
[C:]	*[c:]*
IV	bvii
S	sR
F7M	Ab7M

64	
[C:]	*[c:]*
II	iv
Sr	s
Dm7	Fm7

65	
[C:]	*[c:]*
IV	bvii
S	s6/4
F7M	Bb7

66	
[a:]	**[Eb:]**
ii	**bVI°+**
s/6	**s/3**
Bø	Abm/B

67	
[C:]	*[eb:]*
IV	iv
S	s
F7M	Abm7

68	
[a:]	**[F:]**
ii	**IV**
s/6	**S**
Bø	Bb7M

69	
[C:]	*[d:]*
IV	bvii
S	sR
F7M	Eb7M

70	
[C:]	**[Bb:]**
IV	**bVI°+**
S	**s/3**
F7M	Ebm/Gb

71	
[C:]	*[f:]*
IV	bvii
S	sR
F7M	Db7M

72	
[a:]	*[bb:]*
II	iv
Sr	s
Dm7	Ebm7

73	
[C:]	*[bb:]*
IV	bvii
S	sR
F7M	Gb7M

D - T   Cadential Model (distances among tonal centers)

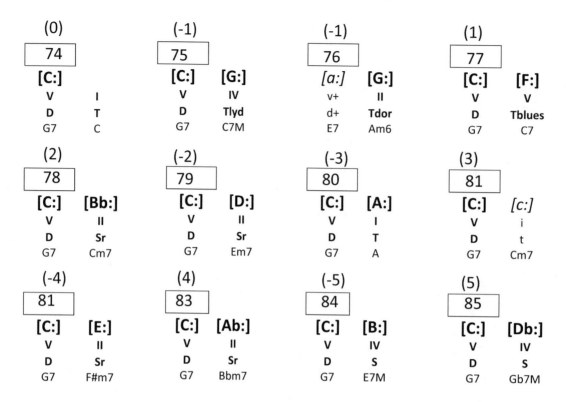

(0)	(-1)	(-1)	(1)
74	**75**	**76**	**77**

(0)

74

[C:]		**[G:]**	**[a:]**	**[G:]**	**[C:]**	**[F:]**
V	I	V	IV	v+	II	V	V
D	T	D	Tlyd	d+	Tdor	D	Tblues
G7	C	G7	C7M	E7	Am6	G7	C7

(2)	(-2)	(-3)	(3)
78	**79**	**80**	**81**

[C:]	**[Bb:]**	**[C:]**	**[D:]**	**[C:]**	**[A:]**	**[C:]**	**[c:]**
V	II	V	II	V	I	V	i
D	Sr	D	Sr	D	T	D	t
G7	Cm7	G7	Em7	G7	A	G7	Cm7

(-4)	(4)	(-5)	(5)
81	**83**	**84**	**85**

[C:]	**[E:]**	**[C:]**	**[Ab:]**	**[C:]**	**[B:]**	**[C:]**	**[Db:]**
V	II	V	II	V	IV	V	IV
D	Sr	D	Sr	D	S	D	S
G7	F#m7	G7	Bbm7	G7	E7M	G7	Gb7M

S - D   Cadential Model (distances among tonal centers)

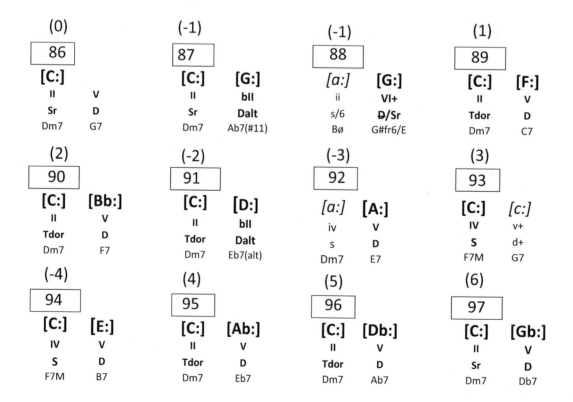

(0)	(-1)	(-1)	(1)
86	**87**	**88**	**89**

[C:]		**[C:]**	**[G:]**	**[a:]**	**[G:]**	**[C:]**	**[F:]**
II	V	II	bII	ii	VI+	II	V
Sr	D	Sr	Dalt	s/6	D/Sr	Tdor	D
Dm7	G7	Dm7	Ab7(#11)	Bø	G#fr6/E	Dm7	C7

(2)	(-2)	(-3)	(3)
90	**91**	**92**	**93**

[C:]	**[Bb:]**	**[C:]**	**[D:]**	**[a:]**	**[A:]**	**[C:]**	**[c:]**
II	V	II	bII	iv	V	IV	v+
Tdor	D	Tdor	Dalt	s	D	S	d+
Dm7	F7	Dm7	Eb7(alt)	Dm7	E7	F7M	G7

(-4)	(4)	(5)	(6)
94	**95**	**96**	**97**

[C:]	**[E:]**	**[C:]**	**[Ab:]**	**[C:]**	**[Db:]**	**[C:]**	**[Gb:]**
IV	V	II	V	II	V	II	V
S	D	Tdor	D	Tdor	D	Sr	D
F7M	B7	Dm7	Eb7	Dm7	Ab7	Dm7	Db7

7.6   CONNECTING CADENTIAL MODELS

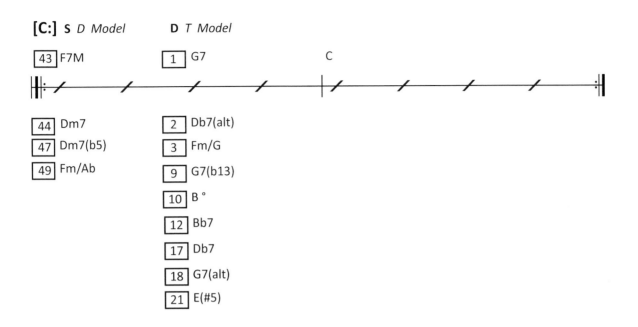

[C:] **S** *D Model*   **D** *T Model*

| 43 | F7M | | 1 | G7 | | C |

44	Dm7		2	Db7(alt)
47	Dm7(b5)		3	Fm/G
49	Fm/Ab		9	G7(b13)
			10	B °
			12	Bb7
			17	Db7
			18	G7(alt)
			21	E(#5)

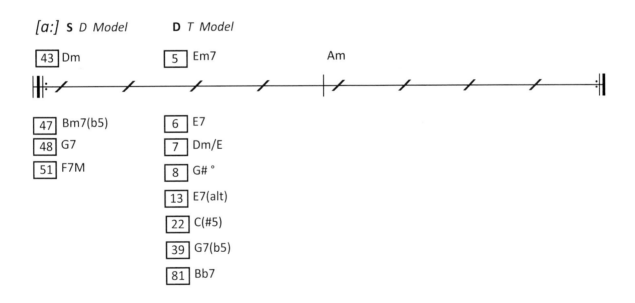

[a:] **S** *D Model*   **D** *T Model*

| 43 | Dm | | 5 | Em7 | | Am |

47	Bm7(b5)		6	E7
48	G7		7	Dm/E
51	F7M		8	G# °
			13	E7(alt)
			22	C(#5)
			39	G7(b5)
			81	Bb7

7.7 CHORD PROGRESSIONS

7.7.1 Same chord type through the Sesquiditone Circle

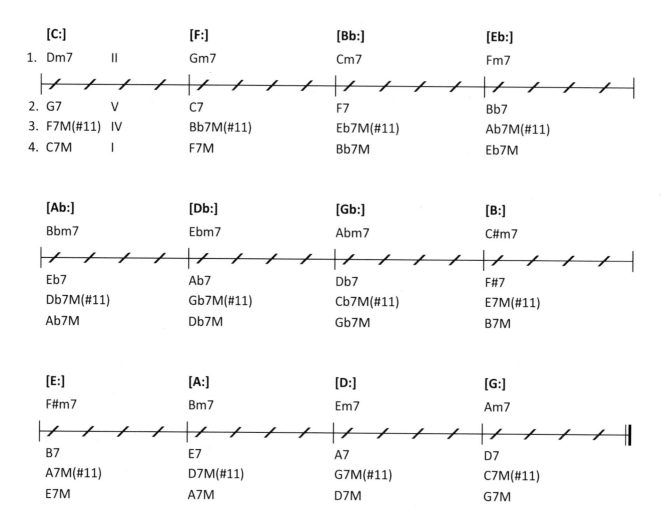

	[C:]		[F:]	[Bb:]	[Eb:]
1.	Dm7	II	Gm7	Cm7	Fm7
2.	G7	V	C7	F7	Bb7
3.	F7M(#11)	IV	Bb7M(#11)	Eb7M(#11)	Ab7M(#11)
4.	C7M	I	F7M	Bb7M	Eb7M

[Ab:]	[Db:]	[Gb:]	[B:]
Bbm7	Ebm7	Abm7	C#m7
Eb7	Ab7	Db7	F#7
Db7M(#11)	Gb7M(#11)	Cb7M(#11)	E7M(#11)
Ab7M	Db7M	Gb7M	B7M

[E:]	[A:]	[D:]	[G:]
F#m7	Bm7	Em7	Am7
B7	E7	A7	D7
A7M(#11)	D7M(#11)	G7M(#11)	C7M(#11)
E7M	A7M	D7M	G7M

COMBINATORIAL HARMONY - BY JULIO HERRLEIN - MEL BAY

7.7.2 V - I through the Sesquiditone Circle

V - I Progression - model 1

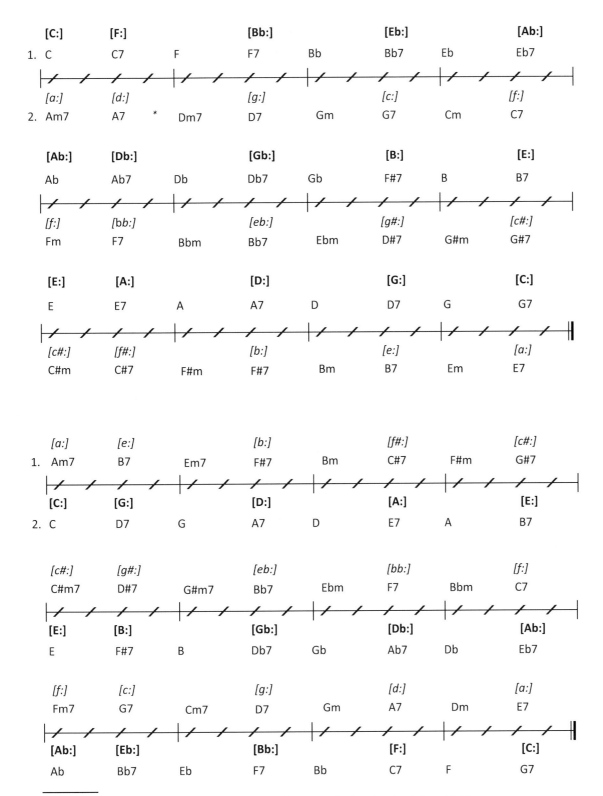

*For all minor tonal center progressions try also seventh chords with b9 and b13,
like A7(b9), A7(b13) or A7(#5).

7.7.3 V - I through the Ditone Cycle

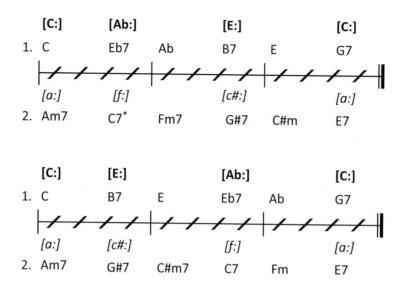

[C:]	[Ab:]		[E:]		[C:]
1. C	Eb7	Ab	B7	E	G7

[a:]	[f:]		[c#:]		[a:]
2. Am7	C7*	Fm7	G#7	C#m	E7

[C:]	[E:]		[Ab:]		[C:]
1. C	B7	E	Eb7	Ab	G7

[a:]	[c#:]		[f:]		[a:]
2. Am7	G#7	C#m7	C7	Fm	E7

7.7.4 V - I through the Sesquitone Cycle

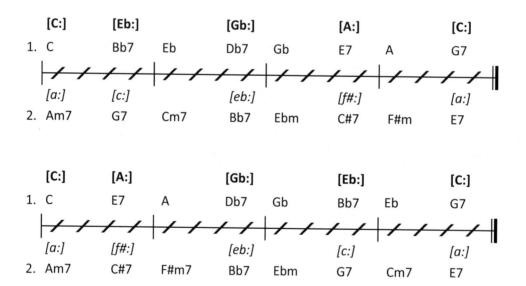

[C:]	[Eb:]		[Gb:]		[A:]		[C:]
1. C	Bb7	Eb	Db7	Gb	E7	A	G7

[a:]	[c:]		[eb:]		[f#:]		[a:]
2. Am7	G7	Cm7	Bb7	Ebm	C#7	F#m	E7

[C:]	[A:]		[Gb:]		[Eb:]		[C:]
1. C	E7	A	Db7	Gb	Bb7	Eb	G7

[a:]	[f#:]		[eb:]		[c:]		[a:]
2. Am7	C#7	F#m7	Bb7	Ebm	G7	Cm7	E7

---

*For all minor tonal center progressions try also seventh chords with b9 and b13,
like C7(b9), C7(b13) or C7(#5).

7.7.5 V - I through the Whole-tone Cycle

down:

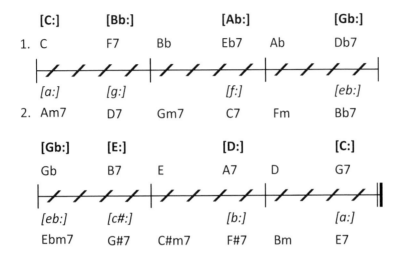

up:

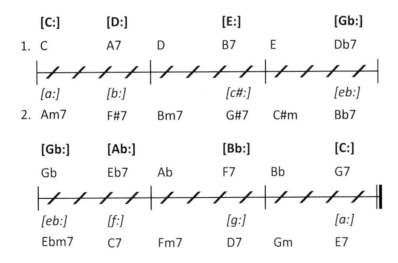

7.7.6   II - V   Progression through the Sesquiditone Circle

II - V   Progression - model   44   and   47

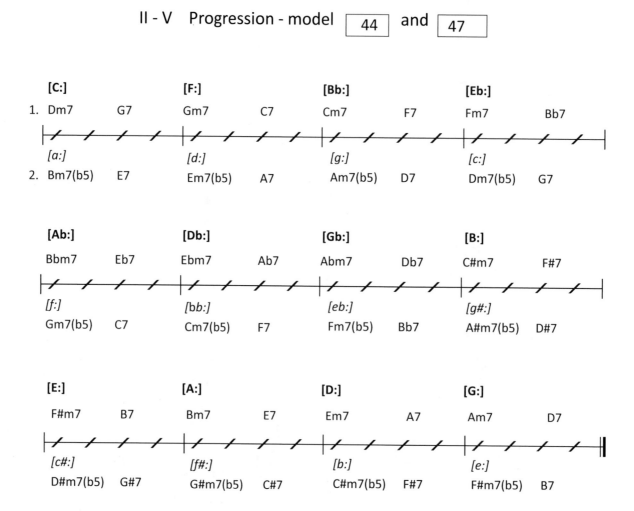

The same chord can have different harmonic functions. For this reason, each chord in Chapters 3 and 4 has its own list of functional possibilities.

We will illustrate the harmonic plurality using a very versatile chord in terms of functionality. This is the 4-16a chord, or F7M (#11-5), simply called F7M(b5).

Harmonic Plurality of the 4-16a Chord

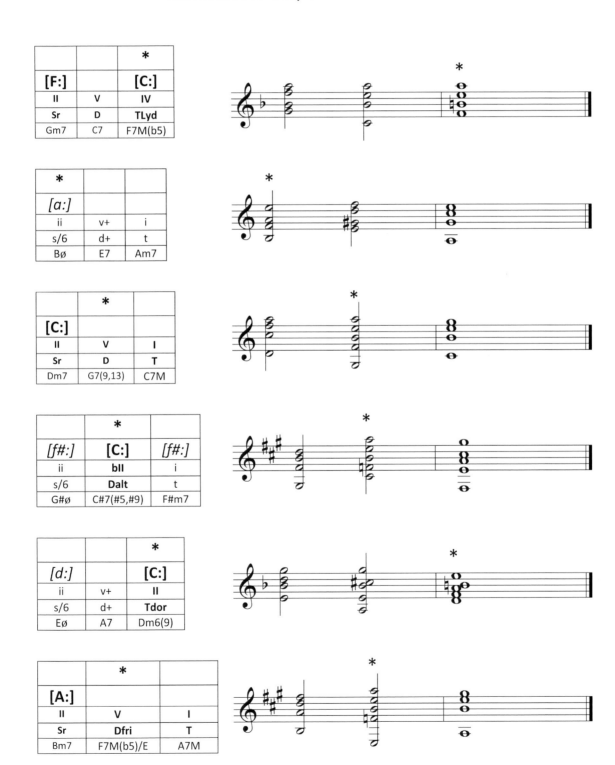

		*
[F:]		**[C:]**
II	V	IV
Sr	D	TLyd
Gm7	C7	F7M(b5)

*		
[a:]		
ii	v+	i
s/6	d+	t
Bø	E7	Am7

	*	
[C:]		
II	V	I
Sr	D	T
Dm7	G7(9,13)	C7M

	*	
[f#:]	**[C:]**	**[f#:]**
ii	bII	i
s/6	Dalt	t
G#ø	C#7(#5,#9)	F#m7

		*
[d:]		**[C:]**
ii	v+	II
s/6	d+	Tdor
Eø	A7	Dm6(9)

	*	
[A:]		
II	V	I
Sr	Dfri	T
Bm7	F7M(b5)/E	A7M

7.9 HARMONIC ANALYSIS

As we have seen before, all harmonic structures can be fit within a single tonal center. This way we can relate any given chord to a single tonal center. In the context of a song with a determined tonal center, any chord that is out of the main tonal center can be understood as belonging to another tonal center.

7.9.1 SECONDARY DOMINANTS

As discussed in item 2.4.2.1, the leading tones contained in the tritone have the attraction feature. The use of this characteristic for the other degrees is what we call individual or secondary dominant. The secondary dominant will be analyzed considering the resolution chord as an independent tonality. The C7 chord can be analyzed as V degree, generated from [F:]. (Note that the F7M chord is still being analyzed as [C:] IV degree). In that case, the A7 chord can be analyzed as v degree generated from [d:]. (Note that the Dm7 is still being analyzed as [C:] II degree).

a) The C7 chord can be analyzed as V degree, generated from [F:]. Note that the F7M chord is still being analyzed as [C:] IV degree.

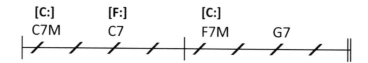

b) In that case, the A7 chord can be analyzed as v degree generated from [d:]. Note that the Dm7 is still being analyzed as [C:] II degree.

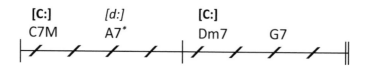

c) Individual dominants for various degrees of the same tonality.

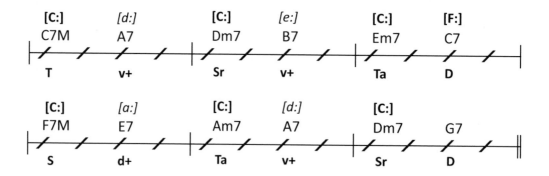

---

* For all minor tonal center progressions try also seventh chords with b9 and b13,
   like A7(b9), A7(b13) or A7(#5).

The so-called SubV chord in [C:] consists of a Db7 chord, bII degree, used instead of the G7 chord, V Degree. These two chords have the same tritone, 'F-'B in [C:] and' F-'Cb in [Gb:]. See the figure below:

Thus, the Db7 chord is closer to the [Gb:] tonal center, as in example 7.9.2b more than in the analysis of the 7.9.2a example) in [C:]. It is common to use the tensions (9, #11, 13) in SubV. So the Db7 (9, #11,13) chord implies the IV mode of the melodic minor scale, called Lydian b7 mode or Mixolydian #11 mode.

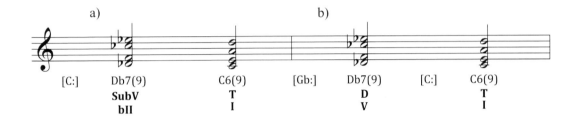

The table in 7.9.2c shows the relation between the tensions of Lydian b7 and those from the altered scale, IV and VII modes of the melodic minor scale, respectively.

In example 7.9.2d, note the proximity of the [Gb:] diatonic scale and the altered scale that generates the G7(alt) chord. The altered scale can be thought of as a [Gb:] scale with the 'G note instead of the 'Gb note (in bold).

c)

	Db7 (9,#11,13)	G7(alt.) b9,#9,b5,#5
Db	T	5D
Eb	9M	5A
F	3M	7m
G	11A	T
Ab	5J	9m
Bb	6M	9A
Cb	7m	3M

d)

[Gb:] Diat 7-35	Alt. 7-34	G7(alt) b9,#9,b5,#5
Gb ↗	G	T
Ab	Ab	9m
Bb	Bb	9A
Cb	Cb (B)	3M
Db	Db	5D
Eb	Eb (D#)	5A
F	F	7m

7.9.2e: The F#7 chord can be considered as V degree, generated from [B:].

e)

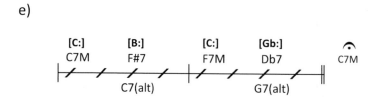

7.9.2f: In this example, the Eb7 chord can be analyzed as V degree, generated from [Ab].

f)

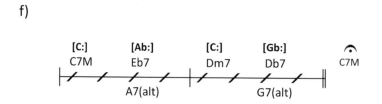

7.9.2g: SubV7 and V7(alt) for different degrees of the same tonality.

g)

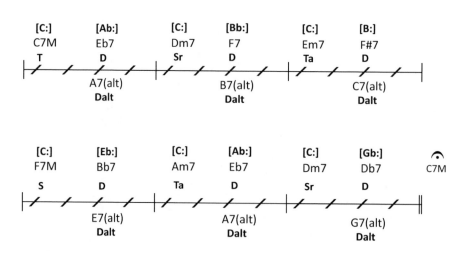

7.9.3   Secondary II - V

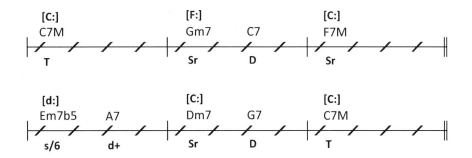

7.9.4   Secondary II - SubV7

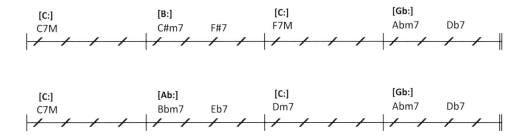

7.9.5   Extended Dominants

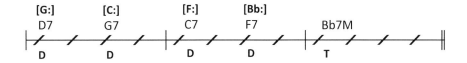

7.9.6   Interpolated Chords

a) Extended dominants with interpolated SubV7´s

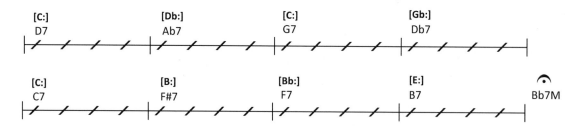

b) Similar to a) but with all V7 chords preceded by their respective IIm7.

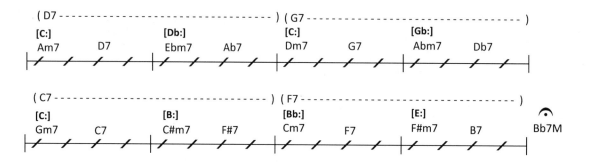

7.9.7   Adjacent II - V´s

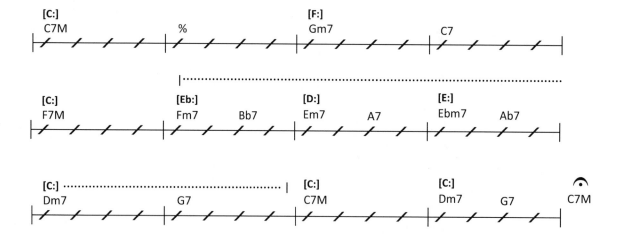

7.9.8.1 MODAL BORROWING

Modal borrowing chords will be analyzed as they belong to other tonalities. The most common case is the iv chord borrowed from the homonymous minor tonality, as an Fm chord borrowed from [c:] in [C:].

7.9.8.2 CHROMATIC MEDIANTS

Similar to modal borrowing, the chromatic mediants will be analyzed as an interchange between different tonalities.

Thus "Mi/T" means major chord built on a minor third down to theTonic chord. For example, Mi/T in [C:] is the A chord, or A7M. Similarly, mS/s means a minor chord built a major third up to the subdominant minor chord. In [a:], mS/s is the F#m chord.

M - major mediant
m - minor mediant
I - major third down
S - major third up
i - minor third down
s - minor third up

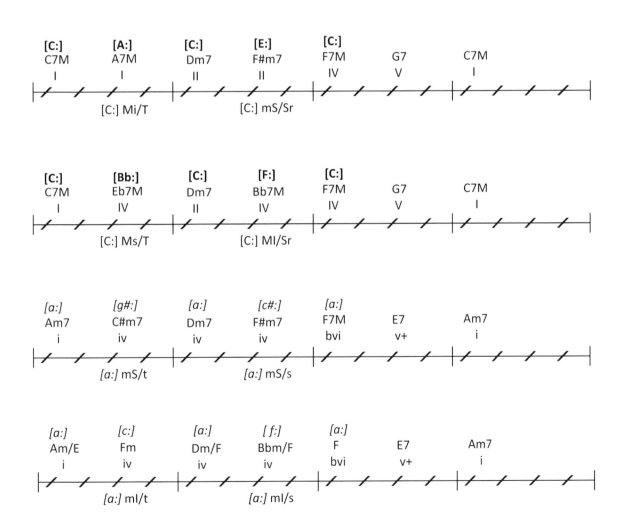

7.9.9a: Ascending diminished: the diminished chord that occurs a half tone down from the next chord, functioning as dominant without the root. In this case, the chord can be analyzed as a vii or VII degree, or simply as generated from the whole-tone/semitone diminished scale (symmetric scale).

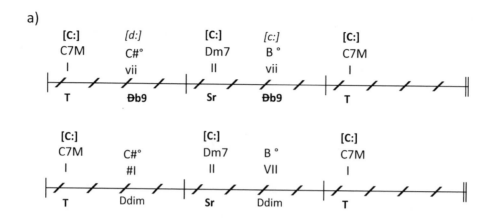

a)

7.9.9b: Descending diminished: occurs a half tone up from the next chord; very common as a link between the **Ta** and the **Sr**.

b)

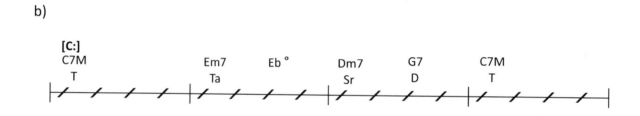

7.9.9c: Auxiliary diminished: used in chromatic function with the same bass of the next chord, usually preceding the **T** or the **S**. It can be disguised due to the chord inversions, as in the second example.

c)

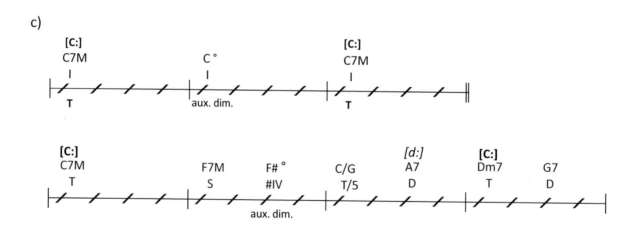

7.9.9d: As a symmetrical chord, the diminished can serve as a modulation bridge to other tonalities.

d)

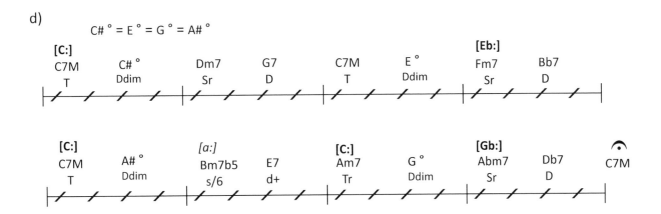

7.9.10 AUGMENTED CHORDS

Augmented chords can have different harmonic functions. Note, in Chapter 3, the functionality of the 3-12 trichord. In a typical progression as the I VI II - V turnaround shown below, the augmented chord can assume the function of any of the chords.

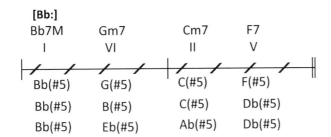

7.10 SCALE FINGERINGS (for guitar)

7.10.1

7-35 Diatonic

Please, also refer to 1.4.2. (CAGED System).

7.10.2

7-32a Harmonic Minor

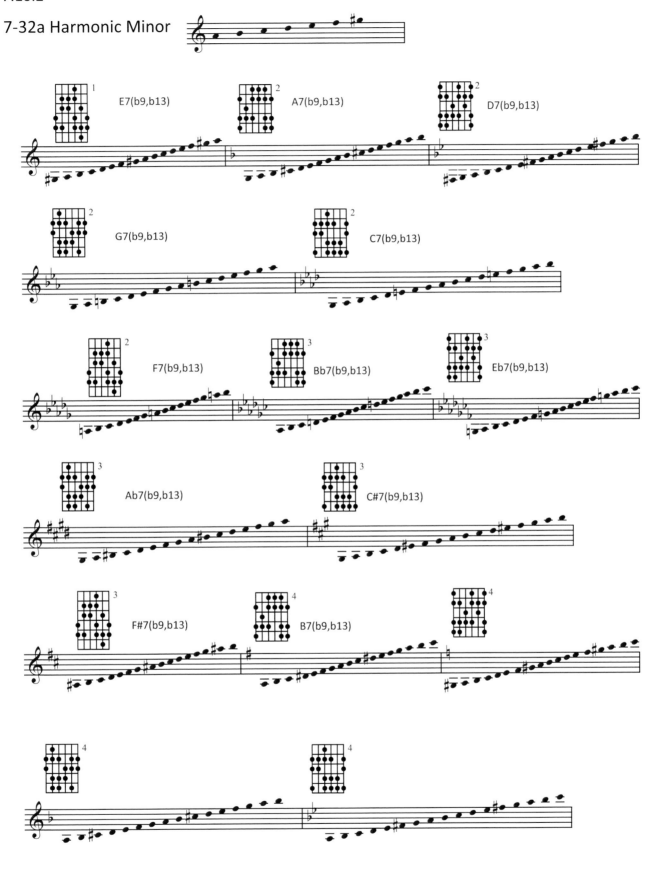

Please, also refer to page 63.

7.10.3

7-34 Melodic Minor

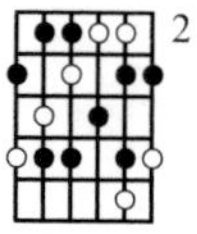

C#7(alt)
G7 (9,#11)
E7,4 (b9,13)

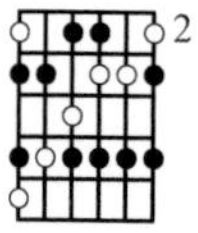

F#7(alt)
C7 (9,#11)
A7,4 (b9,13)

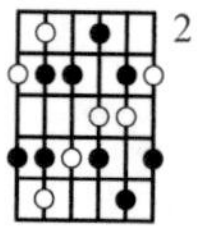

B7(alt)
F7(9,#11)
D7,4(b9,13)

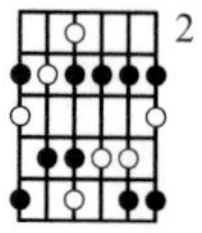

E7(alt)
Bb7 (9,#11)
G7,4(b9,13)

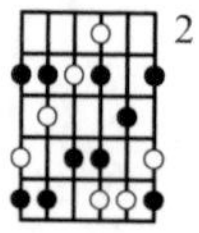

A7(alt)
Eb7 (9,#11)
C7,4(b9,13)

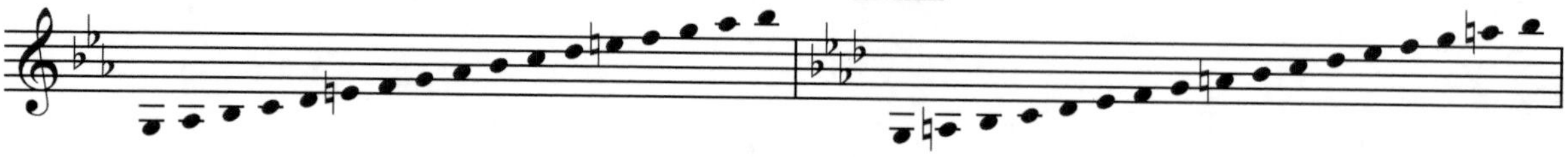

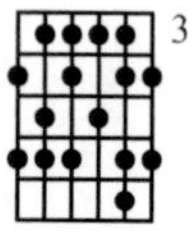

D7(alt)
Ab7 (9,#11)
F7,4(b9,13)

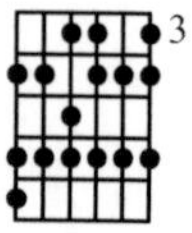

G7(alt)
Db7 (9,#11)
Bb7,4(b9,13)

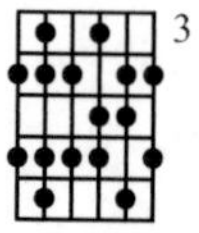

C7(alt)
Gb7 (9,#11)
Eb7,4(b9,13)

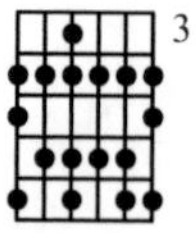

F7(alt)
B7 (9,#11)
Ab7,4(b9,13)

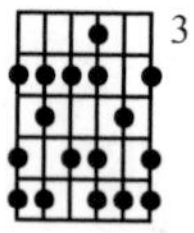

Bb7(alt)
E7 (9,#11)
Db7,4(b9,13)

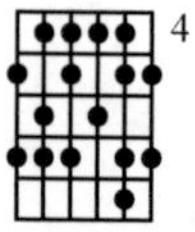

Eb7(alt)
A7 (9,#11)
Gb7,4(b9,13)

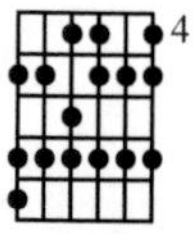

Ab7(alt)
D7 (9,#11)
B7,4(b9,13)

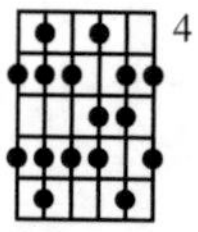

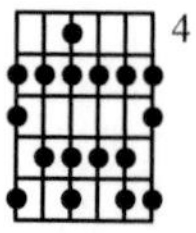

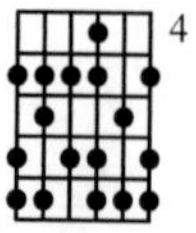

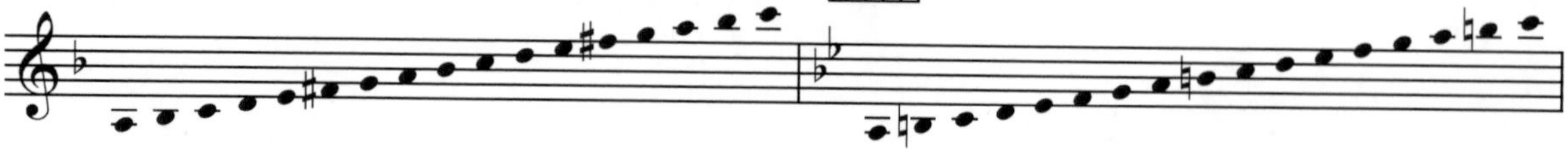

Please, also refer to page 65.

7.10.4

7-32b Harmonic Major

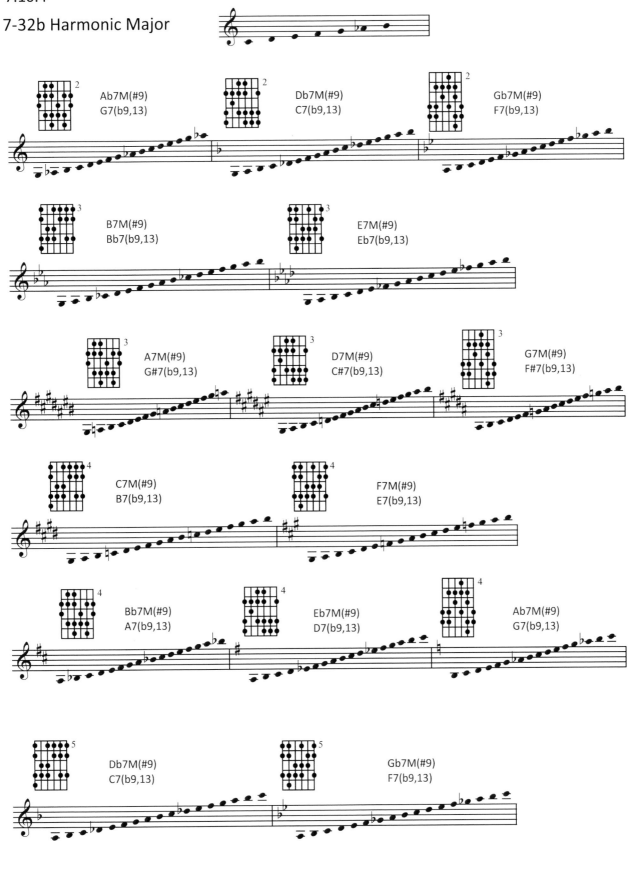

Ab7M(#9)
G7(b9,13)

Db7M(#9)
C7(b9,13)

Gb7M(#9)
F7(b9,13)

B7M(#9)
Bb7(b9,13)

E7M(#9)
Eb7(b9,13)

A7M(#9)
G#7(b9,13)

D7M(#9)
C#7(b9,13)

G7M(#9)
F#7(b9,13)

C7M(#9)
B7(b9,13)

F7M(#9)
E7(b9,13)

Bb7M(#9)
A7(b9,13)

Eb7M(#9)
D7(b9,13)

Ab7M(#9)
G7(b9,13)

Db7M(#9)
C7(b9,13)

Gb7M(#9)
F7(b9,13)

Please, also refer to page 63.

8. COMPOSITIONS

SONATA (Julio HERRLEIN)
(for Electric Guitar)
Dur. 6´

This composition in sonata form was written for electric guitar, but can also be performed on acoustic guitar (on models "cutaway" or "Humphrey"). The composition uses Brazilian rhythmic motifs and many chords with open strings in a free harmonic language, based on the mechanics of the instrument.

AINDA NÃO (Julio HERRLEIN)
NOT YET
(for Acoustic Guitar)
Dur. 4´

This is a non-strict serial composition. The tone row used is presented after the composition, together with the harmonic structures that it generates.

The composition has an expression of anger and impatience, like someone caught in an intellectual trap created by their own ego.

All compositions played by Julio Herrlein.

Sonata

(to Ben Monder)
for Electric Guitar
duration *ca.* 6 minutes

Julio HERRLEIN
Porto Alegre
June / 2009

Sonata   Julio HERRLEIN

right hand damp (palm mute)

right hand damp (palm mute)

Sonata   Julio HERRLEIN

Sonata   Julio HERRLEIN

Sonata   Julio HERRLEIN

Sonata   Julio HERRLEIN

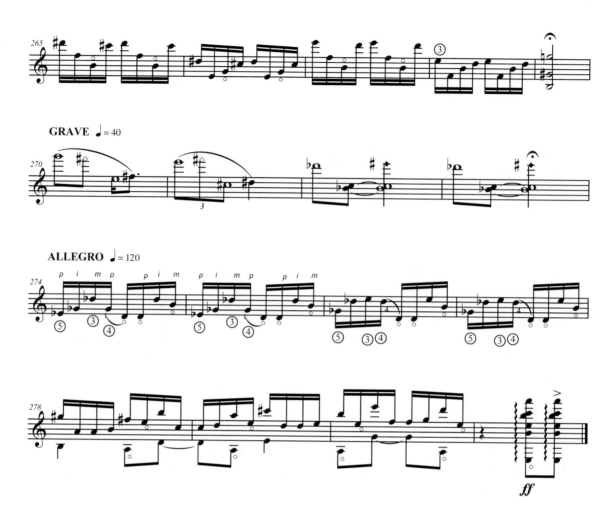

Ainda Não (Not Yet)

for nylon acoustic solo guitar
Duration: *ca.* 4 minutes

Julio HERRLEIN
Porto Alegre / Brasil
May / 2010

Ainda Não - Julio HERRLEIN

Ainda Não - Julio HERRLEIN

5

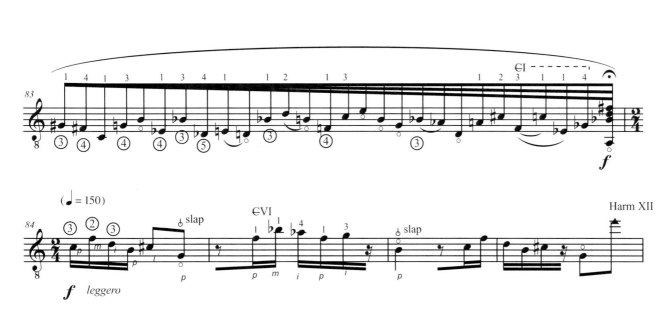

Ainda Não - Julio HERRLEIN

Ainda Não - Julio HERRLEIN

Ainda Não - Julio HERRLEIN

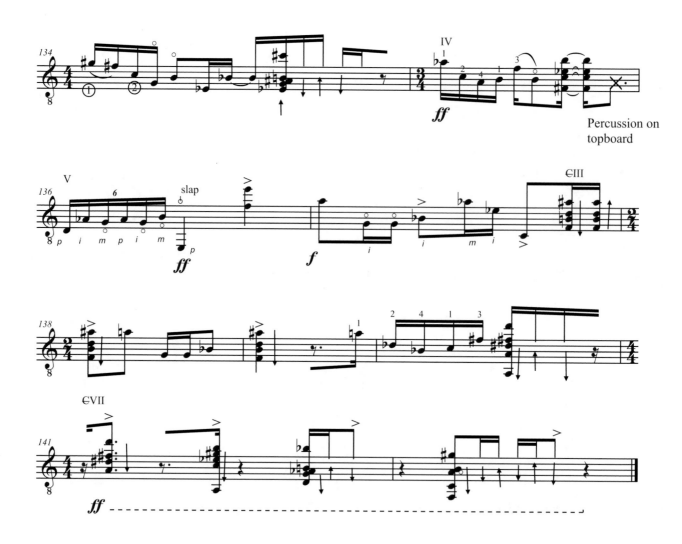

Percussion on
topboard

SERIAL MATRIX USED ON "AINDA NÃO" COMPOSITION

TECHNICAL APPENDIX

MUSICAL SET THEORY

Musical set theory is a way of organizing the 12 musical notes.

This theory was used in this book to map the harmonic (and in some cases also melodic) use of various combinations of sounds. It has proved to be an excellent tool for organizing elements, sets, set classes, etc., and has always been a reference to the completeness of the presented material.

WHY SETS?

There are ideas that can be rationalized based on the notion of sets, subsets, supersets, combinations and permutations: a) a group of notes available to play over a chord, b) a series of chords that are contained within a scale, c) a chord that, when superimposed on a root, generates another chord.

For this reason, the study of set theory can be very useful in applied music.

ALLEN FORTE

The musician Allen Forte was the great organizer of musical set theory.

Forte organized all set classes in the temperament system in a table ordered by **cardinality**, or the amount of notes of each set class. The set classes of cardinality 3 have three notes and are called trichords; the set classes of cardinality 4 have four notes and are called tetrachords, and so successively we will have pentachords (or pentatonics) hexachords (or hexatonics), etc.

Each set has a specific number. Sets of two elements (intervals or dyads) are not listed by Forte but are considered interval classes or building blocks for larger sets.

The cardinality 3 sets are numbered 3-1, 3-2, 3-3, etc.; the cardinality 4 sets are numbered 4-1, 4-2, 4-3, etc. The same goes for the cardinalities 5, 6, 7, 8 and 9. Forte does not enumerate the 10, 11 and 12 sound sets.

ELLIOTT CARTER

Elliott Carter also uses the set theory approach extensively in his music. In his book, "Harmony Book," he presents his own numbering of the same sets, along with "Consensus of Forte and Carter" (p. 23), where the classifications given by Forte and Carter are synchronized. I have decided to use Forte's nomenclature, which is the most current. Throughout the book, each harmonic structure demonstrated has the corresponding Forte number.

a) The pitches in the circle represent the 12 notes of the temperament system.

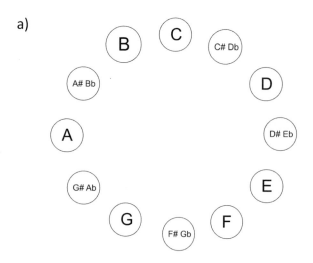

b) The middle ´C is called ‘C3.

B#2 C3 C#3 Db3 D3 D#3 Eb3 E3 Fb3 E#3 F3 F#3 Gb3 G3 G#3 Ab3 A3 A#3 Bb3 B3 Cb B#3 C4

c) This shows the way the octave that goes from ‘C3 to ‘C4 can be written.

´B#2	´C#3		´D#3		´E#3	´F#3		´G#3		´A#3		´B#3
´C3		´D3		´E3	´F3		´G3		´A3		´B3	´C4
	´Db3		´Eb3	´Fb3		´Gb3		´Ab3		´Bb3	´Cb4	

A.2 PITCH CLASSES

If the same note occurs in different octaves, it will belong to the same pitch class, regardless of its octave. Then:

d) 'C0' C1, ... 'C5' C6, belong to the same pitch class, the 'C pitch class.

d)

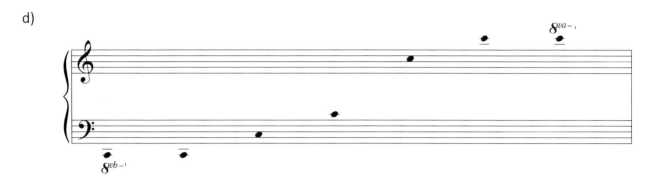

e) Notes enharmonically equivalent to 'C as 'B#, 'Dbb, in any octave, also belong to 'C pitch class.

e)

f) This diagram shows how the 12 pitch classes are numbered. Note that the sequence starts again in 'C pitch class, from the next octave on. For number 10, we will use the letter A and for number 11, the letter B.

f)

0	1	2	3	4	5	6	7	8	9	A	B	0	1	etc
'B#2	'C#3		'D#3		'E#3	'F#3		'G#3		'A#3		'B#3	'C#4	
'C3		'D3		'E3	'F3		'G3		'A3		'B3	'C4		
	'Db3		'Eb3	'Fb3		'Gb3		'Ab3		'Bb3	'Cb4		'Db4	

g) We can see that after the last of the 12 tones, the series begins again. For this reason, we can design a series of 12 tones as circular.

The view through the chromatic circle allows us to observe certain properties:

h) Any note of the circle can be taken as the first of the series, maintaining the same relationships with the other notes (circularity). Notice that the number "0 " can start on any note.

We observe that, being the shortest interval between two notes equal to 1 (one semitone), any larger interval will be measured by the sum of this smallest unit.

g)

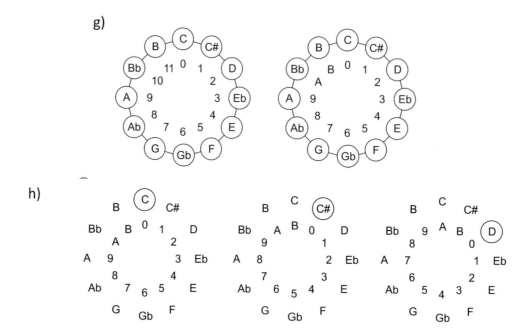

h)

A.4 PITCH CLASS SETS

Several pitch classes form pitch class sets. The notes 'C, 'E and 'G form the set that we traditionally call major triad (0,4,7).

i) The table with the transpositions of (0,4,7), keeping the 'C note fixed (0).

'C 'E 'G	'Db 'F 'Ab	'D 'F# 'A	'Eb 'G 'Bb	'E 'G# 'B	'F 'A 'C
(0,4,7)	(1,5,8)	(2,6,9)	(3,7,A)	(4,8,B)	(5,9,0)
'Gb 'Bb 'Db	'G 'B 'D	'Ab 'C 'Eb	'A 'C# 'E	'Bb 'D 'F	'B 'D# 'F#
(6,A,1)	(7,B,2)	(8,0,3)	(9,1,4)	(A,2,5)	(B,3,6)

j) The representation of the triads C, Db and D (0,4,7) in the chromatic circle. All note sets of the examples (i) and (j) belong to the same set class because, despite the transpositions, they maintain the same relationship.

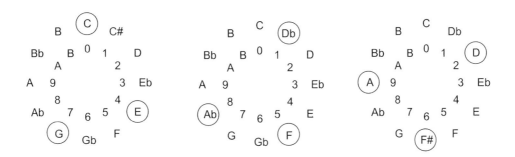

A.5 PRIME FORMS

The prime form is the simplest way by which a whole class set can be represented. Considering the set formed by pitch classes 'C, 'E, and 'G, this set will have the prime form (0,4,7).

k) The table shows the transpositions of this major triad that can be reduced to a single prime form (0,4,7), which represents the set class that traditionally is called major triad.

(0,4,7)	(1,5,8)-	(2,6,9)-	(3,7,A)-	(4,8,B)-	(5,9,0)-
(6,A,1)-	(7,B,2)-	(8,0,3)-	(9,1,4)-	(A,2,5)-	(B,3,6)-

The concept of a prime form reduces the amount of combinations, keeping only the sets that are qualitatively different, providing a more elegant system.

A.6 INTERVAL VECTOR (and inversional equivalence)

Two concepts that are commonly used in the analysis of set theory (END NOTE 9) were not used in this book: the notion of interval vector, or how often each interval class appears in each set, and the idea of the musical validity of inversional equivalence, (END NOTE 10) i.e. that two chords with the same interval vector are equivalent. The reason these concepts were not included is that in a tonal approach of harmony, the chords with the same interval vector do not necessarily have the same tonal function. In addition, the same set can have different harmonic functions (plurality) even when having the same interval vector. Therefore, the tables based on Forte reproduced here do not contain the interval vectors.

Take for example the set 3-11 and its inversion 3-11b (respectively, a major and minor triad). These two harmonic entities, although inversionally related, have the same interval vector. They can be assigned to similar harmonic functions but do not sound the same, having different meanings.

(NOTE) In this edition I decided to include only the interval vector of the Four-note chords (Chapter 4).

All Pitch Class Sets

CARD 2

P.F.		I.F.
2m	(0,1) ST, Semitone	7M
2M	(0,2) T, Whole Tone	7m
3m	(0,3) sesquitone	6M / 7d
3M	(0,4) ditone	6m / 5A
4J	(0,5) sesquiditone	5J
4A (6)	(0,6) TT	5D

Note that Forte does not enumerate these dyads. As stated earlier, the intervals are the "building blocks" of larger sets.

CARD 3

Forte	PF(a)	IF(b)
3-1:	(0,1,2)	
3-2:	(0,1,3)	[0,2,3]
3-3:	(0,1,4)	[0,3,4]
3-4:	(0,1,5)	[0,4,5]
3-5:	(0,1,6)	[0,5,6]
3-6:	(0,2,4)	
3-7:	(0,2,5)	[0,3,5]
3-8:	(0,2,6) lt	[0,4,6]
3-9:	(0,2,7) Q3	
3-10:	(0,3,6) dim	
3-11:	(0,3,7) min	[0,4,7] maj
3-12:	(0,4,8) aug (4)	

CARD 4

Forte	PF(a)	IF(b)
4-1:	(0,1,2,3)	
4-2:	(0,1,2,4)	[0,2,3,4]
4-3:	(0,1,3,4)	
4-4:	(0,1,2,5)	[0,3,4,5]
4-5:	(0,1,2,6)	[0,4,5,6]
4-6:	(0,1,2,7)	
4-7:	(0,1,4,5)	
4-8:	(0,1,5,6)	
4-9	(0,1,6,7) (6)	
4-10:	(0,2,3,5)	
4-11:	(0,1,3,5)	[0,2,4,5]
4-12:	(0,2,3,6)	[0,3,4,6]
4-13:	(0,1,3,6)	[0,3,5,6]
4-14:	(0,2,3,7)	[0,4,5,7]
4-Z15:	(0,1,4,6)	[0,2,5,6]
4-Z29:	(0,1,3,7)	[0,4,6,7]
4-16:	(0,1,5,7)	[0,2,6,7]
4-17:	(0,3,4,7)	
4-18:	(0,1,4,7)	[0,3,6,7]
4-19:	(0,1,4,8) m7M	[0,3,4,8]
4-20:	(0,1,5,8) 7M	
4-21:	(0,2,4,6)	
4-22:	(0,2,4,7)	[0,3,5,7]
4-23:	(0,2,5,7) Q4	
4-24:	(0,2,4,8) 7(#5)	
4-25:	(0,2,6,8) Fr6 (6)	
4-26:	(0,3,5,8) m7, 6	
4-27:	(0,2,5,8) ø	[0,3,6,8] 7
4-28:	(0,3,6,9) ° (3)	

CARD 5

Forte	PF(a)	IF(b)
5-1:	(0,1,2,3,4)	
5-2:	(0,1,2,3,5)	[0,2,3,4,5]
5-3:	(0,1,2,4,5)	[0,1,3,4,5]
5-4:	(0,1,2,3,6)	[0,3,4,5,6]
5-5:	(0,1,2,3,7)	[0,4,5,6,7]
5-6:	(0,1,2,5,6)	[0,1,4,5,6]
5-7:	(0,1,2,6,7)	[0,1,5,6,7]
5-8:	(0,2,3,4,6)	
5-9:	(0,1,2,4,6)	[0,2,4,5,6]
5-10:	(0,1,3,4,6)	[0,2,3,5,6]
5-11:	(0,2,3,4,7)	[0,3,4,5,7]
5Z12:	(0,1,3,5,6)	
5Z36:	(0,1,2,4,7)	[0,3,5,6,7]
5-13:	(0,1,2,4,8)	[0,2,3,4,8]
5-14:	(0,1,2,5,7)	[0,2,5,6,7]
5-15:	(0,1,2,6,8)	
5-16:	(0,1,3,4,7)	[0,3,4,6,7]
5-Z17:	(0,1,3,4,8)	
5-Z37:	(0,3,4,5,8)	
5-Z18:	(0,1,4,5,7)	[0,2,3,6,7]
5Z38:	(0,1,2,5,8)	[0,3,6,7,8]
5-19:	(0,1,3,6,7)	[0,1,4,6,7]
5-20:	(0,1,5,6,8)	[0,2,3,7,8]
5-21:	(0,1,4,5,8)	[0,3,4,7,8]
5-22:	(0,1,4,7,8)	
5-23:	(0,2,3,5,7)	[0,2,4,5,7]
5-24:	(0,1,3,5,7)	[0,2,4,6,7]
5-25:	(0,2,3,5,8)	[0,3,5,6,8]
5-26:	(0,2,4,5,8)	[0,3,4,6,8]
5-27:	(0,1,3,5,8)	[0,3,5,7,8] m7(9)
5-28:	(0,2,3,6,8)	[0,2,5,6,8]
5-29:	(0,1,3,6,8)	[0,2,5,7,8]
5-30:	(0,1,4,6,8)	[0,2,4,7,8]
5-31:	(0,1,3,6,9)	[0,2,3,6,9] 7(b9)
5-32:	(0,1,4,6,9)	[0,2,5,6,9] 7(#9)
5-33:	(0,2,4,6,8) 9#5b5	
5-34:	(0,2,4,6,9) 7(9)	
5-35:	(0,2,4,7,9) penta	Q5

CARD 6

Forte	PF(a)	IF(b)
6-1:	(0,1,2,3,4,5)	
6-2:	(0,1,2,3,4,6)	[0,2,3,4,5,6]
6-Z3:	(0,1,2,3,5,6)	[0,1,3,4,5,6]
6-Z36:	(0,1,2,3,4,7)	[0,3,4,5,6,7]
6-Z4:	(0,1,2,4,5,6)	
6-Z37:	(0,1,2,3,4,8)	
6-5:	(0,1,2,3,6,7)	[0,1,4,5,6,7]
6-Z6:	(0,1,2,5,6,7)	
6-Z38:	(0,1,2,3,7,8)	
6-7:	(0,1,2,6,7,8) (6)	
6-8:	(0,2,3,4,5,7)	
6-9:	(0,1,2,3,5,7)	[0,2,4,5,6,7]
6-Z10:	(0,1,3,4,5,7)	[0,2,3,4,6,7]
6-Z39:	(0,2,3,4,5,8)	[0,3,4,5,6,8]
6-Z11:	(0,1,2,4,5,7)	[0,2,3,5,6,7]
6-Z40:	(0,1,2,3,5,8)	[0,3,5,6,7,8]
6-Z12:	(0,1,2,4,6,7)	[0,1,3,5,6,7]
6-Z41:	(0,1,2,3,6,8)	[0,2,5,6,7,8]
6-Z13:	(0,1,3,4,6,7)	
6-Z42:	(0,1,2,3,6,9)	
6-14:	(0,1,3,4,5,8)	[0,3,4,5,7,8]
6-15:	(0,1,2,4,5,8)	[0,3,4,6,7,8]
6-16:	(0,1,4,5,6,8)	[0,2,3,4,7,8]
6-Z17:	(0,1,2,4,7,8)	[0,1,4,6,7,8]
6-Z43:	(0,1,2,5,6,8)	[0,2,3,6,7,8]
*6-18:	(0,1,2,5,7,8)	[0,1,3,6,7,8]
6-Z19:	(0,1,3,4,7,8)	[0,1,4,5,7,8]
6-Z44:	(0,1,2,5,6,9)	[0,1,4,5,6,9]
6-20:	(0,1,4,5,8,9) (4)	
6-21:	(0,2,3,4,6,8)	[0,2,4,5,6,8]
6-22:	(0,1,2,4,6,8)	[0,2,4,6,7,8]
6-Z23:	(0,2,3,5,6,8)	
6-Z45:	(0,2,3,4,6,9)	
6-Z24:	(0,1,3,4,6,8)	[0,2,4,5,7,8]
6-Z46:	(0,1,2,4,6,9)	[0,2,4,5,6,9]
6-Z25:	(0,1,3,5,6,8)	[0,2,3,5,7,8]
6-Z47:	(0,1,2,4,7,9)	[0,2,3,4,7,9]
6-Z26:	(0,1,3,5,7,8)	
6-Z48:	(0,1,2,5,7,9)	
6-27:	(0,1,3,4,6,9)	[0,2,3,5,6,9]
6-Z28:	(0,1,3,5,6,9)	
6-Z49:	(0,1,3,4,7,9)	
6-Z29:	(0,2,3,6,7,9)	
6-Z50:	(0,1,4,6,7,9)	
6-30:	(0,1,3,6,7,9)	[0,2,3,6,8,9]
6-31:	(0,1,4,5,7,9)	[0,2,4,5,8,9]
6-32:	(0,2,4,5,7,9) m11	
6-33:	(0,2,3,5,7,9)	[0,2,4,6,7,9] 7(11)
6-34:	(0,1,3,5,7,9)	[0,2,4,6,8,9]
6-35:	(0,2,4,6,8,A)(2) WT	

From the sets of cardinality 3, Forte starts the numbering, which is the number of cardinality (number of sounds), followed by an ordinal number. The set of cardinality 3 has 12 elements. If we consider the inversion of each set as a separate set, there are actually 19 trichord classes. For this reason, we will differentiate the original form of the inverted form, adding to the Forte number the letter "a" (to the prime form, henceforth PF) and the letter "b" (for an inverted form, henceforth IF).

The three-note sets are a relatively small and manageable group because they do not present a great amount of combinations.

CARD 7

Forte	PF(a)	IF(b)
7-1:	(0,1,2,3,4,5,6)	
7-2:	(0,1,2,3,4,5,7)	[0,2,3,4,5,6,7]
7-3:	(0,1,2,3,4,5,8)	[0,3,4,5,6,7,8]
7-4:	(0,1,2,3,4,6,7)	[0,1,3,4,5,6,7]
7-5:	(0,1,2,3,5,6,7)	[0,1,2,4,5,6,7]
7-6:	(0,1,2,3,4,7,8)	[0,1,4,5,6,7,8]
7-7:	(0,1,2,3,6,7,8)	[0,1,2,5,6,7,8]
7-8:	(0,2,3,4,5,6,8)	
7-9:	(0,1,2,3,4,6,8)	[0,2,4,5,6,7,8]
7-10:	(0,1,2,3,4,6,9)	[0,2,3,4,5,6,9]
7-11:	(0,1,3,4,5,6,8)	[0,2,3,4,5,7,8]
7-Z12:	(0,1,2,3,4,7,9)	
7-Z36:	(0,1,2,3,5,6,8)	[0,2,3,5,6,7,8]
7-13:	(0,1,2,4,5,6,8)	[0,2,3,4,6,7,8]
7-14:	(0,1,2,3,5,7,8)	[0,1,3,5,6,7,8]
7-15:	(0,1,2,4,6,7,8)	
7-16:	(0,1,2,3,5,6,9)	[0,1,3,4,5,6,9]
7-Z17:	(0,1,2,4,5,6,9)	
7-Z37:	(0,1,3,4,5,7,8)	
7-Z18:	(0,1,4,5,6,7,9)	[0,2,3,4,5,8,9]
7-Z38:	(0,1,2,4,5,7,8)	[0,1,3,4,6,7,8]
7-19:	(0,1,2,3,6,7,9)	[0,1,2,3,6,8,9]
7-20:	(0,1,2,5,6,7,9)	[0,2,3,4,7,8,9]
7-21:	(0,1,2,4,5,8,9)	[0,1,3,4,5,8,9]
7-22:	(0,1,2,5,6,8,9) hn	
7-23:	(0,2,3,4,5,7,9)	[0,2,4,5,6,7,9]
7-24:	(0,1,2,3,5,7,9)	[0,2,4,6,7,8,9]
7-25:	(0,2,3,4,6,7,9)	[0,2,3,5,6,7,9]
7-26:	(0,1,3,4,5,7,9)	[0,2,4,5,6,8,9]
7-27:	(0,1,2,4,5,7,9)	[0,2,4,5,7,8,9]
7-28:	(0,1,3,5,6,7,9)	[0,2,3,4,6,8,9]
7-29:	(0,1,2,4,6,7,9)	[0,2,3,5,7,8,9]
7-30:	(0,1,2,4,6,8,9)	[0,1,3,5,7,8,9]
7-31:	(0,1,3,4,6,7,9)	[0,2,3,5,6,8,9]
7-32:	(0,1,3,4,6,8,9) Hm	[0,1,3,5,6,8,9] HM
7-33:	(0,1,2,4,6,8,A)	
7-34:	(0,1,3,4,6,8,A) Ac	
7-35:	(0,1,3,5,6,8,A) Diat	

CARD 8

Forte	PF(a)	IF(b)
8-1:	(0,1,2,3,4,5,6,7)	
8-2:	(0,1,2,3,4,5,6,8)	[0,2,3,4,5,6,7,8]
8-3:	(0,1,2,3,4,5,6,9)	
8-4:	(0,1,2,3,4,5,7,8)	[0,1,3,4,5,6,7,8]
8-5:	(0,1,2,3,4,6,7,8)	[0,1,2,4,5,6,7,8]
8-6:	(0,1,2,3,5,6,7,8)	
8-7:	(0,1,2,3,4,5,8,9)	
8-8:	(0,1,2,3,4,7,8,9)	
8-9:	(0,1,2,3,6,7,8,9)	
8-10:	(0,2,3,4,5,6,7,9)	
8-11:	(0,1,2,3,4,5,7,9)	[0,2,4,5,6,7,8,9]
8-12:	(0,1,3,4,5,6,7,9)	[0,2,3,4,5,6,8,9]
8-13:	(0,1,2,3,4,6,7,9)	[0,2,3,5,6,7,8,9]
8-14:	(0,1,2,4,5,6,7,9)	[0,2,3,4,5,7,8,9]
8-Z15:	(0,1,2,3,4,6,8,9)	[0,1,3,5,6,7,8,9]
8-Z29:	(0,1,2,3,5,6,7,9)	[0,2,3,4,6,7,8,9]
8-16:	(0,1,2,3,5,7,8,9)	[0,1,2,4,6,7,8,9]
8-17:	(0,1,3,4,5,6,8,9)	
8-18:	(0,1,2,3,5,6,8,9)	[0,1,3,4,6,7,8,9]
8-19:	(0,1,2,4,5,6,8,9)	[0,1,3,4,5,7,8,9]
8-20:	(0,1,2,4,5,7,8,9)	
8-21:	(0,1,2,3,4,6,8,A)	
8-22:	(0,1,2,3,5,6,8,A)	[0,1,3,4,5,6,8,A]
8-23:	(0,1,2,3,5,7,8,A)	
8-24:	(0,1,2,4,5,6,8,A)	
8-25:	(0,1,2,4,6,7,8,A)	
8-26:	(0,1,3,4,5,7,8,A)	
8-27:	(0,1,2,4,5,7,8,A)	[0,1,3,4,6,7,8,A]
8-28:	(0,1,3,4,6,7,9,A) (3)	octa

CARD 9

Forte	PF(a)	IF(b)
9-1:	(0,1,2,3,4,5,6,7,8)	
9-2:	(0,1,2,3,4,5,6,7,9)	[0,2,3,4,5,6,7,8,9]
9-3:	(0,1,2,3,4,5,6,8,9)	[0,1,3,4,5,6,7,8,9]
9-4:	(0,1,2,3,4,5,7,8,9)	[0,1,2,4,5,6,7,8,9]
9-5:	(0,1,2,3,4,6,7,8,9)	[0,1,2,3,5,6,7,8,9]
9-6:	(0,1,2,3,4,5,6,8,A)	
9-7:	(0,1,2,3,4,5,7,8,A)	[0,1,3,4,5,6,7,8,A]
9-8:	(0,1,2,3,4,6,7,8,A)	[0,1,2,4,5,6,7,8,A]
9-9:	(0,1,2,3,5,6,7,8,A)	
9-10:	(0,1,2,3,4,6,7,9,A)	
9-11:	(0,1,2,3,5,6,7,9,A)	[0,1,2,4,5,6,7,9,A]
9-12:	(0,1,2,4,5,6,8,9,A)	

CARD 10

No FORTE Code
(0,1,2,3,4,5,6,7,8,9)
(0,1,2,3,4,5,6,7,8,A)
(0,1,2,3,4,5,6,7,9,A)
(0,1,2,3,4,5,6,8,9,A)
(0,1,2,3,4,5,7,8,9,A)
(0,1,2,3,4,6,7,8,9,A) (6)

CARD 11

No FORTE Code
(0,1,2,3,4,5,6,7,8,9,A) (12)

CARD 12

No FORTE Code
(0,1,2,3,4,5,6,7,8,9,A,B) (1)

Card 3 — 19 *sets*

Card 4 — 43 *sets*

Card 5 — 66 *sets*

Card 6 — 80 *sets*

Card 7 — 66 *sets*

Card 8 — 43 *sets*

Card 9 — 19 *sets*

A.7 FORTE'S TABLE

The table of the previous pages reproduces all possible combinations of sounds found in the equal temperament system. It is a concise, elegant and ordered representation of all possible combinations of sounds. It is surprising to learn that it fits in just two pages.(END NOTE 11) We will analyze it step by step through cardinality.

A.7.1 REDUCING THE SCOPE

As we can see, despite the briefness shown in Forte's table, the total of sets is still quite extensive. The list at the end of A.7 counts the chords in prime and inverted form (when appropriate), considering the inverted form as an independent set, although with the same interval vector.

Notice the eight-note sets in the Forte table (A.7). The prime forms show that most of the eight-note sets begin with the trichord 3-1 (0,1,2). In fact, the only eight-note set that does not begin with (0,1,2) or does not have the (0,1,2) as a subset is the 8-28 set, known as octatonic scale (or as it is usually called in improvisational music, the diminished or dominant-diminished scale).

A.7.2 THE SET 3-1 (0,1,2)

This set is called a chromatic cluster. Its melodic use is common because chromatic melodies are part of the tonal practice.

However, the recurrent use of the chromatic cluster as a harmonic entity comes from the post-tonal period, beginning with the second Viennese school. The term "cluster" was originally coined by Henry Cowell in the twentieth century. (END NOTE 12)

The chromatic cluster (0,1,2) does not belong to any traditional scale, such as the diatonic scale (7-35), harmonic scales (minor, 7-32a and major, 7-32b), or the melodic minor scale (7-34), nor is it a subset of the pentatonic scales (5-35). Not even the symmetrical scales of limited transposition (END NOTE 13), as the whole-tone scale (6-35), the augmented scale (6-20) and the octatonic scale (8-28) contain the trichord 3-1 (0,1,2).

Thus, tonal music (including jazz), even in its most expanded form, does not make systematic use of the trichord (0,1,2) as a harmonic entity. (END NOTE 14) Some scales, called "be-bop" scales, are eight-note sets that contain a trichord (0,1,2), but are used not for harmonic but for rhythmic-melodic reasons. (END NOTE 15) According to Levine, be-bop scales can be thought as the harmonic repository of tonic chords (C6) and dominant (B°) chords. (END NOTE 16)

Moreover, unlike other trichords, the (0,1,2) is the only trichord that cannot be easily understood in a harmonic system that seeks functionality. Its character is essentially ambiguous and non-polar. Polarity is a prerequisite for harmonic functionality and cadential gravity.

This observation led me to the methodological principle that would make possible the handling of a smaller group of sets, and thus, propose a tonal organization. This principle is the elimination of all supersets of the 3-1 set (0,1,2) or chromatic cluster. Any set that contains the trichord (0,1,2) as a subset will be disregarded.

A.7.3 REMOVING THE 3-1 (0,1,2) THRICORD FROM THE SYSTEM

Based on the assumptions on the characteristics of the 3-1 trichord, I have concluded that removing it would make the system manipulation of the extensive number of sets much simpler. As an example, we can mention the case of eight-note sets. With the removal of trichord (0,1,2) we have only the octatonic scale (8-28). We will not deal with nine-note and ten-note sets, since they all contain (0,1,2). In the case of nine-note sets, we will make an exception for the 9-12 set (nonatonic scale or Messiaen mode 3) of limited transpositions (4). The eleven-note set is a defective chromatic scale. The analysis of compositions that contain 3-1 trichord is not, however, impossible. You can perform the decomposition of structures that contain clusters in smaller units, compatible with the tonal system, but this is not the purpose of this book. However, this idea might be developed in the future.

A.7.4 TABLE OF THE SETS WITHOUT THE 3-1 TRICHORD

PITCH CLASS SETS
Without the 3-1(0,1,2)
Trichord

CARD 2 (I. Classes)

P.F.		I.F.
2m	(0,1) ST, Semitone	7M
2M	(0,2) T, Whole Tone	7m
3m	(0,3) sesquitone	6M / 7d
3M	(0,4) ditone	6m / 5A
4J	(0,5) sesquiditone	5J
4A (6)	(0,6) TT	5D

CARD 3

Forte	PF (a)	IF (b)
3-2:	(0,1,3)	[0,2,3]
3-3:	(0,1,4)	[0,3,4]
3-4:	(0,1,5)	[0,4,5]
3-5:	(0,1,6)	[0,5,6]
3-6:	(0,2,4)	
3-7:	(0,2,5)	[0,3,5]
3-8:	(0,2,6) It	[0,4,6]
3-9:	(0,2,7) Q3	
3-10:	(0,3,6) dim	
3-11:	(0,3,7) min	[0,4,7] maj
3-12:	(0,4,8) aug (4)	

CARD 4

Forte	PF (a)	IF (b)
4-3:	(0,1,3,4)	
4-7:	(0,1,4,5)	
4-8:	(0,1,5,6)	
4-9	(0,1,6,7) (6)	
4-10:	(0,2,3,5)	
4-11:	(0,1,3,5)	[0,2,4,5]
4-12:	(0,2,3,6)	[0,3,4,6]
4-13:	(0,1,3,6)	[0,3,5,6]
4-14:	(0,2,3,7)	[0,4,5,7]
4-Z15:	(0,1,4,6)	[0,2,5,6]
4-Z29:	(0,1,3,7)	[0,4,6,7]
4-16:	(0,1,5,7)	[0,2,6,7]
4-17:	(0,3,4,7)	
4-18:	(0,1,4,7)	[0,3,6,7]
4-19:	(0,1,4,8) m7M	[0,3,4,8]
4-20:	(0,1,5,8) 7M	
4-21:	(0,2,4,6)	
4-22:	(0,2,4,7)	[0,3,5,7]
4-23:	(0,2,5,7) Q4	
4-24:	(0,2,4,8) 7(#5)	
4-25:	(0,2,6,8) Fr6 (6)	
4-26:	(0,3,5,8) m7, 6	
4-27:	(0,2,5,8) ø	[0,3,6,8] 7
4-28:	(0,3,6,9) ° (3)	

CARD 5

Forte	PF (a)	IF (b)
5-10:	(0,1,3,4,6)	[0,2,3,5,6]
5-Z12:	(0,1,3,5,6)	
5-16:	(0,1,3,4,7)	[0,3,4,6,7]
5-Z17:	(0,1,3,4,8)	
5-Z18:	(0,1,4,5,7)	[0,2,3,6,7]
5-19:	(0,1,3,6,7)	[0,1,4,6,7]
5-20:	(0,1,5,6,8)	[0,2,3,7,8]
5-21:	(0,1,4,5,8)	[0,3,4,7,8]
5-22:	(0,1,4,7,8)	
5-23:	(0,2,3,5,7)	[0,2,4,5,7]
5-24:	(0,1,3,5,7)	[0,2,4,6,7]
5-25:	(0,2,3,5,8)	[0,3,5,6,8]
5-26:	(0,2,4,5,8)	[0,3,4,6,8]
5-27:	(0,1,3,5,8)	[0,3,5,7,8] m7(9)
5-28:	(0,2,3,6,8)	[0,2,5,6,8]
5-29:	(0,1,3,6,8)	[0,2,5,7,8]
5-30:	(0,1,4,6,8)	[0,2,4,7,8]
5-31:	(0,1,3,6,9)	[0,2,3,6,9] 7(b9)
5-32:	(0,1,4,6,9)	[0,2,5,6,9] 7(#9)
5-33:	(0,2,4,6,8) 9#5b5	
5-34:	(0,2,4,6,9) 7(9)	
5-35:	(0,2,4,7,9) Penta	Q5

CARD 6

Forte	PF (a)	IF (b)
6-Z13:	(0,1,3,4,6,7)	
6-Z19:	(0,1,3,4,7,8)	[0,1,4,5,7,8]
6-20:	(0,1,4,5,8,9) (4)	
6-Z23:	(0,2,3,5,6,8)	
6-Z24:	(0,1,3,4,6,8)	[0,2,4,5,7,8]
6-Z25:	(0,1,3,5,6,8)	[0,2,3,5,7,8]
6-Z26:	(0,1,3,5,7,8)	
6-27:	(0,1,3,4,6,9)	[0,2,3,5,6,9]
6-Z28:	(0,1,3,5,6,9)	
6-Z49:	(0,1,3,4,7,9)	
6-Z29:	(0,2,3,6,7,9)	
6-Z50:	(0,1,4,6,7,9)	
6-30:	(0,1,3,6,7,9)	[0,2,3,6,8,9]
6-31:	(0,1,4,5,7,9)	[0,2,4,5,8,9]
6-32:	(0,2,4,5,7,9)	
6-33:	(0,2,3,5,7,9)	[0,2,4,6,7,9] 7(11)
6-34:	(0,1,3,5,7,9)	[0,2,4,6,8,9]
6-35:	(0,2,4,6,8,A)	

CARD 7 (Scales)

Forte	PF (a)	IF (b)
7-31:	(0,1,3,4,6,7,9)	[0,2,3,5,6,8,9]
7-32:	(0,1,3,4,6,8,9) Hm	[0,1,3,5,6,8,9] HM
7-34:	(0,1,3,4,6,8,A) Ac	
7-35:	(0,1,3,5,6,8,A) Diat	

CARD 8 (Octa)

Forte	PF	IF
8-28:	(0,1,3,4,6,7,9,A) (3)	Octa

Card 3 – 18 *sets (all, except 3-1)*
Card 4 – 35 *sets (43*)*
Card 5 – 38 *sets (66*)*
Card 6 – 26 *sets (80*)*
Card 7 – 6 *sets (66*)*
Card 8 – 1 *sets (43*)*
Card 9 – 0 *sets (19*)*

*before the exclusion
of 3-1 (0,1,2) trichord.

A.7.5 SETS WITHOUT 3-1

After the removal of the 3-1, we begin to see why 7 is the magic number of music. The seven-note sets are the main responsible for the production of harmonic entities.

Moreover, the major scale (7-35) has many special properties, being the only seven-note set that produces another set with the same properties when only one note is changed. This feature, which allows for tonal perspective, modulations, and cadential gravity, was one of the constituent elements of the musical architecture that extends from Bach's "Well Tempered Clavier" to jazz and folk songs, going through the entire tonal tradition of western music.

When looking at the list of sets that do not contain the 3-1 trichord we notice that it decreases considerably, fitting a single page.

From the removal of the 3-1 from the system, the set that presents the largest cardinality will be the 8-28 (octatonic scale).

The 7-31a and 7-31b, from the cardinality 7 sets, can be seen as a defective octatonic scale, or the set 8-28 without one of its elements. For this reason, we will not include the 7-31a and 7-31b among the 7 cardinality sets that produce chords, because the harmonic entities contained in them are already contained in 8-28.

Thus, after removing the 3-1 from the system, we have only three harmonically important sets in the cardinality 7. They are:

7-35 – the diatonic scale (or major scale)
7-34 – the acoustic scale (or melodic minor scale);
7-32 – the harmonic scales (Hm – harmonic minor and HM – harmonic major)

This way, we can infer that the seven-note scales will be the most responsible for the production of chords in our system. As we have seen earlier, the 7-32a, 32b-7 and 7-34 scales may be viewed as a variation of the 7-35 scale. Furthermore, in Chapter 1, we show a superimposition system of these four scales in only one tonal center.

END NOTES

1. Melhdau, Brad. House on the hill (pg. 6). www.bradmehldau.com

2. Hindemith, Paul. *The Craft of Musical Composition*. Mainz: Schott, 1970.

3. This idea of scale superimposition is similar to George Russell's, in his "Lydian Chromatic Concept of Tonal Organization." In the 1959 edition, this procedure is clearer than in the new version (2001). However, Russell makes reference to the degrees from the Lydian mode on, numbering it as I (first) degree. Considering the preceding tonal inheritance and how we get used to practicing the repertoire, I thought it would be more intuitive to treat the degrees the traditional way in which, in the tonal center [C:], the note 'C is the I degree.

4. Freitas, Sérgio Paulo Ribeiro de. "Teoria da Harmonia na Música Popular: uma definição das relações de combinação entre os acordes na harmonia tonal", São Paulo, 1995, UNESP (pg. 22-23).

5. Mattos, Fernando Lewis de. "Sistemas de Cifragem de Acordes", handout, Harmony Class at UFRGS.

6. This type of functional notation is widely used by Koellreutter and other authors, suffering some variation from author to author. Some changes were added, and they will be properly explained.

7. Johnson, Timothy. *Foundations of Diatonic Theory*. Lanham: The Scarecrow Press, Inc, 2008.

8. Degreg, Phil. *Jazz Keyboard Harmony - a Practical Voicing Method for All Musicians*. Jamey Aebersold, 2010.

9. Forte, Allen. *The Structure of Atonal Music*. New Haven: Yale University Press, 1973.

10. Capuzzo, Guy. Review of Robert D. Morris, Class Notes for Advanced Atonal Music Theory (Lebanon, N.H.: Frog Peak Music, 2001).

11. The layout was based on tables created by Paul Nelson. See at www.composertools.com

12. Griffiths, Paul. *Modern Music*. London: Thames and Hudson, 1994.

13. Messiaen, Olivier. The technique of my musical language. Alphonse Leduc, 1956. [781.43 MES]

14. Tymoczko, Dmitri. 1997. "The Consecutive-Semitone Constraint on Scalar Structure: A Link Between Impressionism and Jazz." Integral 11: 135-179.

15. BERGONZI, *Jerry, Inside Improvisation, Vol 3. Jazz Line. Advance Music.*

16. *Levine, Mark.* Jazz Piano Masterclass with Mark Levine. *The Drop 2 Book. Sher Music Company, 2007. Mark Levine.*

REFERENCES

Almada, Carlos. *Harmonia Funcional.*Campinas. Ed. Unicamp, 2009.

Assis-Brasil, Gustavo. *Hybrid Picking for Guitar*. City: Gustavo Assis Brasil Music, 2005.

Carter, Elliott et.al. *Harmony Book*. New York: Carl Fischer, 2002.

Carvalho, Any Raquel. *Contraponto Tonal e Fuga: manual prático*. Porto Alegre. Editora Novak Multimedia, 2002.

Chediak, Almir. *Dicionário de acordes cifrados*. Rio de Janeiro: Lumiar, 1984.

_____. *Harmonia & improvisação*. 2v. Rio de Janeiro: Lumiar, 1986.

Christensen, Thomas. *The Cambridge History of Western Music Theory*. Cambridge: Cambridge University Press, 2002.

Cope, David. *The Algorithmic Composer*. Madison: A-R Editions, 2000.

Damian, Jon, and Jonathan Feist. *The Guitarist's Guide to Composing and Improvising*. Boston: Berklee Press Publications, 2001.

Degreg, Phil. *Jazz Keyboard Harmony - a Practical Voicing Method for All Musicians*. Jamey Aebersold, 2010.

Eps, George. *Mel Bay Presents Harmonic Mechanisms for Guitar, Vol. 3*. City: Mel Bay Publications, Inc, 1982.

Forte, Allen. *The American Popular Ballad of the Golden Era, 1924-1950*. Princeton: Princeton University Press, 1995.

Forte, Allen. *The Structure of Atonal Music*. New Haven: Yale University Press, 1973.

Fux, Johann et.al. *The Study of Counterpoint from Johann Fux's Gradus Ad Parnassum*. New York: W.W. Norton, 1971.

Goodrick, Mick. *Advancing Guitarist*. Milwaukee: Hal Leonard, 1987.

Greene, Ted. *Chord Chemistry*. City: Warner Brothers Publications, 1981.

Guerra Peixe, Cesar. *Melos e harmonia acústica*. São Paulo: Irmãos Vitale, s.d.

Guest, Ian. *Harmonia: método prático*. 2v. Rio de Janeiro: Lumiar, 2006.

Griffiths, Paul. *Modern Music*. London: Thames and Hudson, 1994.

Hindemith, Paul. *The craft of musical composition*. London: Schott, 1970 (ed.original: 1942).

_____. *Harmonia tradicional*. São Paulo: Irmãos Vitale, s.d. (ed. original: New Haven, 1944).

Johnson, Timothy. *Foundations of Diatonic Theory*. Lanham: The Scarecrow Press, Inc, 2008.

Faria, Nelson. *A arte da improvisação*. Rio de Janeiro. Ed. Lumiar, 1991.

_____. *Harmonia Aplicada ao Violão e à Guitarra.Técnicas em Chord Melody*. Rio de Janeiro. Nelson Faria Produções Musicais, 2009.

Koellreutter. *Harmonia funcional*. São Paulo: Ricordi, 1980.

Kostka, Stefan; Payne, Dorothy. *Tonal harmony*. New York: 1989.

Lendvai, Erno, and Alan Bush. *Bela Bartok*. City: Kahn & Averill Publishers, 2005.

Levine, Mark. *Jazz Piano Masterclass with Mark Levine*. City: Sher Music Company, 2007.

Levine, Mark. *The Jazz Piano Book*. Petaluma: Sher Music, 1989.

Levine, Mark. *The Jazz Theory Book*. City: Sher Music Co, 1996.

Messiaen, Olivier. *The technique of my musical language*. Alphonse Leduc, 1956. [781.43 MES]

Pass, Joe. *Joe Pass Guitar Chords*. Van Nuys: Alfred Publishing, 2006.

Paiva Oliveira, João Pedro. *Teoria Analítica da Música do Século XX*. F.C.Gulbenkian, 1998.

Perle, George. *Serial composition and atonality*. Berkeley, University of California, 1981.

Persichetti, Vincent. *Twentieth-Century Harmony*. New York: W. W. Norton, 1961.

Ricker, Ramon. *Technique development in forths for jazz improvisation*. New York: Studio, 1976.

Riemann, Hugo. *Harmony Simplified: or, the Theory of the Tonal Functions of Chords*. City: Cornell University Library, 2009

Russell, George. *Lydian Chromatic Concept of Tonal Organization for Improvisation*. York: Concept Pub, 1959

_____, *Lydian Chromatic Concept of Tonal Organization*. City: Beekman Pub, 2001.

Bergonzi, Jerry. Inside Improvisation, Vol 3. Jazz Line. Advance Music.

Tymoczko, Dmitri. 1997. "The Consecutive-Semitone Constraint on Scalar Structure: A Link Between Impressionism and Jazz." *Integral* 11: 135-179.

_____, 2002. "Stravinsky and the Octatonic: A Reconsideration." *Music Theory Spectrum* 24(1): 68-102.

_____ , 2004: 'Scale Networks and Debussy', *Journal of Music Theory*, 48/ii:215-292.

_____, Forthcoming. "Scale Networks and Debussy." *Journal of Music Theory*.

Schiff, David. *The Music of Elliott Carter*. Ithaca: Cornell University Press, 1998.

Antokoletz, Elliott. *The Music of Béla Bartók*. Berkeley: University of California Press, 1984.

Schoenberg, Arnold. *Harmonia*. São Paulo: UNESP, 2002 (ed. original: 1911).

Freitas, Sérgio Paulo Ribeiro de. *"Teoria da Harmonia na Música Popular: uma definição das relações de combinação entre os acordes na harmonia tonal"*, São Paulo, 1995, UNESP, página 22-23.

Schonberg, Arnold et.al. *Structural Functions of Harmony*. New York: W. W. Norton, 1969.

Slonimsky, Nicolas. *Thesaurus of Scales and Melodic Patterns*. New York: Amsco, 1986.

Weiskopf, Walt. *Intervallic Improvisation: The Modern Sound*. Jamey Aebersold.

Winkler, Todd. *Composing Interactive Music*. Cambridge: MIT Press, 1998.

Wyble, Jimmy and Ron Berman. *Mel Bay Concepts for the Classical and Jazz Guitar Book/CD Set*. City: Mel Bay Publications, Inc, 2000.

Wyble, Jimmy. *Art of Two-Line Improvisation Book/CD Set*. Pacific: Mel Bay Publications, 2001.

ONLINE RESOURCES
www.composertools.com
http://dmitri.tymoczko.com/
http://allenforte.com/

ABOUT THE AUTHOR

Julio "Chumbinho" Herrlein

Julio Herrlein was born in Porto Alegre, Brazil, September 22, 1973 and started playing music at age 11. He has been working professionally for nearly 20 years as a guitarist, composer and arranger.

He earned his bachelor's degree and Master 's degrees in musical composition at UFRGS (Universidade Federal do Rio Grande do Sul, Brazil). In 2006, in Rio de Janeiro, Julio won first prize in the VIII National Composition Contest - IBEU (Brazil-United States Institute) with his composition "Brazilian Maestros Suite," composed and arranged by him for big band. This composition honors three key figures of Brazilian culture: Moacir Santos, Hermeto Pascoal and Maestro Cipó. Among the judges were Carlos Malta (saxophonist, arranger), João Guilherme Ripper (member of the Brazilian Academy of Music and curator of Cecília Meirelles Hall), and Leonardo Bruno (composer, Abel Ferreira's son). In 1996, his composition "Novembro," from the album "Julio Herrlein Quartet," won the I Instrumental Music Festival of Rio Grande do Sul. He has composed, arranged and produced nearly 1,300 pieces, many of which have won awards, for advertising broadcast nationally and internationally.

As a guitarist, he recorded his first album, Julio Herrlein Quartet, in 1996 at age 22, with the musicians Kiko Freitas, Michel Dorfman, and Ricardo Baumgarten. He has also performed in a variety of formations (duo, trio and quartet), sharing the stage with many important musicians of the Brazilian and international scenes. Julio developed the guitar recital "Solo Jazz," performing in many theaters around Brazil.

Julio also works regularly as a music teacher, and is sought out by professional musicians from many genres who want to improve their music. Some of his articles were included in the book and CD ROM "The Art of Improvisation," by the American trumpet player Bob Taylor. In 2010 he was a teacher of the Guitar Course on the XVIII Curitiba Music Workshop (one of the most important workshops in Brazil). There he performed with such important names in Brazilian instrumental music as Fábio Torres (piano), Edu Ribeiro (drums) and André Vasconcellos (bass).

Julio hasalready played with several national and international musicians such as Joris Teepe, Ari Hoenig, Kiko Freitas, Marquinhos Fê, Fábio Torres, Edu Ribeiro, André Vasconcellos, Eduardo Neves, Thiago do Espírito Santo, Sandro Haick, Gustavo Assis-Brasil, Edu Martins, Lucinha Lins, Robertinho Silva, Phil DeGreg, Alegre Corrêa, Maggie Green, Craig Owens, Pata Masters, Guinha Ramires, Glauco Solter, Michel Dorfman, Bebeto Alves, Gelson Oliveira, Alessandro "Bebê" Kramer, Maurício Marques, Paulo Dorfman, Emilio Valdes, Michel Leme, Bruno Tessele, Matheus Nicolaiewsky, Diego Ferreira, Maurício Zotarelli, among others.

www.julioherrlein.com

PITCH CLASS SETS INDEX

CARD 3

Forte	PF (a)	NAME	Pag	IF (b)	NAME	Pag
3-2:	(0,1,3)	^7M(9)	88	[0,2,3]	^7(b9)	90
3-3:	(0,1,4)	^m7M	78	[0,3,4]	^7M(#5)	80
3-4:	(0,1,5)	7M(¬5)	72	[0,4,5]	^7M(5)	82
3-5:	(0,1,6)	QT	68	[0,5,6]	TQ	70
3-6:	(0,2,4)	^7(9)	92			
3-7:	(0,2,5)	^m7	74	[0,3,5]	^7(5)	84
3-8:	(0,2,6)	lt	76	[0,4,6]	^7(b5)	86
3-9:	(0,2,7)	Q3	66			
3-10:	(0,3,6)	dim	62			
3-11:	(0,3,7)	min	60	[0,4,7]	maj	58
3-12:	(0,4,8) (4)	aug	64			

CARD 4

Forte	PF (a)	NAME	Pag	IF (b)	NAME	Pag
4-3:	(0,1,3,4)	m7M(9-5)	146			
4-7:	(0,1,4,5)	7M(#9-5)	147			
4-8:	(0,1,5,6)	7M(4-5)	127			
4-9:	(0,1,6,7) (6)	7Mb5(4-3)	128			
4-10:	(0,2,3,5)	m7(b9-5)	148			
4-11:	(0,1,3,5)	7M(9-5)	149	[0,2,4,5]	m7(9-5)	150
4-12:	(0,2,3,6)	7(b9)	132	[0,3,4,6]	7M#5(9-3)	140
4-13:	(0,1,3,6)	m7(13-5)	133	[0,3,5,6]	7(b9-3)	141
4-14:	(0,2,3,7)	7M(6-5)	134	[0,4,5,7]	7M(9-3)	142
4-z15:	(0,1,4,6) AIT	7(#4-3)	130	[0,2,5,6]	7(#9)	131
4-z29:	(0,1,3,7)	7(13-5)	137	[0,4,6,7]	ø (b9-m)	145
4-16:	(0,1,5,7)	7M(b5)	126	[0,2,6,7]	7M(4-3)	129
4-17:	(0,3,4,7)	m7M(b6-5)	138			
4-18:	(0,1,4,7)	° (b13-b5)	135	[0,3,6,7]	° (b9-m)	143
4-19:	(0,1,4,8)	m7M	117	[0,3,4,8]	7M#5	118
4-20:	(0,1,5,8)	7M	116			
4-21:	(0,2,4,6)	G7(9-5)	151			
4-22:	(0,2,4,7)	m7(b6-5)	136	[0,3,5,7]	7(9-3)	144
4-23:	(0,2,5,7)	Q4	124			
4-24:	(0,2,4,8)	7(#5)	139			
4-25:	(0,2,6,8) (6)	Fr6	125			
4-26:	(0,3,5,8)	m7, 6	120			
4-27:	(0,2,5,8)	ø	121	[0,3,6,8]	7	122
4-28:	(0,3,6,9) (3)	°	123			

CARD 5

Forte	PF (a)	Pag	IF (b)	Pag
5-20:	(0,1,5,6,8)	164	[0,2,3,7,8]	163
5-22:	(0,1,4,7,8)	168		
5-28:	(0,2,3,6,8)	166	[0,2,5,6,8]	166
5-29:	(0,1,3,6,8)	163	[0,2,5,7,8]	164
5-30:	(0,1,4,6,8)	165	[0,2,4,7,8]	165
5-31:	(0,1,3,6,9)	167	[0,2,3,6,9] 7(b9)	167
5-32:	(0,1,4,6,9)	167	[0,2,5,6,9] 7(#9)	168
5-34:	(0,2,4,6,9) 7(9)	164		
5-35:	(0,2,4,7,9) PentaQ5	163		

CARD 6

Forte	PF (a)	NAME	Pag	IF (b)	NAME	Pag
6-z13:	(0,1,3,4,6,7)	C#dim+Ddim	228			
6-z19:	(0,1,3,4,7,8)	Em + F	208	[0,1,4,5,7,8]	E + F	192
6-20:	(0,1,4,5,8,9)	Caug+Dbau	238			
6-z23:	(0,2,3,5,6,8)	Bdim+C#dim	226			
6-z24:	(0,1,3,4,6,8)	G#dim+Am	194	[0,2,4,5,7,8]	C + Ddim	206
6-z25:	(0,1,3,5,6,8)	Bdim + C	184	[0,2,3,5,7,8]	Am + Bdim	182
6-z26:	(0,1,3,5,7,8)	Em + F	178			
6-27:	(0,1,3,4,6,9)	C#dim + Bb	224	[0,2,3,5,6,9]	Ddim + Em	230
6-z28:	(0,1,3,5,6,9)	Bdim + Caug	196			
6-z49:	(0,1,3,4,7,9)	Bbm + G	222			
6-z29:	(0,2,3,6,7,9)	Dm + E	190			
6-z50:	(0,1,4,6,7,9)	Bb + Em	216			
6-30:	(0,1,3,6,7,9)	Em + Bbm	218	[0,2,3,6,8,9]	Db + G	220
6-31:	(0,1,4,5,7,9)	G + Abaug	210	[0,2,4,5,8,9]	Caug +	188
6-32:	(0,2,4,5,7,9)	m7(9,11)	174			
6-33:	(0,2,3,5,7,9)	Dm + Em	176	[0,2,4,6,7,9]	F + G	180
6-34:	(0,1,3,5,7,9)	Em + Faug	200	[0,2,4,6,8,9]	Faug + G	202
6-35:	(0,2,4,6,8,A)	WT	234			
6-z17	(0,1,2,4,7,8)		240			

CARD 7

Forte	PF (a)	Pag	IF (b)	Pag
7-32:	(0,1,3,4,6,8,9) Hm	269, 63	[0,1,3,5,6,8,9] HM	271, 63
7-34:	(0,1,3,4,6,8,A) Ac	270, 65		
7-35:	(0,1,3,5,6,8,A) Diat	268, 61		

CD TRACKS INDEX

CARD 3	Name	Forte #	PF/IF	Page
TRACK # 1	F major	3-11b:	(0,4,7)	58
TRACK # 2	C major (open position)			59
TRACK # 3	D minor	3-11a:	(0,3,7)	60
TRACK # 4	A minor (open position)			61
TRACK # 5	B diminished	3-10:	(0,3,6)	62
TRACK # 6	B diminished (open position)			63
TRACK # 7	F(#5) - augmented	3-12:	(0,4,8)	64
TRACK # 8	F(#5) (open position)			65
TRACK # 9	GQ3 – quartal	3-9:	(0,2,7)	66
TRACK # 10	GQ3 – quartal (open position)			67
TRACK # 11	CQT – quartal/tritone	3-5:	(0,1,6)	68
TRACK # 12	FTQ – tritone/quartal	3-5:	(0,5,6)	70
TRACK # 13	F7M(¬5) F major seventh (no fifth)	3-4:	(0,1,5)	72
TRACK # 14	D^m7 D minor seventh, no fifth	3-7a:	(0,2,5)	74
TRACK # 15	GIt – G7 (no fifth) – Italian	3-8:	(0,2,6)	76
TRACK # 16	D^m7M – D minor maj7, no fifth	3-3a:	(0,1,4)	78
TRACK # 17	F^7M(#5) F maj7 #5, no third	3-3b:	(0,3,4)	80
TRACK # 18	F^7M(5) F major7, no third	3-4b:	(0,4,5)	82
TRACK # 19	E^7(5) E seventh, no third	3-7b:	(0,3,5)	84
TRACK # 20	B^7(b5) B seventh b5, no third	3-8b:	(0,4,6)	86
TRACK # 21	F^7M(9) F with maj7 and 9 added	3-2a:	(0,1,3)	88
TRACK # 22	E^7(b9) E with 7 and b9 added	3-2b:	(0,2,3)	90
TRACK # 23	E^7(9) D with 7 and 9 added	3-6:	(0,2,4)	92

NOTE:

> Tracks #1 to #38
> Left Channel: Chords
> Right Channel: Solo

You can mute one of the sides to play along only with the harmony or only with the solo.

CARD 5	Pentatonic Melodic Exercises	Forte #	Page
TRACK # 24	Subsets of 7-35 (Diatonic)	5-20b:	163
TRACK # 25		5-29a:	163
TRACK # 26		5-35:	163
TRACK # 27		5-29b:	164
TRACK # 28		5-20a:	164
TRACK # 29		5-34:	164
TRACK # 30	Subsets of 7-34 (Melodic Minor)	5-30a:	165
TRACK # 31		5-30b:	165
TRACK # 32	Subsets of 8-28 (Octatonic)	5-28a:	166
TRACK # 33		5-28b:	166
TRACK # 34		5-32a:	167
TRACK # 35		5-31a:	167
TRACK # 36		5-31b:	167
TRACK # 37		5-32b:	168
TRACK # 38	Subsets of 7-32a/b (Harmonic)	5-22:	168

COMPOSITIONS – by Julio Herrlein

TRACK # 39	Sonata (to Ben Monder)	274
TRACK # 40	Ainda Não (Not Yet)	283